Sex, Money and Power

Sex, Money and Power

The Transformation of Collective Life

Bill Jordan

polity

First published in 2004 by Polity Press

Polity Press
65 Bridge Street
Cambridge CB2 1UR, UK.

Polity Press
350 Main Street
Malden, MA 02148, USA

ISBN: 0-7456-3350-1
ISBN: 0-7456-3351-X (pb)

A catalogue record for this book is available from the British Library and has been applied for from the Library of Congress.

Typeset in 11 on 13 pt Berling
by SNP Best-set Typesetter Ltd., Hong Kong
Printed and bound in Great Britain by MPG Book Ltd, Bodmin, Cornwall

For further information on Polity, visit our website: www.polity.co.uk

Contents

Acknowledgements

I would like to thank the many friends and colleagues, all over Europe, with whom I discussed the ideas behind this book, over a number of years.

In particular, I am very grateful for suggestions, comments and criticisms by those who saw parts of drafts of it, or who looked at earlier versions. My thanks go to Phil Agulnik, Alex Allan, Steve Barton, Peter Boxall, Michael Breuer, Fiona Dukelow, Rose Gayner, Peter Herrmann, Charlie Jordan, Sarah Jordan, Mită Kaněrová, Zuzana Ladzianska, Abigail McKnight, Kate Milnes, Jean Packman, Marcus Redley, Bryan Saunders, Andrew Travers and Sue White.

I am also very grateful to Gill Watson for (yet another) fine job in typing the manuscript, to Matthew Losasso for producing the cover photography and to Angie Triner for typing the index.

Introduction

When I lived in Bratislava, the capital of the then newly independent post-Communist state of Slovakia, a friend of my own age commented ironically on her mental engagement in the turbulent public life of her country during her lifetime. She was just old enough to have clear memories of the coup which established a Soviet-style Czechoslovak regime in 1948, and strongly supported that revolution. By 1968, she was in her prime, and an enthusiastic adherent of the reformist ideas that inspired Alexander Dubček's 'Prague spring' and in turn provoked the incursion of Russian troops to restore Soviet orthodoxy. In 1989, she rejoiced in the overthrow of that regime, and now found herself living with the ambiguous results of this transformation in an impoverished and sometimes violent city.

She wryly accused herself of being a sucker for every fashionable new idea in town, always willing to subscribe to whatever vision of 'the good society' was on offer. She had bought into the images of happy Russian citizens under Stalin, of liberated students under Dubček and of prosperous, leisured Americans in 1989. Her ideas and emotions adapted all too readily to each cultural and ideological change in the social landscape.

If we are similarly honest and clear-eyed, there are few of us at my age who can look back on our lives and not accuse ourselves of having been 'cultural dopes' of this kind. Even though the shifts in social relations in the United Kingdom were less sudden and dramatic than those of Slovakia, they have been very striking. After all, when I was born, there was not only wartime conscription into the armed forces, but also direction of civilian labour, a totally planned economy, rationing and billeting, public canteens and fully censored news media. Many of these controls spilled over into the post-war period, making it possible to establish the massive system of social engineering and political regulation that was the welfare state.

Although I was required to be a uniformed cadet during my schooldays, I avoided military conscription by the narrowest of margins and entered university, employment and marriage exactly at the moment when the grey 1950s were being transformed into the swinging sixties, the 'decade of love'. Like most of my generation, I saw the public services as offering the most exciting prospects for a career in which social relevance, professional autonomy and political radicalism could be combined in a heady mixture of personal and collective development.

When one is young, it is easy to attribute cultural shifts to generational change. Although my own parents were rather stylish and dashing (if often unreliable), those of my friends were mainly stiff and stuffy. Fifties' Britain was still full of desperately threadbare bourgeois households, in which faded parents were making huge sacrifices to send their children to third-rate public schools. Among the working class, the equivalent was a life of quiet municipal virtue and restrained privacy, so brilliantly recorded by Alan Bennett in his memoir of his parents' life in Leeds:

> Without being at all pious, neither of them touched alcohol, which limited their social life. He disliked all male company as my mother did the exclusive company of women and they were happiest – only happy really – when together. They were shy, timorous, silly and full of fun. . . . They had a longing to be ordinary – or at least like other people – and not to be perceived as different or set apart.[1]

The 1960s' shift was mainly based on a change in the sexual division of labour. Women had been drawn into the factories and the fields during the war, but sent back to be homemakers and mothers afterwards. By the early 1960s they were beginning – through education, the expansion of public services and a change in work organization – to re-enter the public sphere. More confident and assertive models of womanhood, new media icons and leisure opportunities fed into an altered expectation of relationships. Feminism followed this shift, rather than inspired it.

But there were plenty of casualties of these processes. My own marriage was to the daughter of close family friends, and the commitment to it made before I went to university. My wife subscribed to the new ethos of autonomy for women, but had none of the advantages of education or opportunities of a profession. We had several children in quick succession, and she justifiably felt excluded from the exciting public life which I enjoyed. I became the inept partner to a resentful, highly competent person trapped in domesticity; I was aware of my unmerited advantages, but unable to change the balance of our relationship. Having set out above all to avoid being like my father, who left the family when I was 13, I ended up doing exactly the same thing.

One way of looking at this story is that the 1960s provided me with the cultural resources to make a success of my early public career (as a social worker, an academic, a sportsman and an activist in a social movement), but not to overcome the structural inequalities and injustices in my first marriage. As a good 'cultural dope', I embraced the ideas and practices of the age well enough to thrive in the world of public services, protest movements and social criticism; yet the new model of partnership and equality in marital relationships couldn't deal with the fundamental faultlines of our marriage, or I couldn't make it do so. But this leaves plenty of unanswered questions about how culture and structure of social relations either enable new patterns of interaction to emerge, or generate conflicts that cannot be resolved, and lead to breakdowns in relationships, affecting the parties and those close to them for the rest of their lives.

Like the reflections of my friend in Bratislava, all this is a post hoc reconstruction of events which, at the time, seemed vivid, joyful, painful or frustrating, and were experienced both as having their own internal logic and dynamic and as deeply personal. The puzzle is how relationships and activities which can, from the perspective of a whole lifetime, be reconstructed as characteristic of a certain set of conventions and collective arrangements and shaped by the specific circumstances of the period, on the other hand seem so unique, so engaging and so authentic at the moment they are being lived. This book tries to unravel these questions, in the particular context of present-day social relations, which are very different from the ones of my childhood and young adult life.

One of the biggest shifts since the early 1970s is that individuals no longer feel the need to be part of some larger social movement or collective purpose. At that time, it seemed to me and most of my friends that one essential element in a meaningful life was to be a member of an organization, party or group committed to some social programme – to 'change society for the better'. In retrospect, it is easy to see why this fitted with the way things were arranged in those days. Since the 1960s, the situation of women, black people, gays and some groups like disabled people and people with mental illnesses had been substantially improved through collective action. Often this involved alliances between these groups and politicians, professionals or other members of the elite. Collective action paid; policy- and decision-makers responded to demonstrations, protests, lobbying and representations. The fact that many of these issues concerned people's identities and personal relationships made links between lifestyles and politics through social movements.

It was the clear intention of Margaret Thatcher and all her successors to change this situation. The miners' and printers' strikes of the 1980s, and the anti-poll tax movement (which was actually successful) were the last examples of mass collective action on the streets, in bitter confrontation with the police and courts. Thatcher succeeded beyond her wildest dreams, I suspect. The interesting question is how such collective identification and participation became such a dispensable part of a meaningful identity, and how politics was drained of ideology and participation. The culture shift that started in the late 1970s allowed people to feel affiliation and belonging, without these manifestations of membership and commitment. This book will investigate how the intensely private activities of intimacy and consumption can construct the sense of being meaningfully connected with innumerable others.

The methods I shall use will be eclectic. In trying to explain how we, as individuals, create a sense of coherence in our lives and make ourselves accountable (sometimes excessively so) to public standards, I draw on my own experiences, on psychological research, on social theory, politics and economics. But I claim legitimacy for these methods by constantly referring to the analyses of the Renaissance and Enlightenment philosophers. They deployed exactly such evidence in their explanations of the links between our inner and the social worlds. Indeed, the forms of argument they used were, I shall argue, peculiarly convincing, even to us today.

It is always much harder to analyse the codes and conventions in which one is currently living than those of other cultures or past ages. As Mary Douglas has pointed out, it is characteristic of the institutions that standardize our thoughts and behaviour to seem both natural and rational; they explicitly work by analogy with nature and reason.[2] The most successful institutions are those to which we willingly assent, and which leave us feeling completely free.

In our present age, these revolve around sex and money. Sex is seen as the natural expression for our personal development, and sexual relationships the field in which such development occurs. Consumption is represented as the rational outworking of our chosen identity and the way we perform our inner selves in the public arena. Both are highly voluntaristic and enhance our sense of self-ownership and self-responsibility. Hence the institutions which govern sexual and consumer relations are able to standardize our ideas and actions without us being conscious of them.

TV drama is compelling in so far as it represents these relations in an essential form, portraying the spirit of these principles through characters and situations which distil the key elements in them. UK television series like *This Life*, *Cold Feet*, *Cutting It* and *Clocking Off* portray the essence of sexual and commercial relationships in different segments of our social world. Although there are well-observed and detailed variations, according to geography and income level, the fundamentals are shared between them.

Whether they are young professionals or factory workers, the characters are portrayed as entering sexual relationships in a spirit that is both experimental and highly engaged. However many of these they may try and quickly discard, however hedonistic or exploitative their journey through them, the underlying assumption is that somewhere, somehow, there is the 'right' man or woman for each of them.[3] The worst thing they could do would be to mess up this relationship, or fail to recognize it. Our interest in the characters and their situations, indeed our compulsion to watch such dramas, lies in our hopes and fears around these risks. The characters' personalities develop through the relationships we witness, and we come to recognize, as they do, that they must engage fully, using all their allure and social skills, to be certain not to miss this unique chance of fulfilment.

It is easy, if not watching these dramas with full attention, to suppose that they are nothing more than a series of sexual encounters. The social theorist Zygmunt Bauman, in his book *Liquid Love: On the Frailty of Human Bonds*, sees present-day sexual relations as constructing looser ties, lacking long-term commitments and allowing easy exit.

> Convenience is the sole thing that counts, and convenience is a matter of a clear head, not a warm (let alone overheated) heart. . . . The art of *breaking up* the relationship and emerging out of it unscathed . . . beats the art of *composing* relationships hands down – by the sheer frequency of being vented.[4]

However, the spectacle of such instrumental and mechanistic behaviour would have no purchase in the world of TV drama. We would not be drawn, gripped or moved by a series of such opportunistic encounters. It is precisely the conviction – sometimes denied, sometimes avowed, sometimes only half-acknowledged by the characters themselves – that personal development requires a really satisfying relationship, founded on sex but leading to all-round fulfilment, which drives the complexities of these dramas. Whether it is the suspense of a protagonist risking a 'right' relationship by indulging in a careless fling 'on the side', or the excitement of another breaking out of a secure yet stifling partnership, these assumptions, and this framework, are what make these series dramatic rather than banal and repetitive. The viewer has to believe, and the characters have to convey, that sex *matters*, and matters desperately, because it is the route to and expression of personal identity, fulfilment and destiny.

The other side of contemporary cultural standardization – consumption – is the sub-theme of several of these series. For instance, in *Cutting It* the protagonists' occupations – hairdressing, beauty and bar-keeping – cater for consumer lifestyles and are expressed in their clothes, accessories and working environments. Less central characters are presented as perpetually embellishing their personae by spending money on their appearance, outfits and public postures – being seen in the right clothes and hairstyles in the right places. Celebrities flit in and out of the social scene, bestowing their aura on various venues and drawing admirers and acolytes in their wake.

But it is in the mid-evening programming of the TV channels that the most telling instances of consumer standardization are to be found. The profusion of slots about cooking, gardening, home-ownership and home improvements bears testimony to the hold of image-building through consumption on present-day culture. Here again, the fantasy appears to consist in the notion that money spent on makeovers of cuisine, garden or decor will reveal some inner essence or identity, and allow individuals to develop their public selves to the full expression of their potential.

Thus the focus of interactions in which individuals represent themselves in public and display their contribution to the social world shifts from the sphere of politics, civil society and work to that of the home and garden. Lifestyles and consumption justify and project the person and communicate their inner qualities to those they wish to impress. They also provide the stages on which consumers can interact (in costume), playing out their versions of the dramas of their lives.

It might seem difficult to connect the two parts of the cultural standardization process – sex and money – because the former constructs a fluid world of uncertainty and change, while the latter portrays a rather stable one of domesticity and display (albeit with frequent radical makeovers and shifts of location, location, location). However, they seem able to coexist as different but compatible aspects of the same fantasy lifestyle. Furthermore, they are linked by the bizarre revelation of survey evidence that millions of people find the various gardeners, cooks, decorators and odd-job people who present and take part in these programmes sexually attractive (get a life!).

Even a casual reader of the above pages could gather that, although I am in the thrall of the first element of cultural standardization through TV broadcasting, I am entirely immune to the second. Yet I have to confess that I own a two-acre garden smallholding, have spent many years doing up old houses (most recently converting an old cowshed into a dwelling), and use both these activities to whet my (massive) appetite for good food and drink. In other words, I can address the topic of this book as a cultural insider (at least a semi-dope) without pretending to have any superior detachment.

By implication, both parts of these cultural mechanisms relate to personal development and to the cult of the human individual – identity, expression and fulfilment. Intimate relationships and consumer lifestyles are the means to this end. Durkheim argued that modernity *sanctifies* the individual, as the ultimate basis of value and holiness.[5] What I have suggested about sex and money implies that these share in the sanctity of the human individual. Sex and money are not intrinsically sacred; in some contexts they are portrayed as dirty and degraded, and their combination in the sex industry is morally dubious. However – rather as bread and wine are transformed into holy things by Christian ceremonial – sex and money become the media for present-day sacred rituals of individualism.

However, to an outsider – from Mars, or (say) from a poor Islamic country – our UK prime-time TV programming would scarcely seem uplifting. Given all the suffering and conflict in the world, it might indeed appear shallow, parochial and complacent. So why, despite all the information that is now available about these issues, the opportunities for mind-broadening travel and the interdependence that has come with globalization, do mainstream people in the affluent countries experience the world through the narrow band of mental wavelengths available on these channels?

More important still, how do the organized ways in which we gain access to these wider worlds of other ethnicities, faiths and communities – through the internet, through foreign tours and as members of transnational firms or agencies – actually divide us from these alternative modes of experience more than they connect us with them? How do we, often despite ourselves, feel so much part of a collective world patterned by bonds of sex, money and fee-paying subscription, and so cut off from those whose belonging stems from blood, soil and religion?

It seems clear that some forms of power are at stake in these connections and disconnections, but they are more subtle than the ones with which I grew up. Not only do we no longer mobilize around great ideologies or transformative agendas; increasingly we do not seem to mobilize at all. The rivals for political leadership are all very much like each other, and so are all their programmes.[6] So why is it so much easier to govern us today, in the affluent countries, than it was in the 1960s or '70s – how are we so readily induced to herd ourselves into orderly, obedient and organized units? The collective world of my young adult life was made up of 'action groups' and 'protest days'; now we form 'centres' and 'symposia'.

I am certainly no exception to these tendencies. From the life of a social worker and educator, and a political activist, I now find myself a kind of European scholar-gypsy, moving among a network of (mainly younger) friends and collaborators in many cities. Most of my former colleagues shifted out of public-sector posts into entrepreneurship or consultancy, or moved abroad. All these changes have an economic as well as a personal-developmental logic, and are responses to new configurations of power and resources. I aim to explain these aspects of present-day experience too.

None of this is to suggest that criticism and protest, both individual and on a mass scale, are absent from today's collective world. We have seen an upsurge of resistance, which is both well-informed and well-coordinated, over the war in Iraq and against the whole idea of 'regime change', through military attack on 'rogue states'. But it is, I shall argue, hard to connect up this revulsion from the use of overwhelming force against poor and weak countries with convincing models of institutions for global justice. Opposition lacks a coherent set of ideas for alternatives.

Finally, although the scope of this book is very ambitious, I aim to present my arguments in a way that is accessible through everyday language and experience, and which makes sense of contradictions and anomalies that are familiar from news bulletins and political speeches. Above all, I hope that I can reclaim some of the fascination of social science topics for readers who may have been turned off by the convolutions of recent technical and abstract literature (including my own writing). The advantage of the authors of the seventeenth and eighteenth centuries was that they dealt in evidence that was familiar to all literate people, and argued in ways which were meant to convince this lay readership.

The process of specialization in the social sciences has moved them further and further away from these origins. I am often struck by the fact that I have much more engaged and intellectually challenging conversations on trains and planes going to universities than I do when I get there. On arrival, I deliver lectures and classes of stunning dullness, because of the constraints of the courses, but mainly because of my own lack of courage and imagination. I hope this book will not make those mistakes.

1

Inside the Web

This book is about two issues which have always puzzled social scientists. The first is how to explain the 'joined-upness' of experience – how apparently fragmented events and emotions are organized into some kind of coherent story. It seems clear that experiences are not *inherently* meaningful (for example, people from different historical periods or different cultures would make another kind of sense of them). So how do we reach a more-or-less shared understanding of the meaning of things that happen to us?

The second is how these ways of making sense of the world also limit what we can think and do. It is as if, in order to make experience orderly, safe and manageable, we also contrive to trap ourselves in routine ways of seeing and acting – 'most of us, most of the time, tend to be boring and predictable, not only to others, but even to ourselves'.[1] Born originals, how do we turn ourselves into copies?

It is obvious that these two puzzles are linked. Whatever it is through which we manage to understand and control what goes on around us, and communicate about it with others, also constrains our thoughts and actions. We are, as it were, trapped in the web we spin to capture and digest experiences. But this metaphor is not quite satisfactory, because the web is being spun by millions of us at the same time, and is constantly being repaired and reconstructed; a great deal of our time and energy is spent on joint or reciprocal spinning activities, which in turn transform the web itself. It changes all the time. And yet we cannot perceive what we create, or describe its strings and nodes, or say what holds it all together.

Even this nuanced version of the web analogy fails to do full justice to the diversity of experience. One appealing aspect of the image is the idea that we can move in various directions across the web, but – like spiders – never leave it completely. If we attempt a leap, we remain involuntarily attached by a sticky strand of our own making. But there are also qualitative differences between modes of experience, from the ecstatic or transcendent to the mundane and banal, which show that there are more than two dimensions involved.

Social science has given us an extraordinary number of insights into the processes which enable and constrain our experiences of the world, and our communications about them. But it has not provided a convincing account, either generally or at a specific historical moment, of how either the 'joined-upness' or the 'entrapment' are achieved. Since Hume,[2] the dominant view – first in the Anglo-Saxon world, and finally among most social scientists – has been that the web is primarily 'conventional' (as he would have said), or 'socially constructed' (as we would say today). In other words, we make it up. But why then is it so compelling and inescapable? And what connects our inner, personal worlds with the outer, public one?

To try to illustrate some of the issues, I ask the reader to imagine watching two films, in which the participants speak to each other, but in an unfamiliar language. I shall attempt to describe what is seen in the films as neutrally as possible, and then to anticipate the imaginary viewer's probable interpretation.

In the first film, a woman is digging up potatoes with a kind of mattock, and a young girl is picking them up and putting them in a hessian sack. The soil is lumpy and wet; it sticks to their boots. They wear simple clothes, and their limbs, which are caked with mud, look raw. After a while, they go to a dwelling, open a low door and enter a kitchen. They wash their hands at a sink. They then peel and cut up the potatoes, cook them and add them to a kind of soup or stew, which is simmering on the stove. Finally they sit down at a table and eat the meal, along with pieces of coarse bread.

There is, I would dare to suggest, little problem in the 'joined-upness' of this scenario; the fact that we cannot understand the words they say does little to limit our comprehension of what is happening. The woman and girl may be mother and daughter, or they may not; the father may be out at work, absent, abroad or dead. But clearly there is an assumed coherence and internal necessity in their joint actions, which tends to be confirmed by the sequence of digging, cooking and eating. The whole film seems to reflect a linked set of rational actions, under the constraint of natural necessity (the laws of nature, as they affect horticulture, and the laws of economics, as they concern subsistence production).

Furthermore, the sense of coherence and 'joined-upness' is reinforced by certain continuities of texture, tempo and mood in the film – the lumpiness of the soil, the potatoes and the soup; the steam of the women's breath and the cooking; the coarseness of the hessian sack and the bread; the slow beat of the mattock and the rhythm of the peeling knives; the stoic quality of the work and lifestyle. It is difficult to resist the conclusion that these are rather poor people, living in a less-developed economy or on the far fringes of an affluent one.

In the second film, a man stands in an airport lounge, talking into a mobile phone. He is dressed in smart casual clothes. He boards the plane, and it takes off. He reads some papers in a purposeful way, before turning to the in-flight magazine. The plane lands. He is greeted by a good-looking woman of about his age. They leave the airport building and go to her small, shiny, new car. She drives him from the anonymous outskirts to the historic centre of the city. She parks the car, and they enter a large building and take the lift. She opens the door of a flat. It is bright and well-appointed. He pours two glasses of white wine. They make love.

My point about the second film is that, although there is no obvious coherence or internal necessity about this sequence of events, we are (I would suggest) just as able to 'follow' (or make up) the story and to experience it as natural and rational.[3] Even though it is quite unclear whether this man is on a business trip, a holiday or indulging in sex tourism; whether the woman is his long-term partner, or someone he has 'met' through the internet; or whether they are fellow nationals, associates or strangers – we provide these links almost involuntarily. Furthermore, the people in this film are identifiable (if not identifiable *with*) all over the world. They are, after all, the people in TV advertisements for mobile phones, airlines, compact cars, wines, electric razors, perfumes, deodorants, etc.

But it is not only because of our familiarity with TV adverts for these products that we seem to recognize who these people are and can make sense of what they are doing. They are cultural types (or stereotypes), embodying standards to which we are supposed to aspire and (often in spite of ourselves) somehow do. Unlike the women in the first film, they are not acting under necessity, either natural (climate, soil, growing cycle) or economic (the requirements of subsistence). We can make up a coherence in the vague and disparate elements of the story *because we understand that the man and the woman in the film are making one up for themselves*. They are constructing their identities, their projects and their relationship by choosing from a number of alternative products, air routes, cities, dwellings and other potential sexual partners. It is only by recognizing them as autonomous, mobile agents, acting through choices rather than obeying traditions, customs and rules or the laws of nature and survival, that we can make sense of the film.

What's more, this is not simply a reflection of the commercialization of lifestyles in affluent societies.[4] Imagine that this is not a glossy advertisement, but an 'art' film, deliberately shot in a more grainy, jerky or disjointed, non-sequential way. One of the many differences would be that the continuity, through consumption of items within a particular package of marketed products, would be played down. And this in turn might be reflected in the music accompanying the film. In the advertisement, it would be chosen to heighten awareness of the combined effects of those products, their association with each other, and the desirable features of the lifestyle. In the art film it would be more likely to emphasize the contrasts of pace, mood and emotion between the artificial, metallic, air-conditioned discomfort of the plane flight, the baroque splendour of the city of destination and the sensual intimacies of the sex scene.

Yet these contrasts would probably enhance rather than diminish our capacity to make sense of the story. After all, it takes a good deal of suspension of disbelief to see aeroplanes or city traffic lanes as opportunities for glamorous self-display, or the expression of personal identity. Only the airport encounter and the sexual coupling achieve the necessary links in the advertisement. If the man arrived only to catch another plane, and then another, or got stuck in a traffic jam in the city, the message for consumers might get rather lost. But in the art film, there would be no need to try to forge these connections between commodities, autonomy and emotional fulfilment. The links between freedom, movement, self-development and the reciprocities of sexual release would seem self-evident.

Because it corresponds to a set of linked cultural standards about mainstream people's lives in affluent societies, the second film thus generates its own coherence. But there are also some potentially disturbing aspects of what is joined up in this process, and what is not. We almost automatically assume that the two films are about people who are unrelated to each other – who occupy different circuits of the social world. But what if the older woman in the first film was in fact the wife of the man in the second one, or the sister of his sexual partner? Immediately, moral problems, seemingly absent from the second scenario, make a dramatic entry to the piece.

More generally, on reflection, the links which make the second film's sequence of interactions seem both natural and rational are almost too compelling. They leave too little room for other distractions, excursions or diversions. It becomes all too predictable that, when they rise the next morning, the man and the woman will – either jointly or separately – go out to clinch a business deal, or satisfactorily complete a professional contract. They will then celebrate their individual or associated successes with a meal in a tasteful restaurant, and so on. It is not just that we are conditioned to expect these further developments by advertisements for other products (computer software, business systems, banks); it is also because we know that these are the things that autonomous, mobile, self-developmental people do, in pursuit of their agendas. And also that the world is organized in such a way as to facilitate precisely those processes and outcomes.

In other words, the coherence of the second film reflects something about the web of present-day life which is more stable and structured than the other 'made-up' features of its linkages. The organizations through which the protagonists are able to travel, meet, make love, strike deals and dine out to celebrate are not randomly disposed; they form a kind of order, which spreads across national boundaries. Yet for all that has been written about globalization and the international institutions which sustain it, there is still much to be explained about how personal choice, group affiliation, collective action, economic strategy and political coalition reinforce and consolidate each other, and how they exclude and disempower other forms of social organization.

Above all, what I shall analyse and try to account for are the processes through which these forces combine to make certain ways of thinking and acting compelling, both in the sense of providing strong psychological, social and economic motives for adhering to their precepts and following their pathways, and in that of denying possibilities for coherent opposition or alternative strategy. It feels natural and rational to talk the talk and walk the walk of that culture and its order. By contrast, resistance to it is difficult to articulate; opponents have to struggle for coherence and a clear vision.

It is not that this resistance lacks numerical support or commitment. George Monbiot describes the European Social Forum in Paris on 16 November 2003, in which more than 50,000 mostly young people gathered in some 300 meetings to seek strategies for transforming politics. Although they were united in tracing the injustices they challenged to globalization and capitalism, Manbiot acknowledges the problems of connecting up the fragmented elements of the opposition to these forces in convincing ways, and putting forward a coherent replacement for them:

> By the end of it, I was as unconvinced by my own answers as I was by everyone else's. While I was speaking, the words died in my mouth, as it struck me with horrible clarity that as long as incentives to cheat exist (and they always will) none of our alternatives could be applied universally without totalitarianism.[5]

So this, then, is the really compelling aspect of the web in which we, as participants in affluent, mainstream global culture, live our lives. However much we may deplore the exclusive, unjust consequences of the new world order, and especially the military imposition of 'regime change' on selected states for dubious reasons, we cannot break into (or out of) the tightly sealed links of that web. In particular, the freedoms we prize, even when they are hypocritically defended by our leaders, seem superglued to other ambiguous or unacceptable elements of that order.

What's more, we are struck by a paradox about the relationship between the 'made-up' (interpersonal) and the organized (institutional) elements in the web. Under the previous global order – the stand-off between US-led liberal democracy and Soviet-style socialism, and a world made up of quasi-autonomous nation-states – 'freedom' on the one hand and 'equality' on the other were presumed to be the dispensations of governments. The everyday lives of citizens were regulated by laws, providing frameworks of restraint and fields for cooperation. In that culture, the interpersonal order was assumed to be derived from *rules* (even state socialism presupposed a kind of proletarian 'morality'), which ran parallel to the official rules of the political system. People might not have always done the right thing (in fact they probably seldom did); but we presumed that things worked the way they did because of a known set of principles for doing things right. The political order was supposed to be related to the moral rules.

Nowadays, most commentators and theorists agree that our decisions and actions are, and should be, *choices*; and that these are not derived from stable moral or political traditions. They emphasize the extent to which we make up our own order to fit our personal development and our preferences for public services. Part of what it is to be aware and responsible beings, in charge of our destinies, is constantly and actively to reinterpret the principles which guide our relationships with partners, parents, children, friends and associates, and to reshape the values which sustain the political community. Whether the authors celebrate or deplore these transformations, they see them as characteristic of the culture shift which ushered in the present order. Here, Anthony Giddens and Ulrich Beck give slightly different versions of the transition to 'individualized', 'intimate' and 'post-traditional' social relations, but ones which share these themes.

> The self is seen as a reflexive project for which the individual is responsible. . . . We are, not what we are, but what we make of our-

selves. . . . [W]hat the individual becomes is dependent on the reconstructive endeavours in which she or he engages. . . . The moral thread of self-actualisation is one of *authenticity* . . . based on 'being true to oneself.' . . . The morality of authenticity skirts any universal moral criteria, and includes references to other people only within the sphere of intimate relationships. . . . In contrast to close personal ties in traditional contexts, the pure relationship is not anchored in external conditions of social or economic life – it is, as it were, free-floating. . . . [S]elf-identity is negotiated through linked processes of self-exploration and the development of intimacy with the other. Such processes help create 'shared histories' of a kind more tightly bound than those characteristic of individuals who share experiences by virtue of a common social position.[6]

The individualization of political conflicts and interests does not mean disengagement. . . . Instead, a contradictory multiple engagement is emerging, which mixes and combines the classical poles of the political spectrum so that . . . everyone thinks and acts as a right-winger *and* left-winger, radically *and* conservatively, democratically *and* undemocratically . . . politically *and* unpolitically, all at the same time.[7]

The obvious question arising from these assertions is how such a do-it-yourself, pick-and-mix version of morality and politics can have any binding force on its participants at all. Yet the claim these authors make, and the paradox of our own experience, are that this binding force is in some ways more compelling than that of the older, rule-based order. The rather convoluted language of these quotations describes this paradox without explaining it.

I shall argue that the compelling power of the new order results from the mutually reinforcing actions of interpersonal and institutional elements. In less pompous terms, this means that the way we communicate with each other informally, both verbally and non-verbally, confirms and validates what we experience and do as members of formal groups and organizations, and vice versa. What's more, I shall argue that this mutual confirmation and validation happens in a very particular way, which makes it specially convincing. It follows a kind of formula which – like some potent spell, passed down by our earliest ancestors – exerts a binding force upon us. We seem almost instinctively to recognize the effects of this elixir (just as we know when we have fallen in love, or struck the perfect shot), and this explains its powerful hold over us. We also concede authority and dominion to leaders skilled in manipulating its components.

Let me try to make this abstraction more concrete by the example of my own present life. I spend many hours on public transport of various kinds and, being a sociable person except when in my darker moods, I tend to engage fellow-travellers in conversation. To launch into such exchanges is (at least in my case, and over a longish journey) to open up the possibility of having to give an account of oneself – who one is, where one is going and something about what one is doing there. Particularly if one initiates such a conversation (as is usually the case with me), the onus is on oneself to set the standard of disclosure, as it were. The other person, as respondent, is free to choose whether or not to reciprocate in their accounts. How far I get with my story depends, of course, on the interaction; only if there is an exchange do I perform the whole script.

I have heard myself do this so often (with some variations, I hope) that I can recognize the formula I follow, in trying to provide an engaging, coherent and morally adequate version of myself. As to who I am (apart from strenuous non-verbal exertions to communicate that I am *not* so old, tedious, intrusive or perverted as to cause the other person to change seats), this relies on some account of the family network in which I am embedded. I do my best to describe this tangle of fragmented and discordant relationships in a way which captures the more charming idiosyncrasies of its members and the more fascinating aspects of their grudges and quarrels, as well as the bonds which tie us all together. This is a story of how the sense of family survives (albeit in a somewhat battered form) through three generations of divorce and transcontinental migration. It is also one about how my partnership is rooted in a history of common endeavour, both in our work together as educators of social workers, and in our efforts to give something to children and grandchildren, despite its origins in my delinquency and defection. (The latter aspects are usually only hinted at, I must admit.)

In telling where I am going, I try to give a context that conveys me as someone always on the move, despite my rootedness in

family and farm (see pp. 7–8). This allows me to live up to the
cultural standard described at the beginning of this chapter; I am
pursuing a stimulating and challenging lifestyle, made up of personal choices from the available options, both in the UK and the
wider world. Because I am travelling second class (and now with
an older person's concession) it is important to give this aspect of
the story a democratic flavour. I am an academic, but when abroad
I always make sure I live in modest flats, in culturally diverse inner-
city districts. A few anecdotes can establish my credentials in these
respects, making my journeys seem slightly glamorous, without
being in any way ostentatious.

Since the research and teaching sides of these visits do little to
enhance these features of my accounts, I emphasize the freedom
(nay, licence) associated with the role of visiting professor. I dwell
on the opportunities for new friendships and cultural experiences,
and the aspects of the infrastructures of European cities which
facilitate these delights. I confirm with due modesty that my books
are known in these places, and that my visits stem from my contributions to global wisdom in the social sciences; but I prefer to
emphasize the informal elements of these experiences, and above
all the relationships to which they give rise. This is where my converted cowshed comes into the reckoning, because I can both
illustrate the enduring links created, through my visits, and give a
kind of overall coherence to the disparate elements in the whole
account. I give examples of the (mainly) young people (former
students, other friends, even those I have met on trains or planes)
who have since come to stay in this comfortable facility, thus
sealing the whole circuit of embeddedness and movement in my
story.

Whether or not this version of myself is convincing and morally
adequate, the important question is why I tell it in this particular
way – presumably I am trying to convince myself. It seems always
to take this form (if not necessarily be told in this order), because
the various parts are supposed to reinforce each other and to mesh
in a particular way. This is meant to describe and in some sense
reconcile elements of membership by blood and soil (family,
community and nation), elements of personal development (life
projects, commitments), aspects of wider *chosen* association or
belonging (networks, elective memberships), and economic path-

ways and outcomes (jobs, careers, investments). I shall argue that this combination is in turn required to be connected up in a formulaic pattern.

In the next two chapters, I shall try to trace the components of this formula, and to specify the exact relationships between them which supply the desired outcome. But the broad outlines of the formula I seek to identify are already clear. It addresses the central issue in the social sciences – the mutual influences of individual experience and action on the one hand, and the forms of collective life (cultures and organizations) generated by human groups on the other. Despite the huge variations in these over time, and between different parts of the world and sections of societies, there seem to be common patterns in the most influential theories and explanations, just as there is a recognizable pattern in my accounts of myself to strangers on long journeys. And the formulae for social scientific explanations and those for everyday stories have some important features in common.

The pattern is clearest in the work of those writing in the dawn of the modern era, before the social sciences split between psychology, sociology, economics and politics. At that time, philosophers were still also psychologists, sociologists, economists and political theorists. They did not conduct research in those subjects, but used a combination of introspection, observation, reading and speculation to draw together their analyses of and prescriptions for the changing social worlds in which they lived. Although writers like Machiavelli, Hobbes, Locke, Montesquieu, Hume, Rousseau and Adam Smith used 'evidence' which would not pass muster today, they insisted on combining data from history and 'anthropology' (viz. travellers' tales) with theoretical analysis in order to provide what they saw as convincing arguments and models.

In addition to these similarities of evidence and form, they also all dealt extensively in the problem of how the rivalrous, footloose, quarrelsome and self-sufficient ('private') aspects of human behaviour were reconciled with the cooperative, convivial, reciprocal and social ('public') aspects of communities. It seems that they were striving towards a kind of explanation for how this reconciliation was accomplished, which contained certain features:

1   A pattern of behaviour, or a social outcome, is produced by an
    institution, or set of institutions.
2   This pattern or outcome is beneficial for the individual
    members of a community.
3   The pattern or outcome was not intended by the actions of
    the individuals who initiated or participate in the institutions.
4   The fact that their actions produced the pattern or out-
    come is not recognized by the individual members of the
    community.
5   The institution sustains the pattern of outcome, through a
    'feedback loop', passing through the individual members, by
    their interactions.

The most famous example of this type of argument and demon-
stration is Adam Smith's 'invisible hand' account of the distributive effects of markets.[8] It goes:

1   The best possible distribution of resources is achieved by
    exchanges in markets.
2   This distribution is beneficial for all the members of society,
    even idle beggars.
3   This distribution is not intended by those who trade, since they
    intend only to benefit themselves.
4   Traders do not recognize that they are distributing resources
    in the best possible way.
5   The institution of markets sustains the efficient and fair dis-
    tribution of resources, through the insouciant interactions of
    traders, intent only on turning a penny.

Indeed, it is possible to see many of the features of this formula
in the analyses developed by other Renaissance and Enlightenment philosophers, as if they were attempting, not always successfully, to bring off such an explanation. For instance, Hobbes's
version of the origins of political authority, Locke's of the invention of money, Montesquieu's of the effects of the emotions ('passions') on the conduct of government, Hume's and Rousseau's
of the part played by sexual pleasure and procreation in getting
society started all prefigured aspects of Smith's invisible hand

explanation, and might be seen as early attempts – using similar kinds of evidence – at producing this sort of theory.[9]

It is also worth noting that this same formula has been recognized by three distinguished social theorists, Robert Merton, Jon Elster and Mary Douglas, as being requirements for a successful 'functionalist' explanation of social phenomena.[10] Although the first two were mainly concerned to show that most social scientists who have attempted such explanations (including Karl Marx) have failed to meet these requirements, Douglas argued that functionalist analyses are possible in many more cases than are widely recognized, and indeed are necessary to make sense of the interconnectedness of the social world.

In this book, I shall try to show that we all unconsciously attempt functionalist accounts of the way in which that world works, and our position within it. Furthermore, we tend to try to illustrate and embellish our versions with evidence of the kind brought forward by these philosophers. And in doing so, we tend to bear out their seeming conviction that the 'glue' in the web which reconciles the private and public elements in our experiences and in social arrangements is made up from sexual and emotional satisfactions, material rewards and the skilled actions of political leaders. In stark terms, by sex, money and power.

However, this is only one part of the kind of convincing story which social scientists seek. In addition to the formula, defining the way that story should be told, and the elements in it combined, there is also the equally important matter of how it is communicated between the partners in a conversational exchange, or between the members of a group. If what we are trying to understand is the *social bond*, then this aspect deserves at least as much attention.

To return to my long journeys by train and plane, the original purpose of starting up the conversation with my fellow-traveller was not to tell my life story, but to make a connection and initiate an exchange. This could not be achieved by reciting a version of myself, according to this formula or any other. Communication depends upon the artful threading together of accounts of a shared social world, in which the participants take turns to spin the web, both by recounting elements in their experiences and understandings which confirm or contradict those of the other participant(s), and in extending the jointly spun web to embrace other topics and fields.

Again, in looking back on innumerable such conversations, I am conscious that I offer parts of my story which I intuitively feel may have resonances with the other person's life, as an invitation for him or her to reciprocate, and to develop a version of their own. It is difficult to say exactly how I set out to do this, but I suppose that it is partly to do with having been a social worker for many years that I can tune in to others, on a number of non-verbal as well as verbal wavelengths, to pick up unspoken signals as well as spoken ones. This feels as if it is not so much a 'listening skill' (as it is pretentiously described in the professional literature) as a letting down of the barriers which all of us erect when in public or in the company of unchosen strangers. These barriers serve as defences against the remote possibility of being assailed by a stream of unwanted communications, about how Jesus knows and loves us, or concerning close encounters with beings from other planets.

Instead of protecting ourselves in these ways, we open up the possibility of reciprocal spinning, when each helps the other to develop aspects of their stories about how the world works. The conversation then soon becomes a cooperative enterprise, in which the building of a bond is an inescapable ingredient. Erving Goffman captured the ritual elements in such exchanges, in which the participants 'make and give face'.[11] They bestow social value upon each other by the way they accept and embellish each other's accounts of self. But all this is done within the frame of cultural standards and requirements,[12] of what it is to give an adequate account; they (we) use skills in improvisation and artful adhockery to fulfil the demands of such versions.

The art of having interesting conversations on trains is to establish reliable and secure enough boundaries between the selves which are being produced by these cooperative narratives, but also to maintain just enough ambiguity about one's identity and agenda to sustain communications beyond those of conventional exchanges. As in any other encounter with a stranger that may eventually lead to friendship, the trick is to be just indiscreet enough to be interesting but not alarming, and just idiosyncratic enough to be challenging but not threatening. In this way, the exchange may conjure up a special sort of milieu, with a kind of magical quality; at best, both can see themselves reflected back in an interesting, new and stimulating light, in which they take on lively and original personae. This is also dimly recognized as the product of the exchange itself so that each bestows upon the other a temporary charismatic aura.

It seems surprising that social bonds can be created out of nothing, as it were, and can arise from chance meetings such as those between fellow-travellers. In my experience this does happen; several people I have met on trains have become regular visitors, along with their families, to my converted cowshed.

There are some parallels between social scientific theories of how the private and the public aspects of human behaviour are reconciled and analyses of the social bond. Here the sociologist Thomas Scheff outlines his version of how bonds are created and sustained.

> My model of the social bond is based on the concept of *attachment*, mutual identification and understanding. A secure social bond means that the individuals involved identify with and understand each other, rather than misunderstand or reject each other. I assume that in all human contact, if bonds are not being built, maintained, or repaired, they are being damaged. That is to say that in every moment of contact, one's status relative to the other is continually being signalled, usually unintentionally. . . . Status-relevant verbal and nonverbal signs both signal and determine the state of the bond at any given moment. . . . Threats to a secure bond can come in two different formats; either the bonds are too loose or too tight. Relationships in which the bond is too loose are *isolated*: there is mutual misunderstanding or failure to understand, or mutual rejection. Relationships in which the bond is too tight are *engulfed*: at least one of the parties in the relationship, say the subordinate, understands and embraces the standpoint of the other at the expense of the subordinate's own beliefs, values or feelings.[13]

Here again, Scheff's theory describes a process by which individual emotions and experiences, and those of others, are balanced and reconciled through transactions which create and maintain social bonds. Scheff goes on to develop this model into an explanation of how much larger human collectives, including states, conduct their relationships in terms which mirror these processes and reflect hidden emotions such as rage and shame.[14] His theory is explicitly aimed at reconnecting the separated disciplines of the social sciences, to provide an integrated explanation of how practices, beliefs, judgements and emotions combine to create the 'habitus' of everyday life.[15]

However, this does not account for another dimension of this web, which has not been captured in my story so far. Although the interactions studied by Scheff create, sustain, damage and repair social bonds, they also somehow incorporate into such bonds aspects of the wider institutional world of organizations, the economy and politics. And in so doing they both change that institutional landscape[16] and, in turn, are changed by it.

This book is as much an attempt to analyse the transformation of collective life – of social, economic and political relations – as it is about how intimate and impersonal interactions join up the parts of global society. It attempts to show how the formula for giving convincing versions of the coherence of such relationships, and analyses of the emotionally laden transactions concerning social bonds, must also explain how change occurs at all levels. Ultimately, what we do in our everyday lives is linked into the great waves in the web which shape patterns like the mass migrations of population, and conflicts between power blocs, ethnic groups or religious faiths worldwide.

Social scientists who try to make these connections have very different interpretations of the great transformation of collective life which has taken place in the past twenty-five years. For Giddens, Beck and the other theorists of individualization, intimacy[17] and post-traditional relationships, equality and democratic negotiation, which are required to sustain closely bonded partnership and parenting in the new order of domestic life, spill over into the wider economy and polity. They create new forms of engagement and activism, and even what Ken Plummer calls 'intimate citizenship' (see pp. 30–1).[18]

Others take a much more pessimistic view. The equally eminent sociologist Zygmunt Bauman sees social bonds as consistently polluted and made more brittle and fragile by the commercialization of all aspects of collective life. Through this process, *desire* (the wish to consume everything outside the self, and thus annihilate it) replaces *love* (the wish to preserve, respect and care for the other).[19] Relationships which endure over time are analysed as business links or investments.[20] Although sexual desire 'remains the most obviously, unambiguously, unassailably *social*' of the 'natural' human propensities, consumerism has given it a calculative and exploitative form.[21]

In Bauman's account, the 'spilling over' comes from the institutional sphere into the intimate one, rather than the reverse process of Giddens's, Beck's and Plummer's models. Furthermore, it affects all aspects of human belonging, membership and sharing: 'the invasion and colonization of *communitas*, the site of the moral economy, by consumer market forces constitutes the most awesome of dangers threatening the present form of human togetherness.'[22]

But it is not obvious that traditional and communal forms of collective life were (and are) specifically *moral* in ways that deserve a principled defence. After all, the primary social bonds of past centuries – family, kin, clan, neighbourhood, religion, class and country – all stem from contingencies of birth, unchosen and fortuitous, and often sustained by coercion and violence. Blood, faith and soil can scarcely be presented as *ethical* bases for togetherness; they have historically provided the foundations of many forms of domination and exclusion, from patriarchy, through bigotry to chauvinism. If collective life is being transformed by sex and money, as Bauman claims, then this might well be for the better.

In a recent lament for the passing of the 'golden age of cultural theory', Terry Eagleton blames current scholarship's failure to address issues of morality and truth, preferring to deploy evidence from TV programmes to produce analyses which are 'centreless, hedonistic, self-inventing, ceaselessly adaptive':

Structuralism, Marxism, post-structuralism and the like are no longer the sexy topics they were. What is sexy instead is sex. On the wilder shores of academia an interest in French philosophy has given way to a fascination with French kissing. In some circles, the politics of masturbation exert far more fascination than the politics of the Middle East.[23]

My task in this book is to show how the everyday world of sex and TV advertisements is joined up with the politics of the Middle East, and how this shapes the choices open to both individuals and political leaders. These links are glimpsed through the changes which have transformed my own life, from being embedded in the practices of a British public service, to one of a European scholar-gypsy, with informal networks of friends and collaborators in many cities, maintained by email messages and occasional visits. Meanwhile, my contemporaries in my former professional life have mostly moved right out of social work or academic posts and into consultancy or entrepreneurship, often owning a house abroad, or relocating to a distant country.

These shifts have an economic as well as a personal-developmental logic, and the two reinforce each other, as I shall try to show in the later parts of the book. They reflect a social world made up of more mobile individuals, living for shorter spans in smaller units with chosen others, and grouping themselves in collectives which select through members' preferences and the subscriptions they charge, rather than through birth, proximity or nationality. This mobility and these groupings mean that political authority can no longer claim that its provision of the infrastructure for public life entitles it to rule, tax and mobilize individuals as it did in the past. The togetherness that can be created by sex, and the belonging that can be bought with money, meet many of the needs which used to be served by states.

But only for the lucky few. Although people whose lifestyles are based on moving and choosing set the cultural standard, the great mass of the world's population does not live in this way. The organizational structures which facilitate movement and choice for the global elite exclude them. Hence political authorities increasingly cannot sustain solidarities between the privileged and the poor, because the better-off escape their grasp. While new, commercial units provide the collective goods required for mobile, chosen lifestyles, new social movements and communal bonds join up hitherto separate groupings among the excluded majority.

On one night (20–21 November 2003), as the Israeli government was pressing on with its construction of the so-called fence to separate its citizens from Palestinian enclaves, rockets were fired from a donkey cart at an international hotel in Baghdad where an American envoy was staying; two suicide bombers wrecked an HSBC bank and the British Consulate in Istanbul; and a crowd of around 100,000 demonstrated against the visit of the US President in London. The ways in which these events were joined up, and how everyday life connects to regime change and privatization of the public infrastructure of Iraq, will be the challenges for the analysis presented in this book.

2

Intimate Connections

The idea that sex connects the private world of our fantasies, feelings and experiences with the public, social order is a paradox. 'Intimacy theory',[1] as it has come to be known, holds that new kinds of sexual relationship, involving dialogue between equal partners, give rise to a vital and democratic political culture. As Giddens claims:

> There are remarkable parallels between what a good relationship looks like, as developed in the literature of marital and sexual therapy, and formal mechanisms of political democracy. . . . Dialogue, free from the use of coercion, and occupying a 'public space', is in both cases the means, not just of settling disputes, but of creating an atmosphere of mutual tolerance.[2]

At first glance, this idea seems self-contradictory. The word 'intimacy', apart from being a euphemism for sexual intercourse, denotes the closely personal.[3] It has associations, if not of secrecy, then at least with veils of decency and privacy. Yet Giddens is certainly not alone amongst present-day social theorists in arguing that sex links the personal with the public sphere.[4] For example, Ken Plummer somewhat breathlessly contends that this new version of sexuality (and especially gay and lesbian sexuality) can join up the erotic experiences of individuals with equity in political relations.

> At base, I want to argue that the new politics has one major axis in gender/sexual/erotic politics, and that the workings of such politics is heavily dependent upon the kinds of stories invented about intimacy within it. . . . Moving out of silence, the stories helped

shape a new public language, generating communities to receive and disseminate them on a global scale, ultimately creating more and more spaces for them to be heard. All this must be seen as political – as empowering.[5]

The fact that we are able to think and talk about sex at all implies that we use resources from public language, symbols and culture to connect our deepest sensations with the lives of others. Giddens, Plummer and colleagues argue that this joins up the intimate with the political, specifically the democratic and egalitarian features of the public sphere. They imply that sex is linked to morality and politics in a direct, unilinear, rational, causal way.

But any adult connections between sex and the public world must be made up, at least partly, from our earlier, childhood understandings. In our attempts to make sense of these strange bits of our body, so easily sensitized and so directly connected with our inner worlds of emotion and fantasy, we can then only draw on our immediate relationships, and some media representations. Just how confusing these can be, and what an idiosyncratic form our interpretations may take, will be clear from my own example.

Because my parents were away, involved in the war effort in London, I was brought up for the first three years of my life by my maternal grandparents, who owned a small, private boarding school on the outskirts of Dublin. It was with them that I made my first emotional attachments. They were cast in the neo-Hegelian mould – committed to a serious-minded quest for public virtue and service. From them I learned that all else, including one's personal fantasies and follies, must be subsumed under an ethic of duty, justice and citizenship. The life of the body was one of quasi-religious (Greek Stoic in my grandfather's case, Anglican in my grandmother's) physical activity, especially in horticulture and sport. (My grandfather represented Ireland at cricket, as did his brother, who also played international rugby. They contrived to look like Gary Cooper, but thought and acted like T. H. Green or the young Clement Attlee).

As they were busy running the school, my everyday needs were met by the domestic and care staff – young and robust Irishwomen, who used to take me for long walks by the sea in my pram (despite my subsequent athleticism, I do not appear to have walked much until my fourth year). That there were some sexual fantasies involved in these experiences is indicated by the fact that I obsessively carried with me, not a teddy bear or a rabbit, but a cutting from a local newspaper advertising women's underwear, and known as 'the Brawnies'. This was a subject of much mirth among my minders; on a memorable occasion, one of them reported that 'a gust of wind blew them blessed Brawnies away, and I was after chasing them along the promenade, with himself crying his eyes out'. (Did they just tease me and giggle among themselves, or did they actually physically tweak me? Either way, I am convinced that these were the original objects of my desires, the minders as much as the Brawnies, and the pictures elided with the people.)

In my early school years, the fashionable films (like *South Pacific*) were often set in the Polynesian Islands and my sexual fantasies – which were many – embraced the female inhabitants of this exotic location. Somehow the Celtic merged with the Pacific to make up my prepubescent ideal of female physical desirability. And remarkably, in Shaftesbury (population 3,470) ten years later, I found myself a girlfriend, later wife, of Anglo-Scottish ethnicity, but who had spent her childhood in the South Seas and looked like a figure from a painting by Gauguin in his Tahitian period.

Finally, there was my relationship with my parents, who took over my care towards the end of the war. From my earliest recollections, I perceived in their partnership a powerful sexual chemistry, which might (and eventually did) totally subvert their lives in the public sphere of work and society. From this I concluded that sex was a combustible material, to be kept in a special (private, often secret) container.

All these connections and interpretations were arbitrary and contingent on my circumstances. They joined up the visceral experiences of bonding and loss, the confused sensations and fantasies of involuntary sexuality, and the public and political life of that period. Comparing notes with my brother, who was born seven years later in South Africa, I find that his view of sex was based on quite different elements and interpretations. In later chapters, I shall return to the parental, family and community contributions, to our identities, our projects of self and our intimate relationships. In this chapter and the next, I shall focus on how sex links our inner worlds with the economy and polity.

Surprisingly there is a long and distinguished literature of philosophical theory which asserts that sex has provided an indispensable ingredient, both in the evolution of human institutions for order and governance and in reconciling individual striving for autonomy with the restraints of social organization. Indeed, if theorists through the ages are to be believed, sex has been an essential element in social innovation, stabilization and cohesion. As society developed, it supplied the enzymes for change, the emulsion to standardize culture and the adhesive for collective units.

In this chapter I shall show that Hume and Rousseau, in particular, gave a central role to sex in their accounts of these features of the social world. Sex joined up their stories of how society got started; it also played an important part in Hume's explanation of the social order of his day. I shall demonstrate that the arguments they used to elaborate their theories displayed the features of the functionalist formula (see pp. 21–3). In one instance, Hume pulled off a successful example of the formula, to explain how human beings reconciled their innate rivalry with their unique vulnerability as a species, through the sexual bond.

This will not simply be an exercise in intellectual archaeology. These arguments provide a template for the requirements of a convincing model of how sex connects up the private aspects of individual experience with the public, institutional sphere. If Hume and Rousseau could use sexual relationships as part of the key to resolving the paradox of the 'joined-upness' and 'entrapment' of individual life within the web of culture and structure, then they set standards as well as challenges for those attempting to make these links today.

However, we should not suppose that Hume's and Rousseau's versions, even if they are successful examples of the functionalist formula, provide explanations which can be convincing for us today. First, their arguments reflected the shortcomings of current anthropological evidence about the earliest human communities. Many of their speculations were surprisingly accurate, but others were not. Second, they both projected issues in their current societies back into the past and imagined that cultural conventions of their age were more universal than they turned out to be. So neither their explanations of simple societies nor their theories of contemporary social relations can convince readers in our era.

This shows that the links between the intimacies of sex, on the one hand, and the public sphere of civil associations, economics and politics, on the other, are contingent and constantly changing. While it seems always to be true that individuals, in their erotic couplings, drag down the collective institutions of the public world into bed with them, and that they spring (or drag themselves) up from these exertions to go back into that public world as newly minted agents for change, both the dragging down and the bouncing back take remarkably varied forms in various cultural contexts. Sex really does mean different things for people in different cultures.

For example, as anyone who has been an attentive member of the audience for the opera *Rigoletto* is aware, sex in the Italian Renaissance made strong connections with the institutions of violent, invasive, male power. At the court where Rigoletto is the jester, strutting young bucks compete to deflower virgins; sex is about ritual humiliation and subordination, as part of a struggle for ascendancy within the masculine group. Rigoletto's protectiveness of his daughter, her seduction, and his revenge – all are enactments of the links between sex and domination.

Sex was also one of the means of aristocratic rule, through which families maintained honour and reputation as well as power. In rivalry between princes, nobles and dynasties, sex was not simply part of the politics of alliance and enmity or the accumulation of territory; it was also a way of creating and maintaining a reputation for ruthlessness, terror and calculative cruelty. But the physical and emotional content of sex must have been experienced as some kind of combination of all these elements and the gentler, kinder pleasures. In his classic account, Jacob Burckhardt described the code of intimacy as follows:

The novelists and comic poets give us to understand that love consists not only in sensual enjoyment, and that to win this, all means,
tragic or comic, are not only permitted, but are interesting in proportion to their audacity and unscrupulousness. But if we turn to
the best of the lyric poets and writers of dialogues, we find them
in a deep and spiritual passion of the noblest kind and whose
last and highest expression is a revival of the ancient belief in
an original unity of souls in the Divine Being. And both modes
of feeling were then genuine, and could coexist in the same
individual.[6]

In practice, not only was murder an accepted remedy for a
deceived husband or lover, but women too poisoned partners to
be free to make more desirable matches, as happened in the Borgia
dynasty. Violence and revenge were part of a culture of sexual
intrigue, in which infidelity was a necessary feature of the building of both fame and notoriety. Sadism was valued in its own right.

In Sigismondo Malatesa, tyrant of Rimini, the same disinterested
love of evil may also be detected. It is not only the Court of Rome,
but the verdict of history, which credits him of murder, rape,
adultery, incest, sacrilege, perjury and treason, committed not
once but often. The most shocking crime of all – the unnatural
attempt on his own son Roberto, who frustrated it with his
drawn dagger – may have been the result not merely of moral corruption, but perhaps some magical or astrological superstition. The
same conjecture has been made to account for the rape of the
Bishop of Fano by Pierluigi Farnese of Parma, son of [Pope] Paul
III.[7]

In other words, it seems that sex connected Italian Renaissance
people to an institutional order of ritual religious as well as aristocratic power, and was (among other things) an instrument of
the brutal domination of the linked hierarchies of church and
state, in this whole order. If social scientific theory is to try to
analyse the connections between intimacy, economics and politics, it has set itself a challenging task.

Hume and Rousseau, on the other hand, posed for themselves
a deceptively simple conundrum – how human beings made the
transition from being solitary savages to socialized members of

orderly communities. This is the still-fundamental question of how collective institutions, providing shared understandings, ways of resolving conflicts and restraints on unilateral individual action (cheating, breaking rank), ever get off the ground.[8] It is worth examining Hume's solution and the part played by sex in it, in some detail. I paraphrase.

Human beings, he argues, face a problem which is not encountered by other animals, whose physical characteristics equip them for survival in the natural world. Lions, for instance, need a lot of calorific meat to sustain their muscular bodies and proactive leonine lifestyles; but fortunately they have huge, sharp teeth and claws, and can move swiftly over the ground for short distances. Oxen, on the other hand, are even more bulky; but they have two different advantages. First, their mode of existence is a more laid-back, cud-chewing, stand-and-stare one. Second, they have easy access to a very generous supply of sufficiently nutritious grass and leaves, to sustain this way of life.

The diet required by humans for their subsistence lies somewhere between that of lions and oxen. They are predators, but their physique is relatively puny, and their swiftness comparatively limited. They are also born helpless, naked and exposed to the elements. Hence they need to cooperate, to hunt, build shelters, make clothes, raise their young, and so on. Worst of all, human beings are sufficiently self-aware to be rivalrous over the resources for survival, but not rational enough to set up the enduring systems of cooperation required for complex tasks. They could not, in that savage condition, supply themselves with good enough reasons to give up their individual, competitive strategies, in favour of a cooperative one.

> in order to form society, 'tis requisite not only that it be advantageous, but that men be sensible of its advantages; and 'tis impossible, in their wild and uncultivated state, that by study and reflexion alone, they should ever be able to attain this knowledge.[9]

Hume spells out the general problem in explaining the origins of all collective institutions – that individuals' stake in their own autonomy is too great, in the situation before these come into existence, to surrender part of it to restrictive communal order.

Like the savages he is describing, Hume is stuck, because his philosophical method denies him an easy cop-out. The first principle for his investigation of 'human nature' was that all impressions and ideas were derived from the senses, and hence that reason alone could never supply motives for action. Hence 'reason is and ought only to be the slave of the passions, and can never pretend to any other office than to serve and obey them'[10] – a point of view not dissimilar from the one advanced by the neurologist Damasio in recent years.[11] How can the emotions arising from a competitive, individual struggle for survival give rise to collective forms of life, which he insists are 'artificial' (made up by these people themselves), and based on 'conventions', sustained through 'education' (socialization, participation in that culture)?

What then, in the rudimentary instincts which Hume allows himself to attribute to our ancestors, gets him off this hook? Answer: sex, 'the first and original principle of society'.[12] People need other people, for that if nothing else. 'This necessity is no other than the natural appetite between the sexes, which unites them together, and preserves their union, till a new tye takes place in their concern for their common offspring.'[13]

Hume has thus shown how our savage forebears made up the family, the first social institution and the first building block of societies. He has explained how Stone Age men, following only their passions and not able to reason about the remote benefits of such a conventional arrangement, were turned into reasonably reliable providers for their partners and children. And his explanation follows the functionalist formula identified in chapter 1.

1 Reliable cooperation is a result of stable sexual partnerships.
2 Reliable cooperation benefits individual human beings.
3 Individuals do not intend reliable cooperation when they seek sexual partners; they act out of lust, and love for their resultant offspring.
4 Individuals are not aware that sex and providing for children gives rise to reliable cooperation.
5 Stable partnership sustains reliable cooperation through the sexual coupling of partners and their subsequent care for their children.

Whatever the merits of Hume's anthropology (which are not many on this particular point), this is a clear example of an analysis which uses sex as the link between the private emotions and isolated survival activities of hunter-gatherers, and the public forms of their collective institutions. It is also the first step in his explanation of more complex aspects of social arrangements, and ultimately of the whole structure of morality and politics. His real target is to explain how *property* came into existence, but sex provides the link between private and public which makes this possible. Hume uses the same formula as in his lust-procreation-provision argument to account for individuals' eventual respect for others' ownership of their material possessions.

Hume aims to show that *justice*, that complex system of connected moral rules and political laws, is an 'artificial virtue', resting on the conventions through which property ownership is stabilized and government established. There are four problems here to be overcome. First, people are 'insatiably avid' for material possessions. Second, the history of possession is one of violent seizure, theft, fraud and war. Third, there are many possible titles to possession, including occupation, gift, promise, inheritance and so on. Fourth, although individuals have an interest in granting secure ownership rights to family, clan or friends, these loyalties to small groups actually *increase* the likelihood of conflict *between* such groups in a larger community. 'Limited benevolence', based mainly on sexual and family bonds, actually reduces the chances of getting 'general benevolence' established, because such groups are prone to fight each other for resources. 'It is only a general sense of common interest, which sense all members of the society express to one another, and which induces them to regulate their conduct by certain rules.'[14]

Once again, Hume attempts the functionalist formula to explain how these problems are overcome.

> I observe, that it will be for my interest to leave another in the possession of his goods, *provided* he will act in the same manner with regard to me. He is sensible of a like interest in relation to his conduct. When this common sense of interest is mutually expressed, and is known to both, it produces a suitable resolution and behaviour. . . . [I]t *is only from the selfishness and confin'd gen-*

erosity of men, along with the scanty provision nature has made for
his wants, that justice derives its origin.[15] (Emphasis in original)

In other words:

1 Institutions for justice and good government result from
   people granting each other entitlements to property, under
   guarantees of reciprocal security.
2 All individuals and groups in society benefit from institutions
   for justice and good government.
3 When individuals agree to respect each other's property rights,
   they do not intend to establish institutions for justice and good
   government; they act from motives of selfishness, to protect
   the possessions of themselves and their kin.
4 Individuals who act out of these selfish motives are unaware
   of the consequences, in terms of institutions for justice and
   good government.
5 Reciprocal guarantees of security sustain institutions for
   justice and good government, and are upheld by individuals
   and groups acting merely to protect their possessions.

This is not so convincing as an explanation compared with the
first example concerning sex, or with Adam Smith's invisible hand
account of the connections between distributive outcomes and
markets. It seems unlikely that individuals and groups are completely unaware that reciprocal granting of entitlements and
secure ownership of property will lead to something like justice
and good government, and do not intend it. Hume's claim that
they are acting for purely selfish motives and out of a limited view
of others' interests sounds like special pleading. It is significant
that he takes this line. Partly, of course, he is arguing the con-
tentious view that justice is artificial and conventional rather than
derived from a natural or supernatural law. But partly also, I claim,
he is striving (too hard) to produce a convincing version of the
functionalist formula.
    But there is another weakness in this whole model of how the
web of collective institutions came to be spun and how it holds
us in its meshes. This concerns the linked problems of sexual
rivalry and sexual fidelity. Hume tries to persuade us that sex is

the glue which seals the original social bond, and that the 'natural' urge for sex is the same as the 'natural' urge for procreation. This in turn, he argues, leads spontaneously and inexorably to another 'natural' bond – the love of parents for their children. So Hume's whole account of the origins of society, which allows his explanation of property rights, justice and government to make sense, rests on a set of connections between 'instincts' which we would strongly question today.

Hume was aware of some aspects of this hole in his argument, and tried to deal with them later in the *Treatise*. However, I shall now analyse Rousseau's version, because he was much more willing to confront the issues of sexual rivalry and infidelity. I shall return to Hume's explanation of the relative stability of family units later.

Rousseau recognized that, in order to account for the emergence of stable sexual partnership, and patterns of cooperation, sharing and mutual provision in families, he had to explain the transition from 'savage sex' to 'domesticated sex' (sex practised in the security of a family culture). Unlike Hume, he saw that this meant demonstrating how the promiscuity of sexual liaisons in the savage state of nature was transformed into something quite different: sex as the glue for a conventional social bond. This involved a more sophisticated analysis of how sex linked the private world of the emotions with the public forms of social organization.

Rousseau's savages are (as everyone knows) completely autonomous and, like the noble beasts of the wild woods, accountable to no one. They survive in the absence of any collective infrastructure of morals, or any coercive system of government. And their sexual activities reflect this freedom. Because there is no regulatory framework to restrain or mould the expression of sexual appetites, they are able 'quietly [to] await the impulses of nature, yield to them involuntarily, with more pleasure than ardour, and, their wants satisfied, lose their desire'.[16]

Here again, the social relationships expressed through the sexual act are those of the public world – or in this case, the absence of any collective forms. Because individuals are free and natural, sex is free and natural. (By contrast, we might reflect, in a complex society it takes a great deal of effort, contrivance and regulation to produce a social environment in which promiscuity is the norm, such as the 'swingers' clubs' which flourish in affluent countries.[17])

For Rousseau, the transition from the isolated individual hunter-gatherer's life to the formation of cooperative groups was gradual, ad hoc and low-key. 'Loose associations' formed and dissolved, only slowly taking on any regular patterns, as they began to undertake common tasks of hunting, construction and defence against natural threats. He insists that emotions such as 'love' and 'fidelity' were the *products* of these social interactions, rather than modifications of instinctual drives. Hence the first forms of domesticated sexual activity derived directly from the new infrastructures for everyday life, and the politics of these shared facilities:

> The first expansions of the human heart were the effects of a novel situation, which united husbands and wives, fathers and children, under one roof. The habit of living together soon gave rise to the finest feelings known to humanity, conjugal love and paternal affection. Every family became a little society, the more united because liberty and reciprocal attachment were the only bonds of its union.[18]

Here again we find an example of the functionalist formula, to explain the transition from individual autonomy to a collective form of life, and the role of sex in this process. But in this case, sexual experience is as much what is transformed as what accomplishes the transformation. According to Rousseau:

1 A free and loving association between partners is the consequence of domestic living in a society without unequal property or coercive government.
2 Free and loving associations benefit individual men and women and their children.
3 Men and women did not intend to create 'little societies' of this kind; they were just sheltering together from bad weather.
4 Men and women were not aware that they had created 'little societies' of this kind.

5 Domestic living by families maintained and strengthened free and harmonious associations, simply through the fact that men and women went on building shelters of this kind, and living in them as families.

However, whereas Hume's purpose was to explain how property, good government and institutions for justice could emerge spontaneously from the unplanned and uncoerced actions of our savage ancestors, Rousseau's was quite different. He wanted to explain how inequality, oppression and violent conflict were not consequences of human nature, but of societies with unequal property holdings and unequal distributions of power. Therefore he needed a third stage of evolution, in which not only economic and political relations, but also sexual relations, underwent another transformation – in this case, a corruption.

With the emergence of societies with wealth and poverty, slavery and exploitation, war and tyranny, Rousseau described a pattern of rivalry, shame, rage and revenge, which might have been taken from Burckhardt's account of the Italian Renaissance:

> the jealousy of lovers and the vengeance of husbands are the daily cause of duels, murders and even worse crimes; where the obligation of eternal fidelity only occasions adultery, and the very laws of honour and continence necessarily increase debauchery and lead to the multiplication of abortions.[19]

This might be described as a *dysfunctionalist* formula; sexual conflict and demoralization are explained in terms of the corruption of unequal property and power.

1 A state of perpetual conflict between individuals is a result of exploitation in economic relations, and domination in political relations.
2 A state of perpetual conflict is bad for all individuals in a society.
3 Those who conduct sexual intrigues and vendettas do not intend to undermine society; they are merely trying to uphold their reputation and honour.

4   Those who conduct sexual intrigues and vendettas are not
    aware that they are undermining society; they are just trying
    to uphold what they see as high standards in public life.
5   Exploitation and domination constantly maintain a state of
    conflict, which is in turn reinforced by the everyday actions of
    scheming and vengeful individuals.

In this analysis, Rousseau anticipated some of the arguments put
forward by Marx a hundred years later, and the kinds of critical
theories developed in the latter half of the twentieth century
(including Bauman's and Fevre's demoralization theories).[20]
Hume, by contrast, was required to try to explain how the stability of domestic life, which he saw as deriving from human instincts
for sexual satisfaction, procreation and the protection of children,
survived the transition into complex societies, competitive market
economies and regulatory government systems. How did institutions which evolved under Stone Age conditions survive in early
modern ones?

Hume's solution is rather sophisticated, witty and elegant. First,
he defines the problem of sexual rivalry and infidelity in line with
his original assumptions about human nature. Individual men and
women are programmed, as it were, to want sex, to want to produce
children, and to love *their* children. But they are not programmed
to love *anyone else's* children. The problem of rivalry and infidelity
can be stated quite simply, in terms of human biology. Every woman
knows with absolute certainty which children are *her* children,
because they emerge into the world out of her body. But no man
can know with any certainty which children are his, because of the
gaps in time and space between sexual intercourse, conception and
birth. Why then should men continue to be reliable breadwinners
and protectors of women and children, once they enter complex
societies, with their notorious opportunities for infidelity? And why
should women be faithful, when so many occasions for sexual pleasure, and so many (often more attractive) partners become available to them in such societies?

Hume's answer is that the temptations for the defection by
husbands and fathers, and for promiscuity by women, can only be
reduced to manageable proportions by conventions which achieve
the kind of stability and wide acceptance of 'laws of nature'. The

conventions in question concern the 'natural' modesty and chastity of women. If it comes to be generally accepted that women are by their natures chaste, modest and faithful, then Stone Age domestic institutions can survive in thriving commercial cities, like London and Edinburgh.

In fact, as Hume insists, women are no more 'naturally' modest, chaste and faithful than men. He is quite clear that women are 'naturally' lustful and licentious, just as men are. But the convention works well enough to guarantee acceptable stability.

Hume thinks this is achieved by the education and socialization of women, and the patriarchal role of men. He does not endorse or approve either of these – he simply uses them to achieve his explanation of the contemporary relationship between domesticated sex and the collective order of his society:

> What restraint, therefore, shall we impose on women, in order to counterbalance so strong a temptation as they have to infidelity? . . . [W]e must attach a peculiar degree of shame to their infidelity, above what arises merely from its injustice, and must bestow proportionable praises on their chastity.[21]

Hume considers that this combination of convention and socialization has naturalized the notion that women have 'a repugnance to all expressions and postures, and liberties, that have an immediate relation to that enjoyment [of illicit sex]'.[22] His analysis might be formulated as an attempted functionalist explanation as follows:

1   In complex societies, family stability is a consequence of the norms of chastity and modesty among women.
2   All men and women, and especially children, benefit from family stability.
3   Individual men and women do not intend to achieve family stability; they just come to believe that women really are naturally chaste and modest.
4   Individual men and women are unaware that women really aren't chaste and modest.
5   Norms of chastity and modesty are sustained by family stability, and by men and women behaving according to this set of beliefs.

It is fairly clear that this is not a very good explanation. Apart from the fact that Hume himself (a lifelong bachelor) knows that women are lustful and licentious by nature, we cannot readily accept that men, and especially men in politics, the church, education and moral instruction, do not have a deliberate stake in propagating the myth of women's natural modesty and chastity. In other words, the institution and the norm do not emerge spontaneously as unintended consequences of individual actions, but as part of a concerted, conscious strategy of powerful men in public life and of husbands in the domestic sphere.

I have focused in such detail on the way in which Hume and Rousseau explained the origins of society in terms of sexual relations for two reasons. First, I have used these explanations as examples of what were then considered convincing, as accounts of how the personal world of an individual's private experiences is joined up with the collective forms of life in a group or community. I have shown that both Hume and Rousseau attempted explanations which followed the formula identified in chapter 1 (pp. 21–3). Second, I have set out to provide a standard against which we can judge present-day efforts to explain how sexual relationships either contribute to the transformation of collective life (as in Giddens, Beck and Plummer), or reflect such transformations (as in Bauman and Fevre).

On closer examination, the former do not really attempt to connect up their analyses of the new forms of sexual partnership with their speculations about the emergence of dialogical forms of democracy, and they certainly do not try to follow the functionalist formula. For example, in *Beyond Left and Right*, Giddens acknowledges that the transition to new relationships, not relying on traditional moral rules, does not necessarily lead to these changes in political culture. Instead, he argues that there is simply a tendency of some aspects of the opening up of new aspects of collective life to public dialogue to reinforce these changes in sexual partnerships. First, self-help groups enhance the equal autonomy of individuals of both sexes and promote discussion of female and male sexuality, 'making them matters of public debate';[23] second, formal organizations in general are becoming more flexible, with greater devolution of responsibility; and third, global issues require new forms of democratic governance.[24] These are hints at connections, rather than explanations.

By contrast, Bauman and Fevre *do* develop explanations of the demoralization process which seek to explain how the public world of commercial advertising, consumption and celebrity is joined up with the experiences of sexual pleasure and existential anxiety by individual men and women through sex. In this, they follow the *dysfunctionalist* formula pioneered by Rousseau.

For instance, Bauman in *Liquid Love* argues that looser ties in personal relationships are a consequence of the spread of commercial transactions into the 'moral economy', and of commercial reasoning into the moral sphere. Like shopping, partnership comes to be based on nothing more than preferences, and to be seen as requiring no more skills than those of 'an average, moderately experienced consumer'.[25] This stems from the satisfactions of greater freedom and choice, especially in sexual relations. Long-term partnerships are perceived as oppressive, stifling and causing dependency: 'Bindings and bonds make human relations "impure" – as they would do any act of consumption that assumes instant satisfaction and equally instant obsolescence to the consumed object.'[26]

The loosening of bonds (and consequent demoralization of partnership and family life) are not intentional results of commercialization, and are not recognized as undermining the enduring pleasures of close relationships. Instead, people feel aroused and fulfilled by the joys of shopping and consumer-style sex, and believe that they are following the paths of their desires in the most natural and rational ways. This in turn further consolidates the hold of consumer lifestyles and the spread of commercial relations throughout social life. In sex, couples connect up the parts of this feedback loop, acting as conduits for the whole system.

> 'Purification' of sex allows sexual practice to be adapted to such advanced shopping/living patterns. 'Pure sex' is construed with some form of reliable money-back guarantee in view – and the partners in a 'purely sexual encounter' may feel secure, aware that 'no strings attached' compensates for the vexing frailty of their engagement.[27]

It is obvious, and does not need to be spelled out further, that Bauman's powerful and persuasive analysis follows Rousseau's formula. It is a very clear explanation of how we come to understand and be influenced by TV advertisements for the consumer goods associated with individual autonomy, choice, travel and recreation. It is also a convincing account of how we come to associate sexual satisfaction with freedom and mobility, and how we can understand and identify with the characters in the art film version of the scenario described in chapter 1 (pp. 12–13), as well as the commercial advertisement version.

Bauman's argument explains why a notion of 'recreational sex' has become so attractive, in a global economy dominated by financial products and services which promise personal autonomy, and by commodities associated with a glamorous, mobile lifestyle. This in turn strongly influences our self-identities and life-projects and shapes the way we relate to each other, including our long-term sexual relationships.

However, I shall argue that neither Giddens's 'optimistic' account of democratization, dialogue and negotiated equality through intimacy, nor Bauman's 'pessimistic' account of demoralization through the penetration of commercial dynamics into partnership and sexual pleasure, fully captures how sex connects up the private with the public aspects of our social world. In the final part of this chapter, and in the next, I shall try to find a functionalist formula to explain what I see as the process through which sex glues together these connections.

My starting point is the issue of how our individual identities are made up from the cultural resources available to us, and how we link our versions of who we are into the public world of civil associations, economic units and political bodies. In chapter 1, I used the example of my own accounts of myself to fellow-travellers on trains and planes to illustrate the elements in these 'narratives of self'. We present ourselves to others in a kind of prospectus, which outlines our family and community origins, what we have made of ourselves by way of developing our personal endowments (both physical and intellectual), and with whom we have chosen to build our social relationships. Perhaps because of my background in the public services, my narrative emphasizes informal friendships and membership of collegial groups; for others it might sound more like a mission statement or a business plan.

Within the present culture of mainstream members of affluent economies, these stories are supposed to illustrate how we have expressed our 'inner selves', through our life choices and commitments; and how we have made ourselves into autonomous beings, developing and fulfilling this external, public version of our individuality in our everyday lives. I call what is produced by such narrative accounts our 'projects of self'. The important thing is that we are all required to have such projects, and to be able to give our versions of them, in coherent ways, on appropriate occasions.

Our notions of both our 'inner selves' and what constitutes an adequate account of our public project of our selves have changed dramatically since the time of Hume and Rousseau. We do not think of our internal, private, individual psychic dynamics as mechanistically as Hume thought about the instinctual basis for behaviour. We tend to imagine ourselves as driving a high-performance vehicle which is powered by innate impulses and genetically determined dispositions, rather than as slavishly using reason to steer the chariot of our passions.

Similarly, in relation to our public projects of self, Giddens is right to emphasize the decline of traditional rules like those of honour and virginity. He rightly stresses how much we now take for granted the idea of personal autonomy and choice, and that of individuals' responsibility to themselves for the development and fulfilment of their potentials. He and Beck are also right to draw attention to the central role of intimate relationships in linking projects of self to the wider social environment. Selves are therefore both more agonized about their choices of partners than in traditional cultures, and more vulnerable to others' lack of unconditional and uninhibited appreciation. Sex is the activity in which selves most crucially, riskily and desperately seek recognition, confirmation and endorsement of their inner identities and public projects of self.

Sex is therefore both the opportunity to connect up our private worlds of fantasy and emotion with the public world of other people and organizations, and an occasion for negotiating a bond with another identity, and another project of self. But how exactly can this be achieved, given the subjectivity of our inner selves and the lack of a trustworthy basis for sharing and commitment? We are back to Hume's problem of how institutions for cooperation and mutual benefit get started, given the risks of the other's opportunism or defection.

Sexual relationships today therefore take on many of the complexities and tensions of property relations in Hume's account. Sex is a site of potential exploitation, cruelty and, ultimately, the destruction of the self, seen as a fragile but sacred entity, tragically reliant on the collaboration of others for its nurturing. Individuals have duties to themselves (similar to the duty of self-preservation in Locke or Hume) to develop and express themselves through sexual relationships, both by exploring their potentialities with others, and by recognizing and choosing the partner with whom they can most expansively fulfil these potentials, and express their identities.

Bauman captures this ambiguity of sexual encounters as follows:

> [W]as it an initial step towards a relationship, or its crowning and its terminus? A stage in a meaningful succession or a one-off episode, a means to an end or a one-off act? . . . The entitlements of sexual partners have become the prime site of anxiety. What sort of commitment, if any, does the union of bodies entail? In what way, if any, does it bind the future of the partners?[28]

The world of sexual encounters therefore becomes a bit like the world of property (investments, overseas trade, risk on the high seas) in Hume's time. In order to increase one's stock, one must both invest in others' projects for self development (requiring trust and cooperation) and risk incalculable disasters (from the other's life circumstances, personalities, family relationships and friendship circles) by opening oneself up to hurt and loss. Preservation of the self, through isolation and reclusive retreat, is therefore always at least a temporary option, like putting one's stock in gold bars. Every transaction requires deliberation and interpretation, as part of the project of the self.

In other words, sexual encounters have taken on exactly the qualities that Hume attributed to those between our 'savage ancestors' in pre-social times. The love of self and the desire for satisfaction of 'natural appetites' are in palpable tension with the need for a secure and shared basis for cooperation and trust. Some generalized collective good – what Hume calls the 'common sense' of stability and reliability in these crucial transactions – is required. This 'common sense' is not of the crude and calculative kind that Bauman and Fevre postulate; on the contrary, it resides in a metaphysical belief in the sanctity of the self.

The equivalent of the convention of secure possession of property in Hume's time is the convention of the possession of an inner, inviolable self, which requires others for its development and fulfilment, which can be enhanced or diminished in such encounters, which can indeed be totally sacrificed or destroyed in them, but which ultimately 'belongs' to ourselves. This inner temple, the sanctum of our being and the store of our holy treasure, demands the respect of others, especially when we make it vulnerable in sexual relationships. We rely on the shared belief in some such entity on our encounters with others; there is a common interest in sustaining it, even in the face of the injuries and disappointments we all endure.

So I am arguing that sex makes social bonds, by joining up projects of self, albeit in a risky way, which requires constant spinning of the web of mutuality (see pp. 23–4). It also joins up the private world of personal experience with the collective forms of public culture and public organization. And it does so in ways which have some of the characteristics of Giddens's 'negotiated intimacy', and some of Bauman's commercialized, liquid love. As a first, rough approximation of my version of the functionalist formula, to be developed in much more elaborate and detailed forms in the rest of the book, I would offer the following sketch of an explanation:

1 The present-day culture of mutuality through intimate connections is the result of greater autonomy, mobility and choice for individuals in the social relationship of mainstream affluent economies, who follow consumer lifestyles, hold financial portfolios and so on.

2 Individuals benefit from the new culture of mutuality through intimate connections, as a resource for their projects of self.

3 Individuals who follow projects of self do not intend to make up a new culture of mutuality through intimate connections; they just want to feel free to develop and fulfil themselves in many ways.
4 Individuals who follow projects of self are unaware that they are creating a new culture of mutuality through intimate connections.
5 The social relationships of mainstream affluent economies, made up of interactions between those following consumer lifestyles, holding financial portfolios and so on, sustain the culture of mutuality through intimate connections; this is achieved via a feedback loop through individuals pursuing projects of self.

At this stage, this is just a sketch of the various elements in a functionalist formula explaining how the parts of the present-day order are joined up. First, it is much too vague, as yet, about just what the 'culture of mutuality through intimate connections' actually is, how it classifies and joins up the public world, and how it works to sustain individuals' life strategies. Second, the explanation is as yet unclear about how the culture meshes with economic relationships. I reject the rather crude version given by Bauman – that individuals drag down the market economy into bed with them in their sexual couplings. I shall argue that we are a bit more subtle than this. Third, and most important, it fails as yet to explain how it excludes those who do not pursue autonomous, affluent mobile lifestyles, based on such resources. Nor does it explain the consequences of that exclusion.

In the next chapter, I shall focus on the first issue – a clearer account of mutuality through intimate connections in present-day culture. In chapters 4–6, I shall look at how this culture is both sustained by, and incorporates the codes of, the new collective features of the global economy. In chapters 7–9, I shall explain how the exclusions accomplished by those linking processes in mainstream affluent social relations require the use of power to coerce marginal and poor people – the mass of the world's population.

Sex makes intimate connections; it joins up projects of self, in which autonomous individuals seek to develop and fulfil themselves. But sex also joins up the far larger world of the excluded and oppressed. We are reminded of this by the world's greatest pandemic. In many African cities, such as Gaberone and Addis Ababa, a quarter of the population have HIV/AIDS. The bond made by sex between members of the community of outsiders is a bond of death.

3

Sex and Self-Improvement

Attentive readers will have noticed that I took several short cuts in setting out my functionalist formula for how sex joins up the private and public aspects of experience, how we make sense of both, and how that sense orders our lives. In particular, I smuggled in a concept of 'mutuality through intimate connections', and linked it with 'consumer lifestyles, financial portfolios and so on', by sleight of hand.

There are at least two suspicious moves in this bit of conjuring. The first is that erotic intimacy creates *both* social bonds *and* connections with the formal, organized world of civil society, economy and politics. It is fairly obvious that sex creates informal social bonds, and is one of the most powerful non-verbal ways in which we communicate about our inner feelings with each other. Sex is, in this sense, an essential part of our repertoire for spinning the web through which we sustain the sense of being connected up with others, in ways which are emotionally meaningful. It is the ultimate form of affirmation and recognition, and of giving value and respect, in present day mainstream affluent culture.

But this does not show how these bonds in turn link up with public culture, the organized structure of economic life, or the political order. It would be perfectly feasible for sex to be part of a resistance or counter-culture, and for people to make love as a way of defying consumer tastes, corporate slogans and political ideologies. The idea of sex as resistance is an established one in literature, from Stendhal's *Le Rouge et le noir* to George Orwell's *1984*.

Second, and following on from this, I have not yet made convincing links between sexual relationships and consumer lifestyles, the financial arrangements which sustain them, or the political order. Bauman's analysis in his *Liquid Love* makes strong connections between consumerism and a kind of recreational approach to sex, pursued by single people. But this is not yet the dominant cultural form, even if it strongly influences current partnerships and points the way towards a possible future. And, in any case, my explanation is a kind of functionalist one (how a set of social relationships is sustained), whereas Bauman's is an overtly evangelical *dysfunctionalist* one (how traditional morality and the practice of love in long-term partnerships is undermined by commercial values).

Let's return to the second of the two imaginary short films described at the beginning of chapter 1. In the TV advertisement version of that film, both the man flying to the foreign city and the woman meeting him there were seen consuming various glamorous products, including mobile phones, cars and designer clothes. I argued that the viewer would mentally connect up these elements in the story, and make sense of this as a narrative of freedom, choice and movement. These elements would be glued to consumption of the products by the sex scene at the end of the film. This is how the advertisement is intended to work, by those who paid for it to be made in this way.

But of course this is not necessarily the way in which we experience the connectedness of real life, because we are not living in TV advertisements. Let's go back to the art version of the film. As I pointed out (p. 14), this would probably be shot in a deliberately different way, to emphasize the fragmented, discontinuous nature of subjective experience, and the very varying tone, tempo, mood, texture and feeling of the plane flight, the car journey and the sex scene. In particular, there are cinematic conventions about erotic encounters which dictate the pace and perspective of such sequences. These seem also to be aligned with literary conventions about how authors describe such scenes in novels and poems.

In art films, at such moments in the story the camera tends to linger on the bodies of the lovers, as if trying to record for eternity each curve, contour and crevasse, and to preserve the most fleeting and evanescent of experiences. In the same way, literary versions of sex often read as attempts to hold onto the finest details of touch, feel and rhythm, as well as each pore, hair and bead of moisture on the skin. As Scheff comments,[1] it is particularly in portrayals of sex that writers try to imitate Proust in their attention to such details, their recording of the smallest impressions and their attempts to slow down the passage of time. And this is because it is impossible to recall these deeply felt and meaningful moments in all their richness, however intense they are at that instant.[2] Film and literature thus attempt to capture the immediacy of the present, most vividly experienced in the ecstasy of sexual union. (By contrast, few authors since Tolstoy have tried to encompass the elegiac qualities of physical labour on the land – the subject of the other imaginary film – in such fine detail.)

This might well suggest that my account of the connections between intimate experiences and public forms has been overdrawn. Perhaps it is of the essence of really meaningful sex, the kind to which we all ultimately aspire, that it is transcendent and timeless, in the way that films and novels try to capture, and not cheap and glitzy, as TV advertisements make it. If so, then maybe this is because it is only comprehensible as communication between two inner selves, as the private language of love, which is inaudible to the public world.

At the start of chapter 2, I gave an account of the childhood origins of my own attitudes to sex, and how it related to the public world. I explained that this consisted in a pre-pubescent attempt to reconcile my grandparents' stern neo-Hegelian code of public duty and service, my infant experiences of incoherent sensation and Irish female teasing, the images of South Seas femininity on film and my fear of the socially destructive consequences of my parents' passion. This was an attempt to explain the complexity of the elements that go to make up an individual's inner world, and how it connects with a life lived in family and community.

For each one of us, these early influences provide the resources for our versions of how sex connects to the public sphere, and how they are made up out of personal interactions with those closest to us, by birth, clan or physical proximity – the bonds of blood, guts and soil. The point of my example was to illustrate how particular our interpretations are to the accidents of our birth and upbringing (in my case, the war, my parents' absence, my grandparents' moral education, the female underwear fashions of the day, the shape of the Polynesian body and the institutions of divorce and single parenthood in the 1950s). Even the stories told to themselves by my siblings were made up of quite different elements.

Given the hugely idiosyncratic nature of these personal inter-pretations, how can a public culture influence sexual intimacy, and how can it in turn shape that culture? Again, personal experience teaches me that it does so, in two directions. Collective represen-tations, through the media, novels, poetry and music, and through informal friendships and associations, provide an instant feedback between the physical sensations and the emotional contents of sexual relationships, and the outer world. Even if one wants to protect one's partnership from such invasions, it is impossible to do so, short of a reclusive existence. The words and postures of others, the unconscious manifestations of their physical bonds, reverberate with one's own versions of sex and intimacy. During my first marriage, I (and I'm sure my wife too) could not escape the reproach of others' partnerships, within the new culture of opportunity and freedom for women, and the comparison with ours, of inequality and constraint for her, as a traditional wife and mother.

In this way, sex and intimacy cannot avoid a kind of account-ability to public standards. Some of these, of course, are the inten-tional, normative prescriptions of those whose role involves the attempt to classify, regulate, organize and mobilize the general public – educators, counsellors, therapists, clergy and politicians, among others. In our youth, these figures exercised a more direct surveillance over the morals of the masses, even if their influence was already waning. It was just our bad luck that a historical culture shift accelerated this process, so that their prescriptions, some of which we had unconsciously incorporated into our part-nership, were almost instantly consigned to the dustbin of history, leaving us living an anachronism.

This shift was only in small part led by a 'top-down' vision of a more equal and liberated version of sexuality. Although there were role models for this among the elite, the main impetus came from the new opportunities for women to get higher education, and to work in challenging and stimulating jobs. For professionals and politicians, these changes required new rhetorics of rights, new coalitions of interests and revised frameworks of regulation (such as the legalization of gay sex, and equal opportunities laws).

I do not claim that such discourses, mobilizations and laws shape sexual encounters. If I did so, it would violate the conditions for a successful example of the functionalist formula. People do not intend to create a culture of mutuality. Doctors and politicians do not tell us how to fall in love, or how to enjoy sex – or, if they do, we take little notice. But they do, by picking up elements in widespread lifestyles and articulating them in specific ways, contribute to the shape in which the web is spun. And in doing so, they provide hooks of a kind which allow us to link up intimate experiences with public, shared standards. These hooks are disposed in particular patterns, not randomly. We cannot choose to hook up just anywhere. Our personal fantasies and informal practices can only hook into these public ones in certain ways, leaving other parts unconnected, and sometimes hanging in mid air.

I shall try to explain how the culture of equal autonomy hooks into the top-down political rhetoric of our age. First, it is clear that the notion of a self-generated project of self is itself a standard one, derived from a cultural network of ideas, shared by the sexual partners. Although couples must make their own personal bond, and make up their own capsule of respect and trust for each other's projects and sacred selves, this ideal of the basis for a relationship is not of their making. In fact it is, as I argued in the introduction (pp. 5–7), the very stuff of popular drama and novels – the notion that each of us is a being on a journey through life, a voyage of self-discovery and self-development and a quest to find a soul-mate. This notion is both corny and unoriginal; it is we who must breathe new life into it in our relationships.

Furthermore, although the ideal of equal autonomy between the couple in a sexual partnership may seem new, it is part of a long established tradition – the tradition of individualism. As Emile Durkheim observed at the end of the nineteenth century, the whole of European bourgeois culture and liberal politics rested on the notion that the human person is considered sacred in the ritual sense of the word. Indeed, he argued that individualism (in this sense) had become 'a religion in which man is at once the worshipper and the god'; 'it penetrates all our institutions and our mores'.

> The cult, of which he is both the object and the agent, does not address itself to the particular being which he is and which bears his name, but to the human person wherever it is to be found, and in whatever form it is embodied . . . It springs not from egoism but from sympathy for all that is human, a broader pity for all suffering, for all human miseries.[3]

However, this principle of the sanctity of the individual, as the common standard for all relationships, has been associated with a diversity of collective forms and public organizations. In relation to sex, as the leading theorist of the subject, Michel Foucault, pointed out, the sacred notions of privacy, choice and self-development did not by any means imply that professionals and officials left members of society to their own devices. Indeed, as he dedicated so much of his work to demonstrating, they set standards and prescribed practices in detail, from the eighteenth century onwards. The question thus becomes not one of how external cultural and political notions of the proper way to conduct sexual encounters become established, but how *this particular standard* (equal autonomy between individuals, in conditions of negotiated intimacy) came to find hooks in the official, political culture, to connect it with public discourses and mobilizations, at this particular time.

In his *History of Sexuality*, Foucault sought to debunk the 'Repressive Hypothesis' – the idea that sex became a taboo topic in polite bourgeois society from some time in the seventeenth or eighteenth centuries, that open discussion of it was censored and that its expression was therefore repressed. Instead, he argued that sex was endlessly discussed, by priests, professionals, educators, doctors, psychiatrists and politicians, creating new discourses for describing and analysing sexuality, especially deviant forms and acts. Far from being repressed, he argued:

> There was a steady proliferation of discourses concerned with sex – specific discourses, different from one another both by their form and by their object. . . . A censorship of sex? There was installed,

rather, an apparatus for producing an ever greater quantity of discourse about sex, capable of functioning and taking effect in its very economy.[4]

This was part of Foucault's project for analysing 'power/knowledge' in modern societies – the technologies of the body by which government created, supervised and regulated subjects through its policies, agencies and activities, giving rise to a stricter regime for monitoring and managing all forms of relationships and behaviour.

> [M]edicine made a forceful entry into the pleasures of the couple: it created an entire organic, functional, or mental pathology arising out of 'incomplete' sexual practices; it carefully classified all forms of related pleasures; it incorporated them into actions of 'development' and instinctual 'disturbances'; and it undertook to manage them.[5]

Foucault thus argued that modernity ushered in a regime of regulation of sex, as part of a wider agenda of government, for the

> formation, development and transformation of forms of experience, [which] constitute the human being as a subject of learning [*connaissance*]; in other words, it is the basis for accepting or refusing rules, and constitutes human beings as social and juridical subjects; it is what establishes the relation with oneself and with others, and constitutes the human being as an ethical subject.[6]

The important point here is that the issue was as much the formation of the *self* as *subject*, as relationships with others. Foucault sought to analyse 'the different modes by which, in our culture, human beings are made subjects'.[7] This in turn required an understanding of the state as 'both an individualizing and a totalizing form of power'[8] – government concerned with all aspects of social life, from the economy to the details of intimate relationships.

Towards the end of his life, Foucault recognized that a new transformation in both government of social relations and the form of the human subject was taking place – one which shifted from techniques for 'normalizing' behaviour and creating disciplined citizens to one which focuses on the self as an active, developmental, self-improving subject, and the 'ways in which individuals create their own selves and realise their desires *through* discipline'.[9] Hence, in relation to sex and intimacy, he was concerned with the technologies of the self as

> techniques which permit individuals to affect by their own means, a certain number of operations on their own bodies, their own souls, their own thoughts, their own conduct, and this in a manner so as to transform themselves, modify themselves, and to attain a certain state of perfection, happiness, purity, supernatural power.[10]

This was not simply a matter of 'learning the rules of a moral sexual behaviour', but 'discovering the truth in oneself and defeating the illusions in oneself, in cutting out the images and thoughts one's mind produces continuously'.[11] Self-understanding allows the individual to exercise self-government and self-transformation, and be in a good relationship with oneself.[12] Following this line of thought, which Foucault did not live to pursue to its conclusions, a number of authors have explored the implications of government that promotes subjects' projects of the self, and encourages them to new forms of self-improvement.[13]

In particular, and drawing on policy documents and legislation in the USA, Cruikshank argues that self-esteem, self-worth and self-development provided the themes for social policy in the 1990s, informing Bill Clinton's legislation on 'welfare reform', 'inclusion' and 'empowerment'.[14] Extrapolating from the success of mainstream individuals in managing their relationships and working lives, the policy agenda attempts to inculcate the same virtues and practices in poor people. In the UK context, Rose sees a new style of politics and government:

> [T]he self-government of the autonomous individual can be connected up with the imperatives of good government. Etho-politics seeks to act upon conduct by acting upon the forces thought to shape the values, beliefs, moralities that themselves are thought to determine the everyday mundane choices that human beings make as to how they lead their lives.[15]

So there is clear evidence of how a new cultural standard, of equal autonomy between sexual partners, each with personal projects of self, became part of political rhetoric and government orthodoxy. This was an established feature in the USA by the early 1990s, and in the UK by the late '90s, with the election of the Blair government. As to the links between discourses of self-development and those of intimate relationships, the propagators, apologists and high priests of these have indeed been sociologists like Giddens (Tony Blair's guru), Beck, Weeks and Plummer, but mainly the popular columnists, sex and marital therapists, film-makers and novelists on whom their theories were based. Just as the connections between the mutual security of negotiated intimacy seemed natural and rational to the politicians who first preached self-improvement and self-responsibility, and who joined up the elements in the Third Way, so social theorists in turn played their part in spinning this particular part of the web.[16]

However, the web would not have reached right down to hook into the everyday life of couples and their children if they in turn had not been busy spinning, in their more informal, bottom-up ways. Cultural standards and ways of making sense of the world can never be wholly imposed from above; they work only through the reciprocal activities and exchanges of individuals in unstructured or semi-organized relationships. And here again, the ideal of partnerships based on negotiated intimacy between couples, who are equally willing and able to express their individual selves, is not new. What is new, as I shall demonstrate in the final part of this chapter, is the particular way in which such projects of self are connected to the material resources which sustain them. The Third Way is as much about how we fund these projects as how we formulate them.

I have argued, drawing on the work of Cruikshank and others, that governments are now skilled in mobilizing 'our individual desires to fulfil ourselves . . . to craft our personalities, to discover who we really are'.[17] Sex is the strongest of these desires, moving us to explore our inner worlds through relationships with chosen others. But this in turn causes us, through these very relationships, to make and remake the public world, as we reach shared understanding and develop common projects. And how we remake that public world – both consolidating and transforming it – is in interaction with its existing institutions (organizations and cultural standards).

Let me try to illustrate this from some of the best-known love stories of past eras. How love both reflects and transforms the institutions of society was the central theme of the novels of Jane Austen. Their dramatic force, and their capacity still to inspire us to identify with their central characters, stem from their portrayal of the rival pulls of sexual attraction and the other bonds which connect these characters to their social worlds. Austen's writing conveys vividly the strong influence of those other bonds – of family, kinship, friendship, property and power – and how they are eventually reconciled with the bonds created by sexual attraction. (Minor characters illustrate how this reconciliation is often *not* achieved, and the often disastrous consequences of that failure.)

Jane Austen's skill lies in the fact that both bonds of sexual attraction and bonds of family, kin and property are conveyed as stemming from and sustained by feeling, communication and common experience. Although the novels can be read as being about how the characters deal with dilemmas in squaring their emotional lives with their obligations and principles, she manages to portray the latter as bonds which are *felt* and *lived*, as much as rationally adopted. So the stories never illustrate moral rules; instead they show real people improvising from one situation, while trying to retain some coherence and some capacity to make a consistent sense of their feelings and actions.

Pride and Prejudice is the best of her novels, because the physical chemistry between Elizabeth Bennett and Mr Darcy is in such contradiction to their ideas about social relationships, and about how marriage should be aligned with property ownership and family ties. The novel is about two people reassessing their social assumptions and moral principles, under intense pressure from their sexual desires. By contrast, in *Emma*, for example, the heroine's meddlesome matchmaking and snobbery are simply generalized weaknesses, which do not directly confront her passions, and Mr Knightley is too obviously cast in the role of moral tutor; Emma recognizes her attraction to him only *after* she has learnt her moral lessons. Conversely, his only moral weakness and social fault is a certain fastidiousness, which does not specifically limit his (restrained) desire for Emma. But both books have the same themes – the channelling of the passions, to reassess the characters' place in and ideas about the social order, and transform both them and their social worlds.

At the same time, the love affairs of other characters teach harsher moral lessons. Where unrestrained sex triumphs over other bonds and principles, as in Elizabeth's younger sister in *Pride and Prejudice*, or Fanny Price's cousins Maria and Julia in *Mansfield Park*, the outcome is the woman's ruin. We also learn about the fate of unsound men, such as Henry Crawford in *Mansfield Park* and Mr Wickham in *Pride and Prejudice*, through their sexual conduct. The fact that they are manipulative, shallow and sensual leads to seduction and elopement, in which they too are lost and damned – excluded from the moral world, and marginalized in the world of power and property.

As Scheff points out, Jane Austen's stories about how bonds are made, between the couples whose sexual attraction results in a reconciliation between intimacy and their other social bonds, demonstrate close emotional, moral and intellectual engagement.[18] This bonding involves highly charged discussions about issues of feeling, personality, temperament, relationship and public role, which also concern profession, property and public responsibility. While teasing, flirting and challenging, they also debate the ethics and politics of family, kinship, friendship, duty and citizenship. And they do so in a spirit of radical equality, despite differences of gender roles and property holdings.

On the one hand, this leads to a mutual sharing of inner experiences 'in which the two people are able to share their private worlds with each other', with 'virtually no limits'; 'it extends into the very core of the lovers' beings, into their whole selves'. This requires equality and openness, and produces self-knowledge and mutuality, based on 'the never-ending interest of both partners in each other'. It produces a social bond as well as a sexual one, because these are 'mutual understandings and acceptance of each other's thoughts, beliefs and feelings. That is, a secure bond exists when two persons accurately understand each other's interior life.'[19]

But on the other hand, within the intimacy of such mutual understanding and acceptance, the couple also negotiate their shared arrangements of their public life of social relationships, property holdings and public duties. The details of their private bond are worked out among these other ties of mutuality and obligation. Jane Austen's novels are so complete because they show how, in a society of great inequality of wealth and power (including inequality between men and women), these issues are simultaneously addressed by people in the grip of violent sexual feelings and conflicting emotions.

However, in George Eliot's novels these issues are more agonizing, and the reconciliations between personal passions and public duties not so happily achieved. The same tensions have different elaborations and outcomes. In *The Mill on the Floss*, Maggie Tulliver and Stephen Guest, under the strong influence of sexual attraction to each other, but committed to other partners, are swept out to sea in a small boat – a contingency which Maggie accuses Stephen of having contrived. When he proposes that this is an act of fate, and that they should elope together, they argue about the opposing principles of duty to others, and authenticity to their passions.

> Her heart beat like the heart of a frightened bird, but this direct opposition helped her. She felt her determination growing stronger.
>
> 'Remember what you felt weeks ago', she began with beseeching earnestness, 'remember what we both felt: that we owed ourselves to others and must conquer every inclination which could make us false to that debt. We have failed to keep our resolutions, but the wrong remains the same.'
>
> 'No, it does *not* remain the same', said Stephen. 'We have proved that it was impossible to keep our resolutions. We have proved that the feeling which draws us towards each other is too strong to be overcome, that natural law surmounts every other; we can't help what it clashes with.'
>
> 'It is not so, Stephen; I'm quite sure that is wrong. I have tried to think it again and again, but I see, if we judge in that way, there would be a warrant for all treachery and cruelty; we should justify breaking the most sacred ties that can ever be formed on earth. If the past is not to bind us, where can duty lie? We should have no law but the inclination of the moment.'[20]

Thus duty prevails, but the struggle is far more even. Maggie returns to her commitments, and although her brother accuses her of having 'disgraced the family name', she is redeemed in death. In George Eliot's novels, the passions are instruments for personal development, and for moral and social criticism. Tom's condemnation of Maggie reveals his obstinate narrowness of vision. Her experience allows Maggie to learn. And, of course, Eliot herself did elope, with a married man. In her narratives, those who follow their sexual passions are potentially transformative agents; the morally irredeemable are cold, dry prigs, like Mr Casaubon in *Middlemarch*.

But by the turn of the century, writers such as Thomas Hardy and D. H. Lawrence had tilted the balance towards the passions; in the latter, sex became the principle and the emblem of authenticity, which relegated older versions of social sincerity and public duty to the traditionalist trashbin.[21] Their central characters, or at least the ones who espoused an ethic of autonomy and authenticity, were pioneers, often aesthetes or rebels. In the Bohemian world of the Bloomsbury set, who lived deliberately unconventional lifestyles, these standards were reflected in their novels; and Virginia Woolf was to become the dominant influence on subsequent women novelists, who adopted the consciousness and sensibility of the self-directing self – often suffering, but driven primarily by the duty to develop herself and express herself through exploration of her true nature.

While much was gained in this transition – which later embraced the psychodynamic insights of Freud and his followers – a great deal was lost also. Above all, Jane Austen's great strength, as a writer and as a moralist, lay in her capacity to locate her heroines' romantic dilemmas in the social relations of her time. The moral principles with which they struggled were closely related to the distribution of property, the organization of power and production, and the subordination of women. This gave the sexual dynamics of her novels a convincing context in the social order, one which was largely lost in the work of Virginia Woolf. In Jane Austen (and even in Thomas Hardy), poor people, labourers and servants are real, have characters and feelings. For the Bloomsbury set, they have become objects for disdain. It comes as little surprise when new notebooks reveal Virginia Woolf as anti-Semitic as well as snobbish.[22]

So the bonds spun in sexual relationships between individuals in their informal partnerships do connect with the top-down institutional web of the public world. But the way they do so varies with the patterns of economic and political relations in that sphere. The bottom-up can only join and link with the top-down strands of the web where the latter allow these connections to be made.

The central problem for the present model, increasingly espoused by mainstream individuals but gradually adopted from the early twentieth century avant-garde, that intimate relationships should be based on negotiated equality and authenticity between autonomous individuals, each pursuing projects of the self, is that there is nothing to connect these with wider social relations. However much the partnerships of self-improving selves may come to realize higher standards of emotional truth and shared enlightenment, they simply cannot inform, or be responsive to, issues of equality, freedom or justice in the wider order. Even if they are able to resolve many of the tensions between sexual chemistry and commitments to others (by insisting that notions of duty are altruistic in ways that are patronizing, and ultimately insulting to the autonomous, self-improving selves of those others), they cannot supply a basis for the distribution of resources, roles and responsibilities in other sectors of social life, or link directly with any principles which can. They therefore allow their protagonists to engage in the wider world without a sound basis for ethical treatment of their fellows.

This was vividly demonstrated in research that I and colleagues conducted on mainstream (above-average income) couples in a provincial English city in the early 1990s. These couples were committed to a view of partnership derived from their projects of self – of equal autonomy between individuals with a duty to develop their potentials (as it happened, the educational attainments of men and women in the couples recruited were exactly equal). In practice, this had different implications for men and women. Men invested in *careers* – long-term, incremental projects, involving promotion, pensions and perks, and the accumulation of job-specific human capital and organizational power. Women, by contrast, eschewed the notion of careers, and took work that was consistent with 'supportive' roles in households: primary responsibility for child care, the school run and domestic management. Thus their employment was mainly part time and subordinate, but often more self-developmental and fulfilling than that of men. They were certainly more interesting to interview, as they described combinations of work and family roles that were complementary, demanding and challenging. For example, one mother of three teenage children described her working life since having her family as follows:

> *Mrs Oak*: Well, after the children were born . . . I got into breast-feeding counselling, because I had quite a few problems breast-feeding the first two children, and I decided because of that I wanted to help and do some of that. So I got into counselling in that way – I've got a little bit of training there with the counselling and I just took an interest in it. . . . So through that I got an interest in counselling, marital counselling . . . and I just walked in [to a voluntary agency] and said I was interested in doing that. And I helped in the office for a bit and through that I got into training and just got into that. And the sex therapy I got into because I just think it's a very important area of relationships, and I liked the area of work they were doing and it seemed to tie up very, very well with the basic counselling. . . . And then it started paying its counsellors . . . but I used to find the amount I did earn would vary quite a bit from month to month. . . . And I think I saw that I would actually like a job with a little bit more security.[23]

Her account of her work is clearly based on a project of the self, arising as it did from her experiences of caring for her children, of voluntary work and of following a professional line of employment which allowed for simultaneous personal development, but which enabled her finally to return to a job (as a researcher) in line with her educational qualifications (she had a higher degree by research). Like most other women among the interviewees, she sought to explain not only how she reconciled her employment with her responsibilities as a caregiver and manager of the household, but also how the work she did, even if poorly paid (Mrs Oak earned less than £5,000 per year) was both in line with her personal interests and values, and part of a trajectory of self-improvement and self-fulfilment.

The other side of these interviews was the way in which both parents spoke of their roles in enabling their children to become individuals capable of forming a project of the self, of planning and implementing such a project, and of developing the qualities and skills that would ensure its flowering. It was interesting that, in explaining this, none of them said that they wanted their children to make an adult relationship with a partner who would love them, and encourage them to be happy and fulfilled people – an apparently obvious, perhaps too self-evident, point to make. Instead, they focused on their children's acquisition of the cultural resources to form a project of self, and the environment in which they could best do so.

This meant that they must learn to aspire to psychological and economic autonomy. One part of this entailed suitable experiences, in an educational environment conducive to such values. It was not just that children should gain the 'A' levels required to go to university, though this was a necessary condition; it was also that they should be part of a peer group with comparable projects, whose members interacted as selves within the ethic of this whole set of moral and social commitments.

As parents, they indicated that their children should make their own choice of occupation as part of these projects of self, but only *after* they had been through the experiences and educational environments necessary for developing such identities and projects. More than one took the example of selling ice cream as emblematic of an unusual, counter-intuitive or non-professional choice, and insisted that they would support such an option, but only when it was made by a fully prepared and well-qualified self with other opportunities.

> *Mr Linden*: If Reub [son, aged 4] went to school and he got a degree in whatever and then decided he wanted to be an ice-cream salesman then my view would be, he's being an ice-cream salesman, because that's what he wants to do, not he's selling ice creams because that's all that is available to him. And I think that's quite important.[24]

In an interesting example of cultural standardization, another interviewee mentions the same occupation to illustrate a similar point about a teenage daughter:

> *Mr Palm*: Beatrice is the younger, she is a very good mathematician, for instance, but is not – I'm sounding a bit unfair on her – but as I say she is not steady, but she's not as conventional as her elder sister, um, she wants to run an ice-cream parlour. I'm very happy about that, but I think she ought to be properly trained – I mean I think she might go to polytechnic and read economics for instance, and her mathematics might be part of that, for instance.[25]

The other side of the process of preparation for a project of self, and for fully autonomous selfhood, was the parents' concern that their offspring should associate with the right kind of youngster at school and develop in the right kind of cultural milieu. It was important that they did not interact with others who rejected, or were not properly socalized for, such identities and commitments:

> *Mr Redwood*: I would hate either of the boys to have fallen into a group of friends where working at school became in some way uncool.[26]

> *Mr Mahogany*: I think a lot of the success of a business is sort of the people you're mixing with. You try to keep up with them, don't you? If you're going to a council school and all your friends are farm workers, maybe you'll only want to be a farm worker.[27]

The subtext of these comments is obvious; not only should their offspring avoid associates who devalue education, they should also be careful not to become involved in a culture of sex, drugs and rock 'n' roll. One reason for staying on in a sixth form at school and going to university is to meet prospective sexual and marital partners who are forming, or have formed, projects of the self, and who are therefore autonomous agents, capable of relationships based on the sophisticated negotiation between selves demanded by this ethic.

The anxieties that parents felt when their efforts to keep their offspring on the pathway to university, and within a group of friends who accepted their moral framework for a trajectory of youth, were very evident in an interview with a couple whose teenage son had been getting into 'bad company' at a state school. They had removed him from this school, and sent him to a fee-paying one, as a boarder – but this had gone wrong also:

> *Mr Laburnum*: I think it was disastrous, yes. I think it proba-
> bly was on most levels really, certainly academically. . . . He
> didn't fall in with any sort of norm of private/public board-
> ing school at all, did he?
>
> *Mrs Laburnum*: It did teach him a few things, but I mean he
> was thrown out actually in the end, but we put him some-
> where else because he was in the middle of exams, and
> that's been even worse. . . . Academically none of them have
> worked, but then nowhere would have worked really. . . .
> When he left we should have sent him to a tutorial college
> in [city] and kept him at home really, because the last
> little effort has been even worse really. . . . But we
> were trying to provide him with the things he wouldn't
> have got, like sport, which he was good at . . . but it was
> a mistake.[28]

In this passage of the interview, Mr and Mrs Laburnum became both very intense and very uncomfortable, recognizing that they were unable to give a 'morally adequate' account of their performance of their roles as parents, in enabling their son to develop to the point where he could 'make something of himself'.[29] Even the interviewer, becoming aware of their perplexity as they sought to explain and justify their 'mistakes', and being increasingly uncertain what to say, changed the subject. Both parents' capacities to sustain a creditable version of themselves in the interview seemed to be faltering, because they had not made decisions which led to their son passing his GCSEs and embarking on the next stage towards a satisfactory project of the self.

But other interviewees faced a rather different problem in accounting for their decisions as parents. Several mentioned the dilemma they encountered when their children reached the stage of entering secondary schools and taking public examinations, because they saw it as essential that they attained good enough 'A' levels to go to university. A surprisingly large proportion of the couples, even those on quite modest incomes, contemplated or actually chose private education for their children at this point. For example, Mr and Mrs Rowan (working as a manager in an accountancy firm and a school meals and classroom assistant) said they would sell their house and move into a caravan if he became redundant (as he feared he might) rather than take their two children out of private education, because 'regardless of what we think of the money, the main priority as far as we're concerned is the children's education'.[30]

For this couple and several others, such choices posed no cultural problems, because they were politically conservative and accepted the idea that fee-paying schools were appropriate for the children of those who could afford them; parents had the duty to help their offspring gain advantages in competition with others in labour markets. Mr Lime, for instance, said he felt 'sorry for the others' who did not get the same head start as his children were receiving through this form of schooling, because it allowed his offspring to escape from those who might distract them from the quest for higher education and labour-market advantage.[31]

However, there were other couples who recognized that such choices had implications for their political commitments and ran against their ideals for comprehensive education. Not only was the advantage they would gain by doing this unfair; it also undermined the principle that state schools could only hope to achieve excellence if *all* parents, including those of the most able children, supported them:

Mr Redwood: (a local politician): [T]he political party of which we are members have no particular hang-ups about private education. OK, the party policy is in favour of comprehensive education rather than selective education. But the party . . . has always been one of freedom of choice for individuals, and therefore if that is the way in which any individuals choose to spend their money, well that's fair enough. . . .

> *Mrs Redwood*: I basically don't think it's fair, but I think at the
> end of the day Bruce and I always agree that the children,
> the family comes first. I suppose that's rather wet really but
> that's what we feel. If politics interferes, that has to go.[32]

In similar vein, Mr Yew, talking about his children's private education, said that it was something that was contrary to his principles as a socialist (he came from a working-class family and was formerly a strong trade-unionist). However, he said, 'When it comes to a clash between your politics and your family . . . you put the family first.'[33]

Finally, those parents living in districts with schools whose pupils performed badly in GCSE and 'A' level exams faced a similar decision over whether to move house, to make their offspring eligible to attend more successful schools.

> *Dr Conifer*: What is worrying us, we're coming to the decision
> point with our eldest, with that it looks to us that if we stay
> here, particularly here, then the only option we have to
> make sure she gets the best she needs is to send her to
> private school . . . because there are no alternatives in [city]
> of the same, or even adequate calibre. . . . We're socialists
> [laughs] and don't believe in private schools.[34]

What these extracts show is that the morality of the autonomous self, with its requirement on parents to equip their children to 'make something of themselves', cannot provide an adequate guide to the wider world of decisions which affect the life chances of others in the same society. In so far as it supplies any guidance, it justifies an ethic of self-development and self-improvement under conditions of competition in labour markets, in which others will get left behind and will suffer bad consequences from this. 'Equality of opportunity' of this kind is recognized as unfair, and no solutions are offered.

> *Mrs Quince*: So I think we possibly thought that he [son]
> would have a better opportunity in the private sector [of
> education]. Whether we're right or wrong I don't know, but
> we'll find out at the end of the day, won't we?[35]

Mrs Blackthorn: I think they [privately-educated children] are more advantaged in society, rightly or wrongly, therefore one wants to do the best for one's children.[36]

Others commented quite cynically on the decisions of those with political views of a different kind:

Mr Hazel: I think it's a false argument, I mean one is interested in choice, and seeing the contortions one's friends are going through, while good practising socialists, in order to make . . . to make sure that they get the school of their choice. I mean the so-called equal-opportunity state system would have you in fits of laughter.[37]

Mr Larch: It's like all these socialist councillors. Mrs [name] – she said 'Private education is appalling'; yet one child went to [boys' private school] and one went to [girls' private school].[38]

This failure of the project of autonomous selves to provide adequate links with a wider political framework for choices in relation to the needs and rights of others was evident in other decisions. On the question of private health insurance, Mr Lime, a self-employed architect, recognized the shortcomings of such schemes over emergencies, for which the National Health Service was best suited, but chose to subscribe to one rather than risk being on a waiting list for a 'routine' condition:

Mr Lime: And I actually decided, for fairly selfish reasons, because I thought if I've got to work hard and be the bread-winner as such, I don't want all the hassle of being worried if one of my family ever needed some kind of operation which they wouldn't get on the NHS. So it's really for my own peace of mind.[39]

Mrs Mahogany recognized that her subscription to a private health care scheme was not to get better care ('I think the care in hospital was probably better on the National Health') but 'it's just the speed of getting in, I suppose'.[40] In other words, it was worth paying to gain the advantages of a quicker treatment than others not able to pay.

In another area of decision-making, many working mothers employed child-minders, whom they often described as if they were family members, using terms such as 'supergran'. Mrs Lime said that her child preferred to sit on the child-minder's lap at a birthday party, 'and I thought that can't be a bad thing because she obviously gets on well with her'.[41] Mrs Hazel praised the dedication and professionalism of the child-minders in the city, and had chosen hers to suit the needs of her very active small daughter.

> *Mrs Hazel*: [T]hey have to be active people, and when I interview them I make sure of that.... Unfortunately the little one seems to have exhausted two of the child-minders. One had a bad back from lifting her so much eventually, and the other had a nervous breakdown [laughs].... But while they were on top form it was great, and the children seem to have adapted to each one extraordinarily well.[42]

Mrs Hemlock had employed one of her husband's former students to look after her children: '[A]lthough I didn't realize it at the time, it was a disastrous thing to have done for her . . . to have these two small children . . . and she obviously found it difficult to cope.'[43]

These casualties of the interviewees' projects of self through employment and responsibility for self-developing care of their children were described with some compassion, but little sense of possible fundamental injustice. Similarly Mrs Ash told of the flexibility of her working time requirements.

> *Mrs Ash*: I'm supposed to work 17½ hours a week: in fact I tend to work more like 20, 21 . . .
>
> *Q*: Does the child-minder have any limits? Does she ever say, 'No, hang on, I can't do that?'
>
> *Mrs Ash*: No, I think she's fairly short of money, which is handy. . . . So if I need to, thankfully, 'cause my job demands that.[44]

Whereas the social relations described in Jane Austen's novels are ones of great inequality, both in property and power and between classes and genders, the accounts given by mainstream

British couples gave a picture of partnerships between autonomous selves, each with a project of self-development and self-
improvement through employment and family life. But this did
not supply a set of standards and principles linking the ethic of
partnership with wider social roles, or prescribe ways of treating
others fairly. Interviewees either giggled in describing manifest
inequalities and injustices, or sailed on in their descriptions of how
such arrangements suited their projects of self-fulfilment or of
responsible parenthood, without noting their adverse effects on
the life chances of others less fortunate than themselves.

A rather different version of the potential contradictions
between projects of self and partnership, initially entered through
sex, and their wider social relations, is the controversy that arose
over the appointment as Bishop of Reading of the openly gay
Jeffrey John. In this case, John's public pitch appealed to an ethic
of love between himself and his long-term partner, and was based
on the convention of a relationship between two autonomous
individuals, originally engaged in a bond of sexual commitment
which had matured to non-sexual mutual fidelity. He explicitly
adopted the norm of heterosexual partnership, and in this way,
sought to resist the attack of Anglo-Catholics and evangelicals,
who argued that gay sex was contrary to biblical teaching and
traditional church morality. Canon John tacitly invoked the
secular religious standards of everyday non-Christians, agnostics
and atheists alike – that the self is sacred, and that all relationships of long-term partnerships based on mutual projects of self-
development between loving, autonomous and self-responsible
individuals are therefore sacred. (In the USA, a similar justification was put forward by the first Episcopal Church bishop who
is openly gay, Gene Robinson. Canon John's appointment was
later rescinded.)

The quarrel about the sinfulness of actual sexual acts between
men was therefore relegated to a doctrinal issue, made all the
more marginal in Canon John's case by the claim that no such
acts were currently taking place. Sex as the pathway to a sancti-
fied relationship (the universal norm), and long-term partnership
as the relationship in which the sanctity of self-improving selves
is best protected, thus become the foci of the moral issues; but
this approach cannot settle the question of how homosexuality

should be integrated into a predominantly heterosexual society, or how clergy should live amongst a predominantly unbelieving populace. As in issues of property, class, exploitation and economic domination, the morality of self and sex cannot provide standards with which reliably to uphold and justify or criticize and condemn current patterns and lifestyles; nor can it be reconciled with traditional religious morality.

In the chapters that follow, the implications of this lack of coherence between moralities of intimacy and partnership, rationales of private consumption, and principles for justice in social relations, will be explored in depth. What has to be explained is how private relations of equality and autonomy give rise to wider social formations of inequality, exploitation and coercion, not solely (or perhaps even mainly) through the actions of governments, but also through the choices of individuals.

4

The Nature of Change

It is time to return to my very first formulation of the issues addressed in this book. At the start of the Introduction, I pointed out how strongly engaging and engrossing our lives are, especially when we are young, and how deeply we experience all their elements. But these same ideas, lifestyles, relationships and commitments often seem alien and odd to us when we look back on them. The web in which we live changes imperceptibly but relentlessly; we change it, and it changes us.

In this chapter, I shall try to make convincing links between these processes of change and the account of the connectedness of the web which I have developed so far. In my lifetime, there has been a transformation of the collective institutional order which provides the context for our individual projects, family patterns and group strategies. My generation grew up in welfare states, which aimed to restrain the ambitions and reduce the advantages of their ablest citizens for the sake of solidarity with the rest. They supplied a context in which almost all members of a society shared certain often mediocre facilities (as the National Health Service and comprehensive schools then were, in retrospect), in order to foster bonds and mutual loyalties between them. This in turn made us willing to pay our taxes, so that we and our fellow citizens could be looked after (usually rather unceremoniously) when we were old, sick, unemployed or down on our luck.

Let's focus on the part played by the actions of individuals in changing the institutional landscape of their lives; and let's start by considering the more dramatic transformations that took place in the state socialist countries of the Soviet bloc – say Slovakia[1] –

in the late 1980s. In the official histories, most Slovak citizens were busy going about their socialist tasks, in a frustrated state of repressed self-responsibility, stifled entrepreneurialism and democratic desire, in the years up to 1989. Dissidents criticized the Communist Party and its repressive order, but few heard their voices because they were put in prison. Then suddenly, events, first in Berlin and then in Prague, triggered mass demonstrations and that order collapsed. People greeted these changes with varying degrees of enthusiasm (poor Slovaks still refer to 'the coup'[2]), and started the process of building new institutions, and living new lives.

In reality, of course, the experience of this transformation was not like this at all for the people who went through it. Under socialism, most citizens pursued a parallel, hidden existence to the compliant, public one which they lived out under the eye of officialdom. They had second jobs or small businesses, and they exchanged illegally acquired goods, and informally produced services, between networks of friends. When the big change happened, they felt alarmed or elated, but soon recognized that those other activities, furtively followed, were the ones out of which their new projects and strategies might be developed. The more they had been secret entrepreneurs, and the better the links in their covert networks, the greater chance they had of success in the new order of capitalism, markets and democracy.[3]

The point I want to make with this example is that our individual actions often contribute to change, without us being aware of this or intending it. Under state socialism, Slovaks who stole from the state, traded with friends and ran unofficial businesses were not consciously preparing the way for global corporate enterprise or membership of the European Union. The vast majority of them did not want such outcomes and – ten years later – a great many of them regretted most aspects of the big change which had transformed their collective lives.[4]

Although the processes of transformation in the UK and Western Europe were very different from these, there were some common features. In the UK, for instance, Margaret Thatcher was elected in 1979 more because of the failures of the Labour administration than because the voters accepted her ideology for radical market reform. Throughout the 1980s, survey evidence repeatedly indicated majority loyalty to the welfare state and even a preference for more extensive redistribution of resources towards the worse-off.[5] Her success in being twice re-elected was the result of luck, political skill and the ineptitude of the opposition. But in the meanwhile, acting within the new institutional structures she created, millions of ordinary people were pushing through versions of the transformations she championed, without really wanting to or knowing they were doing it.

They did this through their everyday activities and interactions – dating, drinking, leisure, shopping, tourism, mass entertainment and so on. Simply by doing these things, within an emerging new infrastructure provided by commercial firms (often international companies, like Asda, McDonald's or Microsoft), they changed their social world. As change agents, they did not directly challenge the morality or political orthodoxy of the post-war years, nor did they try to overthrow its organizational frameworks. By and large, they just bypassed all of them, developing their own more fluid and flexible ways of doing things, and having more fun. Thus innovation and change took place through the actions of anonymous agents, without conscious principles or programmes, going about their everyday lives.

These phenomena seem to demand an explanation in something like the functionalist formula set out in chapters 1 and 2. But functionalist accounts have always been seen as explaining order and stability, not change. Indeed, the standard criticism of functionalism is that it is far too deterministic, and turns individuals into the most dopey kind of cultural dope – dancing like puppets to the tune of the collective, institutional order.[6] Functionalism turns individuals into zombies, not agents of change.

But wait a minute. If we turn from social to biological science, the world's most famous functionalist theory immediately springs to mind. Darwin's account of the origin of the species, through evolution or 'natural selection', is just such a theory. Individual members of species take actions and pursue strategies in order to survive. They choose mates to which they are attracted. They do not intend to promote genetic adaptations, or to select the fittest for the ever-changing environments; they are not aware of symbiosis or mutation. Evolution, and the transformations of the

environment and the species that it wrought, took place spontaneously, through natural processes of 'blind instinct'.

Of course, the standard objection to the application of the
methods of the natural sciences to human behaviour is that
human beings have intentions, plans and strategies,[7] and can perceive causes and trajectories, so they can act with long-term outcomes in view. They can also consciously take account of the
effects of their actions on others, even others remote from themselves, so they can deliberately aim to help or harm them. Hence
they never act out of instinct alone, and always have some kind
of broader view and longer-term purpose.

But, as the examples of both the Slovak and the Thatcher
'revolutions' show, people in fact have very little awareness, at
the time, either of what their individual actions are doing to the
collective infrastructure or how those actions are influenced by
collective institutions. However hard and long they may reflect on
morality, culture, art or politics, and however committed they may
be, either to conserving the collective landscape or to its violent
destruction, it often seems in retrospect that their casual or banal
actions were actually more meaningful than their grand designs
and programmes. What they did fairly automatically, without
thinking about its social significance, turned out to have been
more influential, for themselves and for their societies, than what
they thought they were doing.

To give another example: South Africa, during the final years
of apartheid, was under strong pressure, both from the boycotts
and campaigns of the world's great powers and from the ANC
(African National Congress) resistance movement at home and
in its neighbouring states, to reform or abandon its regime. But
if the factors which finally brought about sudden change in the
late 1980s are closely analysed, they can be seen to relate to more
humble processes. The inconveniences and inefficiencies of the
petty rules segregating the 'races' and, above all, their damaging
effects on the economy supplied the catalysts for change. Skills
shortages and the rapid growth of the prosperity of black consumers demanded transformation. The silent (and technically
illegal) march of black purchasers into white housing markets, and
black workers, traders and service providers into white consumer

markets, were ultimately the factors which brought the old order down.[8] Of course, the change demanded an alternative vision, which was provided by Nelson Mandela and the ANC. Apartheid had been transformed from within by the individual actions of millions of citizens, following their immediate interests, long before its formal structures were abolished.

Among the social sciences, it is economics, of course, which comes closest to the natural scientific form of explanation. Many criticisms of the 'dismal' aspects of economics stem from its claims to offer 'iron laws' and deterministic theorems. But although we may justifiably object to its more grandiose claims of accounting for the 'spontaneous order of freedom' through market relations, it has an excellent track record in capturing the unintentional aspects of collective forms. In the New Institutional Economics,[9] it has also developed specific models of collective continuity and change, which have much predictive value.

How then can we combine the rather formal, mathematical and deterministic powers of economic theory with the more human and accessible insights of the other social sciences to understand our experiences of living in a changing social environment? How do its axioms help us grasp the paradox of being so engrossed in our present projects and values, and later being so glad that they, and the world we now live in, did not turn out as we hoped and planned? I shall use an early and clever example of an attempt to provide such an explanation to examine what economics can and cannot contribute to a convincing story about the transformation of collective life. It is Locke's account of the invention of money, and how it justified unequal holdings of property. Again, I paraphrase.

According to Locke, our earliest ancestors, living in a state of nature, shared all things in common. They pursued simple, pastoral, communal lives, grazing their animals in the meadows and gathering the berries of the forest, with only the most rudimentary private possessions. At this time, everyone was entitled to the fruits of their individual labours and to acquire anything, so long as they left as much and as good for the rest. It was pointless for anyone to try to get much more than everyone else had, because the foodstuffs they produced would quickly rot and be wasted.[10]

But then someone had the bright idea of using 'a little piece of yellow metal', both as a means of exchange, and as a store of wealth.[11] This meant that the foresightful and industrious few could hoard up something of lasting value, a surplus from what they produced for immediate consumption. These prudent individuals were able to partition off bits of land and increase their output still more. When all the land was divided up in this way, and some people were left with no land, it became necessary to create a political society, with laws and courts to guarantee property rights.[12]

On the face of it, this process seemed to violate the laws of nature under which everyone in the communal society had a right to everything, on that one simple proviso. After all, the invention of money had led to very unequal holdings, with some having no alternative but to work for wages, since they lacked the means to produce enough for their subsistence. But Locke resisted this conclusion. He insisted that the wealth derived from the privatization of the world's natural resources had so much increased productivity and wages that a day labourer in Devon lived better than a king 'in the wild woods of America'.[13] Since everyone was better off in a society run on commercial principles, no injustice had been done. Anyone who refused to work, or who stole or used violence, was acting like a wild animal and deserved to be punished, if necessary by death.[14]

This story contains some slippery shifts and tricky moves. On the one hand, it presents the invention of money as a kind of happy accident, all of whose consequences were therefore to be regarded as unintended. On the other, as soon as the ignorant masses chose to use money, because of its convenience, they were taken to have *consented*[15] to *all* those consequences, including the unforeseen and unforeseeable ones, such as capitalism, factory employment, the criminal justice system and the death penalty for property offences, 'they having by a tacit and voluntary consent found out a way, how man may *fairly* possess more land than he himself can use the product of, by receiving in exchange for the overplus, Gold and Silver, which may be hoarded up without *injury to anyone*' (emphasis in original).[16]

Locke's simple rural yokels were not cultural dopes; they were victims of a con-trick. It is perfectly plausible, indeed ingenious, to trace all the complex trappings of the early modern state to the invention of money, the enclosure of the commons, the privatization of natural resources and the development of employment, wages and prices. But it is disingenuous to claim that the first step in this 'institutional evolution' was enough to spark off all the others – that the trappings of wealth and power were all the spontaneous, unintended consequences of that naive experiment. Somewhere along the line, individuals, groups and coalitions were acting strategically to gain advantages for themselves over others, just as surely as if they had armed themselves for robbery. And the gallows and gibbet were not erected to guarantee fair shares for all.

Although some scholars still insist on reading Locke as a kind of radical, who justified the widening of property holdings and a society of equal independent producers,[17] his track record in power under William and Mary does little to confirm this view.[18] And this piece of philosophical enquiry serves as a warning of the problems of combining economic with ethical reasoning in social scientific issues. Locke's is not a very good model of how to explain the evolution of collective institutions through the unintended consequences of individual actions, because it tries to encompass too much. But the basic idea was a very clever one, and social scientists have been trying to do something similar ever since, to explain social change and the transformations of collective life. Indeed, I shall argue, we all try to do this all the time, in explaining our decisions and strategies to ourselves and each other.

In explaining change, we have to take account of the legacy of the past, which provides the context for our starting point. In everyday stories of our lives, such as the one I give to my fellow-travellers on long journeys (see pp. 19–21), this usually takes the form of a version of our family of birth, the community in which they lived, and (if we are abroad) where this fitted into our country of origin. In other words, it is an account of who we are, in terms of the accidents of birth, kinship, blood, faith and soil – the unchosen but inescapable elements in our identities. All these give rise to bonds, loyalties and duties from which we never really escape; they travel with us through our lives, in the way we look, speak and act.

The theoretical equivalent of this is how one tries to capture the legacy of collective forms in which individual lives are led – the institutional heritage, with its mixture of customs, values, laws, practices and structures. In Locke's justification of property, the moral origins of contemporary (English) society were traced to a kind of Anglo-Saxon utopia of woods and commons, full of deer and acorns, to which such truly English values as the love of freedom, the respect for the individual and the demand for consensual systems of government are traced. This is his version of the historical community of blood and soil, and it is an ethical rather than a political community. English people get from it their sense of justice and the right order of things, as well as their sense of rootedness and belonging, before any political society was established. As a story, it is a kind of model for how we try to explain ourselves to others – our principles, totems and taboos.

The second part of Locke's justification of property is an evolutionary account of how the English economy came into being. He seeks to explain the current distribution of wealth, work and status, in terms of a process of change, in which human institutions were adapted to the unintended (but benevolent) consequences of the invention of money. Although this account is only partially successful (Adam Smith's a century later was much better), it is once more a kind of model of how we tell others what we have made of ourselves, through our projects and commitments. But – like Locke's evolutionary story of commercial and political relations – it is often one of accidents, coincidences and unintended consequences. It is a tale of the unexpected, full of surprises, as well as an account of how we have fulfilled our purposes. We tell of a stumbling journey, rather than a well-planned route march.

In telling the story of our lives, the collective contexts in which we develop our projects of self are usually left implicit. We do not often spell out the changes which were happening in the world around us as we were making our way, unless these were dramatic ones, like wars or revolutions. But I would suggest that we stand ready to do so, if required by an interlocutor. We would expect ourselves to be able to give an account, for example, of how the steps in a career related to major shifts in market conditions or global patterns of employment (if we work in the private sector), or path-breaking innovations in government policy programmes (if we work in the public sector). I have also shown (pp. 68–73) that we expect ourselves to be able to explain such decisions as how we choose schools for our children, and will show this in relation to plans for providing for our old age (pp. 94–8). A convincing version accounts for these in terms of significant shifts in opportunities, advantages and barriers, but also of their moral and political implications.

Suppose, for example, a fellow-passenger on a train or plane challenged me to explain the sudden shift in my 'career' pattern in about 1990, from commitment to high standards of practice in and training for British social work, to swanning around the Continent as a visiting professor. I would expect myself to be able to offer an explanation which included at least the following elements:

1   How I reconciled this with my family responsibilities – in this case, telling how my children had grown up, and how my partner (who had travelled in her youth, which I had not) both generously encouraged me to take the chance and wanted to do justice to her elderly parents' needs at home.
2   How this represented a rational response to the new set of opportunities, advantages and barriers, presented by Margaret Thatcher's ten years of institutional reforms – in this case, explaining my disagreement with the fundamental shift in public policy, structure and management of the social services in the UK, my search for fresh inspiration in other European countries and my (Quixotic) attempt to encourage people in the former Communist countries to identify, value and conserve the good elements in their legacy.
3   How this radical change in the direction of my project of self was consistent with my political and personal values – in this case, how the breach in solidarity with former colleagues, ex-students and service users, and the apparent maverick individualism of my quest, could be reconciled with my espoused views on social policy and social work.

Finally, if I was in a mood to confide such a morally ambiguous conclusion and evaluation, I might admit that in retrospect I was (shamefacedly) rather grateful to Margaret Thatcher for saving me from what might otherwise have been a slightly dull (if worthy) life, and for forcing me to challenge myself in new ways.

So, if we want to give a full account of our projects of self, which makes sense of the way we have spun together their private and public aspects and which explains how they have both reflected and contributed to changes in the collective life of our societies, we take on a quite sophisticated task. We require ourselves to say in what respects we were ahead of the game (in terms of institutional changes) or behind the game. In my case, I was behind the game in my first marriage. It was almost immediately a cultural anachronism, because I totally failed to anticipate the feminist revolution or see how frustrated my wife would be by the differences in our opportunities of access to the wider public sphere. I also failed to find any remedies for this. With my recent mobile lifestyle, I was slightly ahead of the game, and surprised to find that the collective world seemed to be adapting to my requirements, even as I developed my project.

An explanation of this complexity and sophistication, if successfully accomplished, would meet many of the demands of a social scientific explanation of how individuals achieve agency within collective structures and cultural contexts. In other words, people telling each other about their life stories, in trains, pubs or other informal settings, are being do-it-yourself social scientists, reflecting on the collective world and how their individual projects are influenced by (and influence) changes in it.

To understand why these requirements of a convincing story of oneself are so engaging, despite their complexity – why we try so hard to live up to them – is to grasp a great deal of the hold the collective world has over us. We are aware that the social units in which we live our lives do in many ways determine the way we think, and hence the choices we make. They provide the concepts, categories and classifications in terms of which we make sense of the world around us, of other people's behaviour and of our own actions.[19] But we are also aware (more dimly) that some of these patterns of thought have fundamental significance for our identities and values, and others are merely the products of minor organizational routines, petty alliances and loyalties or highly artificial customs.

This distinction between what is conventional and shallow and what is meaningful and deep, about the hold which the collective world exerts over us, works on at least two dimensions. We often experience those aspects which come from our families and communities of origin as bindingly deep, because they arise from biology, from upbringing and from subsistence. Since they come from blood, guts and soil, they seem to be part of our natures, and to be *natural*.[20] By contrast, we are conscious that political and economic institutions are artificial and changeable, but certain aspects of their influence on us make such strong and convincing sense that they appear to be *rational*. They must, it seems, correspond to scientific laws, or permanent features of the material universe.[21] So, while recognizing that our ancestors and we ourselves have collectively made up these institutions, and that we are constantly adapting them, we try to find aspects of their mindsets and regulations which can be relied upon to make sense of our experiences over a longer period – at least for our lifetimes.

When we can convince ourselves that the natural aspects of our collective worlds coincide with the rational ones, or are highly compatible with them, we will be sure that the ideas derived from these features will be the ones to which we should orientate our stories of ourselves. Within our social worlds, our formal and informal exchanges constantly spin versions which test these core concepts, categories and classifications, and reinforce the ones which seem to work best and be most convincing, on these two dimensions. But we subtly modify them also, through these very processes.

Like Locke, in his account of the invention of money, we try to identify those artificially created aspects of collective life which turned out to be most influential, just as we attempt to explain to ourselves how actions and choices which seemed trivial at the time had the most enduring and unexpected consequences. We then seek to line up those unintended outcomes (both in the collective landscape and in our own lives) with the features we regard as fundamental, because natural and rational. Locke tried to show how benefits such as wealth, increased productivity of labour and stable institutions for political justice, arose artificially and accidentally, but how they were consistent with the moral principles which applied in the state of nature. We try to explain how the unanticipated twists and turns in our individual lives, which came about through accidents and coincidences or by casual choices, turned out to make sense in terms of our fundamental commitments to our inner selves, our closest relationships and our most lasting beliefs.

The collective world, of course, is made up of several different kinds of unit. It contains the 'natural' ones of family and informal community; the more organized associations of civil society; the collectivities of the economy, such as firms and trade unions; and the political world of parties, governments and international institutions.[22] In all these units, we make social bonds of different kinds with other members, which will be analysed below (see chapter 6). The way we assist, depend upon, influence and make demands on others in each of these types of social unit varies considerably. Processes of change take place in each, and in the interactions between them.

Trying to make sense of how these changes happen to us, we select chains of events, sequences which seem to be causally linked, and reconstruct the connections. We attempt to trace them to shifts in another part of the collective landscape, and to the intentional or unintended consequences of the actions of others. But we are not necessarily seeking to smooth out all the wrinkles and creases in the web in which we live. On the contrary, our accounts frequently reveal or point to tensions or contradictions between the concepts, categories and classifications which are so useful in one sphere, and the principles and values which apply in another.[23] We saw this in the mainstream interviewees' accounts of how they chose their children's schools (pp. 68–73).

In this way, change comes about because the web is cobbled together in ad hoc ways, and not spun by a machine, or a single giant spider. Those of us who want change, and think we can see a way of bringing it about (through a coordinated coalition, or by opportunistic individual action) can recognize gaps and tangles in its structures, and take advantage of them.[24] But many more of us will simply, by our everyday, unthinking use of the web, make the gaps larger, and the tangles more dense. And this will change the shape of the web, and create new gaps and tangles. So change in the collective landscape happens both by design and by the unre-flective, routine actions of masses of individuals.

Such change, even when it occurs by attrition and very slowly (like ants crawling over a surface, and gradually compressing it, or causing it to crack imperceptibly), eventually causes discomfort. Like the ants, we start to slip on the shiny parts of the path, and trip over the cracks, bumping into our colleagues. We recognize this in the accounts we give to them of ourselves and our pro-jects. We find that some of the concepts, categories and classifica-tions which have proved so useful in our sense-making no longer fit well together. Or we suddenly have difficulty in reconciling our principles with our choices. And even our taken-for-granted ideas about the social units to which we belong seem no longer to match the routines of our lifestyles or the demands of our relationships.

For example, in our research study the mainstream inter-viewees' versions of their decisions on certain key topics displayed both great variations and considerable perplexities. We have seen how, on the question of children's education, they used certain standard concepts, categories and classifications. The most striking examples of standardized thinking lay in the use of the same words, phrases and even examples – such as Mr Palm's and Mr Linden's choice of selling ice creams to denote a non-professional choice of employment by their children (see pp. 68–9).

But some concepts (such as 'household') and some relationships (such as 'family') posed them difficulties, because they required them to make a bridge between 'natural' ties and obligations, and the ethic of choice and self-development which they espoused. Whereas in traditional societies households and families would be groupings perceived as both natural and rational, legitimized by reference to both degrees of kinship and common economic func-tions, in the social order of mainstream UK relations these cate-gories often cut across actual living arrangements and personal connections.

One of our research questions was about the respondents' rela-tionships with their parents, and their plans for the possibility that they might become frail and dependent in their old age. Some of them were already caring for, or offering support to, parents who lived nearby. They described in detail the ways they cared for them, and the ethics that informed this care. But most lived far from their parents, and saw them only occasionally. Their versions of 'household' and 'family' did not include taking in such kin, and their duty to develop themselves as individuals did not easily accommodate such obligations.

Our research study indicated that the way most couples squared this circle was to attribute to their elderly parents (some of whom were already very frail) an extraordinary will, and almost supernatural capacity, for the exercise of autonomy. These were selves who, having developed their independence within a culture of freedom and choice, now insisted on remaining within this ethic to the bitter end.

> *Mr Redwood*: And my mother is one of those totally indomitable people who would almost rather die than ask for help. . . . As I say, my mother for her age is amazingly fit and is very capable of looking after and sorting my father out.[25]

> *Mrs Teak*: My mother's 70 and she leads a very active life. She lives in Sussex on her own, and we see her from time to time – she comes here and we go up there – but she's fiercely independent. . . . Yes, she's emphatic that she's making provision for going into some sort of home or something like that.[26]

> *Mrs Laburnum*: Well, one of them's dead so . . . I mean my father is 70 [indistinct], he's got a wife who's younger. . . . No, I think he's got adequate means, and I'm sure he'd want to be as independent until he dropped really.[27]

> *Mrs Oak*: They're both married again [after divorce]. They come in and out of our lives, without any great sense of responsibility . . . and everybody seems fairly fit and independent and responsible for themselves at the moment.[28]

The slightly nervous tone of these remarks turned to near panic when the interviewer pressed the point, and asked how they would act if their parents asked to come and live with them. For example,

Mrs Laburnum: I mean I can't see him, I can't see that happening but . . . God, I'd leave the country [laughs].[29]

Mrs Hemlock: There's only my father – fortunately I think it's unlikely he's going to need looking after anyway – but there isn't any way I'd be able to.[30]

In mainstream UK culture, it appears that the dominant ethic is one in which older people are conventionally seen as wanting to sustain trajectories of self through retirement and widowhood, and into the final stages of their lives. Autonomy is so strongly prized, as a feature of self-development and self-fulfilment, that it is attributed even to those with severe illnesses and disabilities, requiring daily assistance to live their lives. Clearly, such aspirations for 'independence' involve the classification of reliance on others as compatible with autonomous selfhood, if it is a strictly commercial relationship. Self-developmental and self-fulfilling selves are allowed to *buy* care from strangers, but not to claim it from their offspring or other kin.

This indicates the importance of material resources for maintaining the social relations of equal autonomy between those engaged in projects of the self. As Mrs Laburnum commented, having 'adequate means' was a precondition of her father's independence 'till he dropped'. As in relationships between partners, this convention – that individuals prefer stranger care to family care, because it is more consistent with the sanctity of their selves – presupposes that each member of the moral community has access to sufficient resources to sustain a life on their own, and is unwilling to demean themselves by falling as costs on other family members.

If collective units like families and kinship systems did not provide the binding standards for relationships with others, which social groupings did? The discussion on pp. 86–9 suggested that the answers to this question would not always be obvious. If institutions are effectively 'doing our thinking for us', and if these ideas are seen as natural and rational, we are unaware of their influence, and of the classifications they impose on our thought and action. Douglas argues that institutions are at their most effective when they are invisible.[31] Since the convention that was shared between all the interviewees in our research on mainstream couples was that they had a duty to develop themselves through free choices, they were unlikely to be aware of such constraints. They saw themselves as subscribing to self-generated standards and principles, not external or traditional ones.

However, there were some important clues about how cultural standards operated in the explanations they offered for a whole range of decisions. We became aware that their answers had certain *design features*, which the interviewees took to be characteristic of a meaningfully rational account – features that were 'artfully accomplished' in their interactions with the interviewer, but not consciously noticed by him (nor, we thought, by them) at the time. What was also recognizable on subsequent analysis was that we as interviewers seemed to respond to answers which had these features in the same way:

> [W]e noticed that there was a design feature of accounts of decisions (as rational and meaningful choices) that seemed to lead us to signal our acceptance of the respondent's version (by a positive interpretation or a different question, rather than further 'probing' or seeking further clarification).[32]

One neat example of this was the following account by Mrs Alder, a craft worker who also did the books for her husband's building business, in answer to a question about how she had decided to be self-employed, rather than just staying at home or having a full-time job.

> *Mrs Alder*: I chose self-employment because it's convenient. I've got three children and if I'm working here from home then I'm available if they're sick or whatever, and I enjoy the freedom of it. [My craft] is something you either do self-employed or you don't do at all because otherwise the commercial equipment means sitting in a factory making [artefacts] and that doesn't appeal to me at all. I like the variety and I like being able to organize my own timetable.[33]

This answer had all the necessary elements to 'satisfy' an interviewer who had come, through interactions with others answering our questions, to share the self-imposed cultural standards of our respondents. On the one hand, it accounted for her working life in terms of choices and creative freedom, within the terms of her responsibility for her children (as developing potential selves): we called this 'quality reasoning'. On the other hand, it explained her decision by reference to the economics of production – investment in equipment, factory organization and commercial marketing: this we called 'quantity reasoning'. This combination of 'value rationality' and 'economic rationality' seemed to satisfy both the interviewee and the interviewer. We noted that in fact the 'reasoning' in relation to values and other family members was often so brief and pithy as to be cryptic (Mrs Alder was unusually clear), but even in the face of apparently incomplete accounts (for instance, a sentence tailing off unfinished, or the mere mention of 'family reasons') we as interviewers seemed predisposed to 'accept' answers with this design feature.[34]

It was important for us also to recognize that the cultural standards at work here did not prescribe particular outcomes, such as specific choices for the women over household roles, full- or part-time work. What was required was 'to be artful in managing the non-contradictory dual reasoning in their versions of decisions since, once given, this takes on the character of an external and obligatory "social fact" against which the rationality (or otherwise) of the decision is to be assessed'.[35] So the cultural preference for versions of such decisions which had these design features became something like an imperative when interviewees had trouble in achieving this (for instance, they could not make quality-of-life and economic factors non-contradictory). Under these circumstances, they reconstructed their choices as 'irrational' and sought psychological reasons for them in themselves and their situations (see also pp. 69–70). Here Mr Alder, a builder, was trying to explain why he did not train his son, who wanted to join him in the family business, even though it would be economically advantageous for him to do so. Failing to give non-contradictory quality and quantity reasons, he blamed his irrational feelings:

Mr Alder: Yes, he starts next year. So he's looking elsewhere for somebody because I say I will not train him. He gets his training elsewhere and then when he's trained he can come in with me.

Q: The reason for that being?

Mr Alder: Well I think, when I actually analyse my attitude towards him I'm very hard on him, I'm very analytical of his every move, and you probably have the correct word for it, but I think I'm going through a stage with him where I actually resent him becoming a man. It's strange, I hate myself for it. I can feel myself bubbling and yet because he's actually developing and getting bigger, I tend to shout at him but I don't really want to. It's something I'm really struggling with at the moment. I find him really annoying and yet with my apprentice, who's the same age, I'm far more tolerant of the kid and it really baffles me.[36]

Here Mr Alder was unable to reinforce his decision not to train his son himself with an economic reason, so he was forced to look for an interpersonal, psychological explanation. This, and countless other examples, led us to conclude that the cultural standardization process demanded this particular combination of elements in a satisfactory account. Those who positively chose state schools for their children often argued that this was an issue of (public) economics as well as a political decision. Although it was a matter of principle to uphold the non-selective, comprehensive ideal, the aim of doing so was partly to get proper government funding. By the same token, interviewees had most trouble, and experienced most discomfort, where they were unable to combine quality and quantity reasons in this way.

The cultural standard of autonomy and material self-sufficiency which most interviewees attributed to their parents was also, of course, one which they expected themselves to meet. This meant that they had to explain how they were providing for their own old age, using similar quality and quantity reasoning for their decisions. Their trajectory of selfhood included provision for this period of their lives, when their autonomy could no longer be linked to their earning power. For example, Mr Box, a self-employed professional, described how he was contributing to a private pension in addition to a long-standing occupational scheme:

Mr Box: The feeling that the Company one was inadequate, I suppose, and I don't necessarily look forward to retirement or feel it's something I've waited years to tick away until it arrives, but we began to feel that we ought to make better provision, and that's what we've done.[37]

Most women in our study did not require themselves to give such accounts of planning ahead for retirement, but Mrs Fieldmaple made her reasons for taking out a private pension (even though she was not currently earning) quite clear:

> *Mrs Fieldmaple*: But yeah, I would like to have a bigger private pension. I would like to feel more independent in that respect, I think.
>
> *Q*: This is independent of the state, you're sort of saying . . . ?
>
> *Mrs Fieldmaple*: Well, independent of Jonathan [partner] in a way, because I'm not suggesting I'm going to rush off next week or anything, but if there came a situation when we weren't together then I mean he will have contributed to his university pension for years and have a really good income when he's retired whereas I shall be there with my little [bank's name] pension [laughs] . . . so that I would like to feel that I could be separate and have a reasonable income.[38]

Those quotations show how interviewees anticipated trajectories of autonomous, self-improving selves, sustaining the fulfilment of their life projects. They sought to continue their personal development beyond middle age, either within their existing partnerships or – if these proved disappointing – outside them. Although few of them were able to sustain 'rational economic accounts' of their pension plans (in the sense that they could explain how they had invested and saved so as to provide an income in retirement which could support their projects), all attempted to do so. Women's versions of themselves as autonomous were almost all compromised by the fact that they had 'invested' in their partners' careers, sacrificing part of their own potential earning power (and incremental gains from promotion and perks) to be 'supportive' of partners' strategies for advantage in their employments. Most women had taken major responsibility for child care and household management. Significantly the exceptions were women whose partners' career plans had stalled or collapsed, and those who had experienced divorce.

Mrs Silverbirch's husband's business had been bankrupt, and she described (in front of him) the financial arrangements they had made since.

> *Mrs Silverbirch*: No, we don't trust each other, not with joint accounts, do we dear? [laughs] We have a completely separate account . . . We don't even share the same bank.[39]

Mrs Birch's husband had not been successful in his new business venture. She was openly critical of his methods.

> *Mrs Birch*: We haven't actually planned for retirement, no . . . obviously over the years the fact that Adrian has changed jobs drastically has meant that any retirement schemes he's belonged to have either been cashed in or added to one another, something like that. We realize that our prospects for retirement are not as rosy as they could be. . . . Certainly, I mean although my salary is hardly magnificent, it certainly is enough to live on, and that's always been in the background that no matter what else happens there will always be that and of course the property as well.[40]

Later, Mrs Birch added that it might be a 'good idea' to have separate bank accounts, and asked rhetorically, 'Why haven't we discussed this earlier?'[41]

Ms Blackthorn had two children, was divorced from her first husband, and had recently set up a joint household with Mr Spruce, also divorced, with his children living at their mother's home.

> *Mr Spruce*: [W]e've talked, and because of our experiences in the past, we've talked about retaining separate [bank] accounts but, of necessity, creating a joint account which pays for joint living.
>
> *Ms Blackthorn*: With a look to the future if anything does go wrong, as it's done in the past. You know, I have dependent children; Dave has children to support, so you have to

think of that in the worst scenario as well. Setting up a
mortgage, setting up a house – what happens if there
should be a split and the home to be sold, and that sort of
thing.[42]

The link between personal autonomy and adequate (individual) material resources became fully visible in the interviews only in relation to previous marriage break-ups and possible future ones. But it did make explicit the assumption behind the partnerships investigated – that men and women should both have enough (in earnings, savings and housing stock value) to sustain their projects of self-development and self-fulfilment, if necessary on their own. Ms Blackthorn was the only interviewee who had experienced claiming social assistance following divorce, and hence had experienced loss of autonomy.

Only one of the interviewees' accounts of their plans for income in retirement seemed watertight, in economic terms. Mr Mahogany, a farmer, gave a highly reasoned version of why he had chosen to invest in his farm, rather than a pension fund; he read the *Financial Times* each day, tracking the returns on pension funds and comparing them with his farm accounts. He found that none of the latter could match the returns from his own business, so he continued to buy land and put up new buildings. All this seemed impeccably rational, yet the interviewer appeared not to be satisfied with his account, probing for weaknesses in his answers. Towards the end of the interview, he asked Mr Mahogany whether he would consider a business in computer software, if it could be proved to be more profitable.

Mr Mahogany: No, I wouldn't be interested in that.

Q: Because?

Mr Mahogany: I just think that some things that look as if
they're more profitable in the short term don't always turn
out to be that way.

Q: Say I could convince you that it could be, suppose I could
produce a hard and fast case, to take you right out of the
farming way of life, and give you a completely different life,
then what?

Mr Mahogany: It would obviously depend very much on the circumstances. I don't think I'd be very keen to do that, to be honest. My goal has always been to have lots of acres I can look out over and I'm here on the job every day, and sometimes it can get over-burdening, but I think I'd still put up with a lower income in farming than . . .

Q: But it's a lifestyle thing as well?

Mr Mahogany: It is a bit as well, yes. You certainly wouldn't do it just for the money [laughs].[43]

Here the interviewer pursues the topic, even paraphrasing what Mr Mahogany says to put it into an 'acceptable' quality-of-life reason, which Mr Mahogany finally adopts. It is only after he confirms that he has both quality and quantity reasons for his decision on pensions that the topic is dropped and the interview ends. At this stage of the research, the 'design feature' of 'satisfactory' answers had not yet been recognized; the interviewer was, in effect, coaching Mr Mahogany in how to construct an artfully accomplished version of a rational decision, within the cultural standards of mainstream UK society, without being aware that he was doing so.

Drawing on examples from our research project, I have argued that current social relations construct some kind of balance between the freedom and change associated with self-development by individuals, and the stability and predictability of a reliable order. This is not unique to post-traditional cultures; there is plenty of evidence that the institutions of other societies have sustained a similar balance (see pp. 104–5 below). What is specific to present affluent Western social relations is the way in which 'value rationality' and 'economic rationality'[44] are combined to sustain this, within the shared assumptions of equal autonomy between 'sacred selves'.

Although family and kinship continued to supply many of the classifications that interviewees used in justifying their decisions, and some still drew on the cultural standards of the era of the welfare state, the social groupings which supplied the economic rationale for their accounts were of a rather different nature. They did not have fixed memberships, nor did they in any obvious way impose their norms on those who affiliated to them. But the logic of commercial organizations, supplying such collective goods as pensions and healthcare, supplied many of the categories and exclusions on which interviewees' 'quantity reasoning' relied. In the next chapter, I turn to these membership organizations.

5

On the Move: Mobility as the Basis for Freedom

If spiders span their webs cooperatively (some may, for all I know), they would need an instinctive way of coordinating their movements with those of others. Because we have no such biological programming for our social behaviour, human beings experience life in the web as in constant tension between individual autonomy and collective constraint. On the whole, we associate movement with freedom (with escaping from the strings which bind us), and staying still as being 'tied down'.

This psychological propensity is reflected in the English language, as well as Anglo-Saxon culture. The dynamic for our decisions and actions is supplied by 'emotions', implying movement. This gives rise to the idea that it is motion, not rest, which is our natural state. Or, as Thomas Hobbes put it, 'life itself is but motion', 'a continual process of the desire, from one object to another', which is 'perpetual and restless' and 'ceaseth only in death'[1] (Rest in Peace).

As I shall show, this may have something to do with the nomadic life lived by our Stone Age ancestors. But nowadays it is also connected with the opportunities to change affiliations which are afforded by markets. If we don't like a product, a company or a group facility, we can just move on – if we are lucky enough to have the resources to do so.

In our stories of our projects of self – how we develop and fulfil ourselves, making something of our potentials – movement (including travel abroad) is a constant theme.[2] In my case, my traveller's tales are bound to include this element, because I tell them when I am on trains and aeroplanes. But the mobility which sustains the momentum of our projects also consists in choosing the organizations to supply the infrastructures for our lives, and the residential districts to live them in. We don't just accept the constraints of our current environmental and social contexts; we actively search for the ones which allow us both the best settings to live out our projects and the best value for our money. (How else to make sense of the endless TV programmes about people relocating themselves and setting up small businesses, usually in other countries?)

So movement implies leaving one collective infrastructure for another, as well as moving geographically – and we may achieve the former without physical relocation. The economic transformation of collective life has allowed us to choose suppliers of goods which in the old days went with the territory, quite literally. There was a time when we got our gas, electricity, telephone connections and social services from the local or regional public provider. Now we are constantly reminded that we can get a better deal on gas from an electricity company miles away, or vice versa; that the cheapest phone calls are routed through the USA, or bounced off the moon; and that our grandmother is being cared for by a company based in the Cayman Islands, whose complaints department is a call centre in Bangalore.

How do all these switches and shifts fit into the patterns made by projects of self, and their connections with the public world? How does the economic transformation of the collective landscape both reflect and enable more mobile lifestyles? And how does economic analysis complement and supplement the explanations of our autonomy and restraint, within the web of social relations, which I have developed so far? These will be the subjects of this chapter.

In fact, there has already been a good deal of economics in my review of how philosophers have tackled these questions, and in my own speculative hypotheses. The theories of Locke, Hume, Rousseau and Adam Smith all connected developments in the economic relationships between individuals and groups to the evolution of political institutions, with sex providing the missing links. And in my own hypothesis, the culture of mutuality through intimate connections is the result of greater autonomy, mobility and choice for individuals in the social relationships of mainstream affluent economies, who follow consumer lifestyles, hold financial portfolios and so on (see pp. 50–3). Individual autonomy depends on economic advantages, which most populations of the world lack.

The explanatory links in my hypothesis are still far from complete. How do consumer lifestyles of mobility and choice come about, and how do people get the financial portfolios to follow them? Why has it been possible to adapt the collective infrastructure so as to allow such people to switch and shift as well as move from country to country? And why were these infrastructures so locked into territories and their jurisdictions before, but are no longer so?

We have already seen the ways in which the Renaissance and Enlightenment philosophers presented their analyses of past transformations in collective life. The common characteristic of their explanations, to which I have drawn much attention, was their links between spontaneous technological innovations or economic developments, and the evolution of institutions of government. Roughly speaking, they all accounted for the emergence of political societies in terms of the domestication of sex, *plus* the development of exclusive private property and commercial relations.

They then went on to link specific forms of government with particular kinds of property holding and productive system. In the case of Adam Smith, this took the shape of a sophisticated 'stages of society' analysis of the origins of various kinds of regime, culminating in a case for a leaner, meaner administration, with fewer regulations, taxes and tariffs, to allow free trade. And he claimed the reverse causal effect, that this would allow all countries to be more peaceful and prosperous, and hence in turn to enjoy better governance.[3]

But there was also a minor sub-theme to all their theories, which is highly relevant to the topics of this book. The theories all insisted that, under certain specific economic conditions, societies could function with little or no government, or at least in the absence of any coercive systems for the enforcement of rules and rights. It is worth examining these arguments in more detail, because they have a considerable bearing on the emergence of nomadic individual lifestyles, based on personal autonomy and financial independence, in an environment which maximizes choice, even over the supply of collective, infrastructural facilities.

It may seem fanciful to look at these theories of economic and political relations 'in the beginning of things', and trace common features in their explanations of autonomy, mobility and the lack of political authority. But I am not alone in seeing parallels between Stone Age economics and our present-day lifestyles of switches and shifts between fluid groupings and ad hoc infrastructures. A. O. Hirschman, an economist rightly hailed as the pioneer of analyses which used his discipline's methods to address political and social phenomena,[4] made exactly the same comparison. In a little-known essay, he summarized anthropological evidence about the collective institutions and economic practices of hunter-gatherer tribes in the Amazon and Congo regions, focusing on movements between groups ('exits'). He then drew the following remarkable conclusion:

> The exit behaviour characteristic of the societies just reviewed, particularly when exit from one band involves entry into another, 'better managed' one, is remarkably similar to what has been called 'voting with one's feet'. Because it resembles the working of the market where a buyer is free to switch from one seller to another, some quarters have celebrated this mechanism as far more 'efficient' than the 'cumbersome' political process for the redress of people's grievances or the fulfilment of their demands.[5] Unfortunately, because of differences in income and wealth, the ability to vote with one's feet is unequally distributed in modern societies. . . . It is possible that a more satisfactory approximation to the neo-laissez-faire economist's political dream is found in the societies of the forest people in Central Brazil and Central Africa.[6]

To understand why Hirschman considered that hunter-gatherer bands were 'a more satisfactory' version of a society whose collective infrastructure arose from the choices of autonomous, mobile individuals, we need to go back to Locke, Hume, Rousseau and Adam Smith. All of them agreed that the conditions required for this kind of society to arise were a plentiful supply of accessible food and water and a simple way of life, with equality of possessions. Under these circumstances, political authority was unnecessary. As Locke put it:

> The equality of a simple poor way of living, confining their desires within the narrow bounds of each man's small property, made few controversies, and so no need of many laws to decide them, or variety of officers to superintend the process, or look after the execution of justice, where there were but few trespasses, and few offenders.[7]

Despite the differences in their initial assumptions about 'human nature', and about the form and ethical status of the lives lived by our 'savage ancestors', all agreed with this conclusion. Hume thought that the most important factor was the lack of incentives to compete for resources or to steal meagre possessions, when nourishment and the tools for hunting came so readily to hand.[8] Rousseau pointed out that conflicts could be settled by a brief bout of fisticuffs, followed by the loser sloping off to join another band[9] – so where was the need for political authority, or even moral rules?

In fact, modern anthropological research has borne out many of these speculations, as Hirschman noted.[10] In the sphere of subsistence activity, forest people do indeed move easily between groups, and this does contribute to the lack of coercive power structures. If anyone tries to impose irksome rules, or make them work harder, they just leave. But, in order to make parallels with present-day lifestyles, we need to take account of another dimension of these societies' collective worlds.

It is, after all, not only that these hunter-gatherers have very few private possessions (whereas we have many), but also that they create very little shared infrastructure, beyond a few modest huts and a larger communal shelter. There is therefore little to quarrel about in the 'public sphere', whereas we have a much more elaborate infrastructure of shared amenities. And there is little need for sanctions against aboriginals who fail to contribute to the common effort, since little such public energy is required. But we have to pay substantial sums, under threat of punishment, to sustain our collective facilities (or, if we are poor, we are forced to do welfare-to-work tasks, in exchange for benefits).

But, as Mary Douglas points out, hunter-gatherer societies did have elaborate shared 'collective goods', in the form of beliefs (such as ancestor-worship) and ritual practices (dances, feasts), which expressed the common aspects of their cultures – their creation, lineage and belonging together.[11] The important point about these beliefs and practices was that they *sustained* individual autonomy, movement and flexibility of organization, and *undermined* all forms of strong authority, except religious, ritual leadership.[12] Ancestors were conjured up to put down upstart, bossy bigwigs; so the culture itself, upheld by priests, seers and shamans, brought people together to settle disputes and heal splits in a way which in turn maintained a balance of power between individuals, based on the threat of secession from groups. The whole community ran on a constant process of rational bargaining and negotiation, ensuring weak leadership and few controls.

If there are parallels to be made between the explanation of some features of these societies, and a convincing analysis of our own, then we must look at both individual and collective aspects. On the individual side, we must consider how the equal autonomy of self, each with a personal project for self-fulfilment, is upheld by a balance of power in relationships, based on the threat of exit, to join another partnership, group or community. On the collective side, we must investigate whether changes in the wider culture, which promote the values of choice, self-improvement and self-responsibility, are reflected in and reinforced by organizations which enable and advantage mobility, through switches, shifts and relocations.

We might summarize these preconditions as follows:

1   Individuals must be strongly committed to psychological and economic independence, of each other and of any authority structures.
2   Opportunities to move between economic units, in search of more advantageous terms of membership, must be available.
3   Individual investments in collective goods can be withdrawn on demand, and transferred elsewhere.

The recent transformation of collective life has certainly witnessed strong trends in all these directions, especially in the USA and UK. For individuals, both commercial developments and legislative changes have emphasized the move towards more flexible, transferable skills ('human capital', which can be shifted from one organization to another) and portable assets (property rights, which can be switched from one fund, insurance plan or public scheme to a different one, or between any of these).[13] But in this chapter I shall focus more on the collective landscape, and how this has been transformed to favour mobility.

What Hirschman realized (and criticized) in the early 1970s was that a group of very able and influential economists[14] were putting forward a whole new model of how to make decisions about what kind of collective infrastructure and public services were needed. Instead of electing central and local governments to make such decisions, they recommended that the choices should be made by millions of well-informed, mobile and resourceful citizens, paying subscriptions to membership organizations or 'voting with their feet' by moving to the jurisdiction with the best value (in its bundle of amenities) for their tax dollars.[15] Hirschman argued against this school (public choice theorists, or 'fiscal federalists',[16] as they were called) that these decisions should balance exit rights and opportunities of this kind with 'voice' rights for political participation and democratic choice.[17] These issues will be more fully explored in chapter 6.

At around the same time, another economist, Mancur Olson, was addressing another puzzle which had an important bearing on these same issues.[18] He asked how groups could ever form and take action in political societies which were also market economies. Since all choices in such societies were either made by governments, and then imposed on citizens by law, or by individuals in markets, where they followed their preferences for private goods, how could loose coalitions of producers, workers or citizens ever get together and mobilize around common issues and interests? This was obviously the obverse of the public choice question, which asked why we need governments, when individuals can form themselves into groups and provide their own infrastructures. Olson was asking how anything like this could happen (for instance, how citizens could form clubs, associations and trade unions) if all resources were allocated by states, or bought and sold in markets.

The answer, he suggested, was that groups could form around the goods stemming from certain facilities, amenities and material assets, which they then distributed to members, to the exclusion of those who did not subscribe to their association, coalition or cabal. In this way, groups could find ways of providing 'selective benefits' to members, and could thus cooperate for their common interests, against those of outsiders. This was simply a different way of formulating the public choice model of 'clubs'[19] and 'exclusive jurisdictions'[20] (see pp. 113–15); people could form groups to supply collective goods and infrastructures if they could stop non-subscribers from benefiting from those goods and infrastructures.

All this is clearly relevant to the question of how autonomous, resourceful, mobile individuals, in pursuit of projects of personal development, and seeking the best-value contexts available, might reduce or eliminate the need for coercive government institutions, public services and regulatory laws. It plays straight into the psychology of autonomy and movement, through the economics of exit, and the politics of public choice. More movement, more freedom. Less politics, more power for the individual.

There are, of course, several things missing from this stripped-down model of the collective world, and its prescription for a drastic reduction in restraints on individual choice. Above all, it provides no convincing explanation of how certain groupings, which do not resemble Olson's clubs and coalitions, survive. Olson called these 'latent groups',[21] and thought that they could only flourish briefly, around specific issues, because they could not define card-carrying, fee-paying memberships, or confine benefits to insiders. But Mary Douglas points out that this fails to explain the long-term stamina of many traditional collectives – of clan, tribe, caste, ethnic and faith communities – in modern conditions.[22] This can only stem from some form of mutual reinforcement between private, individual behaviour and belief, and the collective spheres of these units. This will be more fully investigated in chapter 9.

Meanwhile, throughout my adult life, the everyday activities and long-term strategies of mainstream individuals and households have been wearing away the fabric of welfare states. We have seen examples of this in the quotations from the interviewees in chapters 3 and 4. People – even those who believed in the solidarities and restraints of comprehensive, non-selective education, the National Health Service and National Insurance pensions – have been trying to get advantages over others by subscribing to private, commercial systems, or moving to the districts with the best schools, hospitals and care facilities.[23] First in the USA, then in the UK, then in Continental Europe and, finally (most dramatically), in the former Soviet bloc and in the developing countries, these actions and strategies have undermined post-war institutions, and transformed the collective landscape.

At the same time, the explanations of the economics of groups and collective goods developed by public choice theorists and fiscal federalists have gained influence. What started as an abstract model of how membership organizations like swimming clubs,[24] cartels and trade unions[25] were able to provide benefits for their participants, turned into a powerful explanatory tool for analysing social phenomena. Economic analyses were increasingly applied to political institutions and behaviour, and to social phenomena, such as the flight of white people and the black bourgeoisie from inner city districts to the suburbs.[26] Finally, this school of thought and its methods became a political programme and eventually a government orthodoxy, and the model for reform of the public sector, even for militarily imposed 'regime change'. It is reflected in the policy documents of the International Monetary Fund (IMF), the World Bank and (above all) the World Trade Organization (WTO).

Part of its appeal is that it can easily be framed in terms of the functionalist formula, as follows:

1   Universal value for taxpayers' money is the result of decentralized systems for collective goods of all kinds, consisting of self-selecting 'clubs' for paying subscribers, and self-selecting local communities, providing various facilities in their infrastructures.
2   Individuals and households benefit from universal value for their taxes.
3   Individuals and households do not intend to universalize value for taxpayers' money when they make informed choices over collective goods, and move to the best infrastructures they can afford; they are just seeking their own advantage.

4   Individuals and households are not aware that they are universalizing value for tax money when they seek their own advantage.
5   Systems for collective goods sustain universal value for taxpayers' money, by a feedback loop passing through the self-interested actions of individuals and households.

However, the appeal of this argument would not have been convincing, nor would the political programme derived from it have been successful, if there had not been a parallel technological transformation. We would not have been able to buy our electricity from distant gas companies, our gas from foreign water companies, or put our grandparents in care homes run by entrepreneurs in the Cayman Islands, without these technological shifts.

In the 'golden age' of the post-war welfare state, the collective landscape was a legacy of past struggles to build a *public* infrastructure for shared use by groups with potentially conflicting economic interests. The creation of societies based on property and commerce, well explained by the Enlightenment philosophers, had divided communities into new classes, organized around capital and labour. Conflict between them had proved deadly. At best, it led to the stalemate of economic stagnation, as in the USA and UK between the two world wars. At worst, it led to fascism (as in Germany) or state socialism (as in Russia). The welfare state was supposed to create a set of public institutions which avoided all these outcomes, and supplied a context for solidarity and social justice between citizens.

Seen from the perspective of that era, the problems demanded action by governments of nation-states. They alone could mobilize the necessary political and moral authority, and the technological means. The trouble with private property, commerce and capitalist production was that they could not supply enough 'public goods'. There were no incentives for those who produced goods for private consumption and for profit to create a social environment suitable for safe, orderly, harmonious and equitable human conviviality.

Indeed, market forces and profit motives made a world of *hypermobility* – of hectic, never-ending shifts and switches. The whole language of market economics reflects this; everything is in perpetual motion. Markets are supposed to achieve efficient allocations of capital, raw materials, technology and labour power because they all move (or are moved). In the simplest economic models, with perfect information, zero transaction costs and an absence of legal barriers, everything responds to the laws of supply and demand. In this sense, capital and labour, which move to wherever their marginal product exceeds their marginal cost, are like any other commodities which are traded in markets. People just follow the signals given by prices, wages, job vacancies and accommodation costs, endlessly moving on.

This kind of economy has no boundaries. The whole world has to be a market, and every organization must reflect the needs of producing, buying and selling. But people do organize themselves, to try to gain advantages over others, and to protect themselves from the relentless logic of 'creative destruction'.[27] These organizations give rise to titanic class struggles and world wars, unless some big actor, with legitimacy and clout, steps in to create the missing 'public goods' for peace and stability. Enter the social democratic state.

From a theoretical standpoint, the first requirement for a system to supply sufficient public goods to allow a human context for production and exchange was legitimate government. This meant drawing boundaries around territories, defining populations and empowering citizens with collective authority (democracy). The second requirement was the technological means to mobilize resources, to build an infrastructure. For instance, public health demanded the construction of water supplies and sewers, transport demanded roads and railways, and communications demanded posts and telegraphs. Only the state could drum up the funds required for these massive projects, through systems of taxation.

But once these systems had been built, they established precedents for other projects of social engineering, aimed at raising public standards of education, health and housing, for the sake of economic efficiency, as well as to assuage social divisions and conflicts. At a theoretical level, a whole branch of economics, 'welfare economics', considered how the state should supply new public goods, regulate markets, allocate and redistribute resources,[28] using such criteria as the Pareto one (that no one could be made better off without making someone else worse off), or the Hicks-Kaldor one (that those who benefited from a shift in allocations could in principle compensate those who lost, and remain better off). The relevant individuals in such calculations were citizens and legal residents; foreigners didn't count. Even policies which directly affected the interests of foreigners, such as those concerning import tariffs, export subsidies or immigration quotas, could be made without reference to their effects on outsiders.

In the welfare state in which I grew up, these ways of thinking were very difficult to challenge (even intellectually, for the sake of argument). It seemed to make perfect sense to be exclusively concerned with the welfare of fellow citizens, because other countries were supposed to have welfare states of their own. It took almost thirty years after the foundation of our welfare state for people like myself, who were committed to the best standards of practice in the public services, to recognize how we discriminated against immigrants, and specifically black immigrants, in much of our work.

What all this accomplished (and what stopped us from recognizing these things sooner than we did) was to make states the arbiters of individual welfare, and to make decisions about these issues political ones. Of course, there was plenty of room for individual projects and strategies in markets for *private* goods, for individual and household consumption, but little scope for choice over *collective* goods. Only the rich could choose their infrastructures, or design their own education and health plans. All the rest of us had to accept the standard state dispensation, or campaign within action groups and social movements to improve it – as I spent much of my young adult life doing.

But the existence of such a polarized, economic system (public/private) and theory (micro/macro) was entirely artificial. There was no inherent reason why collective goods should not be supplied by private firms (directly, or under contract to states), or by hybrid organizations (public/private partnerships), so long as the technology existed to identify those eligible for services or benefits, to measure the costs of each individual unit of provision and to exclude those who did not qualify. The microelectronic revolution made just such a technology available. All it needed was the administrative and cultural revolutions (Thatcherism, Reaganism, Clintonism, Blairism) to translate this into a new collective landscape.

In the meanwhile, economic theory had caught up with the evolving patterns of individual behaviour, which responded to new opportunities for exclusive memberships, closed clubs and selective communities, already becoming available through this new technology. People were willing to switch and shift, if they thought they could join groups, enter clubs, create facilities or establish enclaves in which they and their children got a better quality of service, and mixed with a better class of fellow member. They were willing to pay to do this, so long as they could be convinced that they were paying for these advantages, and not to support those they regarded as undeserving, feckless and idle.[29]

The new method of analysis was designed to define the circumstances in which firms might, after all, find it profitable to supply such collective goods to subscribers and affiliates, because they excluded needy (hence expensive) and unworthy (hence offensive) members. It also aimed to explain the economics of competition between residential districts, each offering distinctive packages of infrastructural goods (from schools and libraries to parks and playing fields), and trying to attract both households and companies. In both cases, the eventual patterns of membership and residence would be the result of individual choices, not the decisions of governments.

This extended the spontaneous growth of exclusive clubs and selective communities to the heartlands of welfare states. In the present phase of globalization, it is the public sectors of states, which had been monopoly suppliers of infrastructures and welfare services during the past century, which are now the targets of transnational firms. Under the WTO's General Agreement on Trade in Services, governments will progressively be required to open up these sectors to competition from commercial companies from all over the world, rather as in the European Union water, electricity and gas supplies have been privatized and contracted out to international bidders.

These developments follow the economic logic of new markets in products which were formerly state monopoly 'public goods'.

The obvious example of this process is telecommunications. The original telephone networks were expensive and complex to create, and it made sense for national governments to bear the costs of establishing them, become monopoly suppliers of the services and make standard charges for installation and access. But technological innovations such as satellites and mobile phones now allow the development of commercial networks, through which subscribers, by dialling codes or purchasing cards or instruments, can join transnational systems, with their own special charge rates and access facilities.

Schools, hospitals and prisons are clear examples of services where similar shifts from public to private provision are possible, either by the direct recruitment of subscribers, or under contract to governments, for their citizens. Each of these particular goods has different economic properties, in relation to the technologies for excluding non-affiliates, sharing costs among subscribers and involving them in governance. So there is no reason why the same size and structure of organization should be optimal for each good,[30] or why they should recruit from the same overall population. Above all, the most efficient pattern of such new 'clubs'[31] for each of these goods bears no relation to national boundaries; some optimum membership systems are larger than nation-states, some smaller, and they may overlap (see chapter 6).

The other part of this transformation, and the corollary of club formation, is that individuals and households should be free to switch between these organizations. New technology makes these shifts easy. Choice among firms, funds or facilities which are made by the click of a computer mouse make decisions about collective goods much like other market choices. But decisions about geographical relocations have slightly different implications, because the boundaries of organizations supplying bundles of infrastructural goods are territorial and jurisdictional.

The analysis of geographical mobility between competing jurisdictions (modelled as small cities) was first developed by Charles Tiebout in 1956, and is based on a number of unrealistic assumptions: excludable collective goods produced with congestible technologies (districts could become overcrowded); costless movement by perfectly informed households between a potentially infinite number of such jurisdictions, each with the capacity to reproduce the most attractive features of its competitors; and no jurisdictional externalities (costs generated by economic agents who do not compensate those who lose through their activities). Under these assumptions, mobile populations can spontaneously generate a configuration of jurisdictions which is technically efficient, in that it minimizes the average cost per household of their chosen infrastructures.[32]

Despite the unrealistic nature of this model, it has been – along with the other principles of 'fiscal federalism' – extremely influential on public policy. In the UK, for example, the setting up of inspection teams to assess the outcomes of local agencies' activities, to publish league tables and to involve private companies in the finance and management of public services can all be seen as reflecting aspects of the Tiebout model. Well-informed households are encouraged to move to those jurisdictions in which they will find the best schools, clinics and care homes, given the accommodation prices and council taxes they can afford to pay. The creation of foundation hospitals makes explicit the idea that public services should operate as 'clubs', with card-carrying members, electing their governing bodies. Specialist and faith schools, each with their own distinctive ethos, encourage choice based on refined preferences and mobility.

As in Hobbes, therefore, the theory of 'club goods' and 'voting with the feet' between competing jurisdictions sees people as pursuing the objects of their desires and the power to satisfy these desires repeatedly through movement, a movement that is as much about collective goods (Hobbes called them 'systems'[33]) as about private goods for personal consumption. So the basis for freedom in personal relations is made up partly of money to purchase consumption and lifestyle items (portable assets), and partly of subscriptions to the best quality of collective goods that can be afforded. Since the supply of collective goods is now explicitly related to geographical mobility, through the Tiebout model, this raises important questions about social relations between mobile and sedentary populations, and how mobile people participate in territorial social units.[34]

Most modern social and political theory takes 'societies' as its units of account, more-or-less explicitly assuming these to be nation-states. The theory deals in bounded communities with relatively fixed populations, treated as systems of cooperation for production and distribution and for collective decision-making. For example, Rawls's theory of justice, 'freedom of movement and a free choice of occupation against a background of diverse opportunities', is part of the 'basic structure of society'.[35] But such fundamental rights are assumed to be generated in the 'original position', where membership of society is already determined. 'Political society is closed: we come to being within it and we do not, and indeed cannot, enter or leave it voluntarily.'[36] In his last book, Rawls dealt in international issues, and treated 'migrating into other people's territories without their consent' as akin to acts of 'conquest in war' – a form of 'irresponsibility'.[37]

But, present-day 'societies' have none of these characteristics. They are penetrated by many large and powerful international organizations, both those concerned with global governance (such as the United Nations, the International Monetary Fund and the World Bank) and those conducting global business. These organizations now recruit staff in all countries, and transfer them between branches continuously. Hence the movement of people across political borders, for purposes of trade, administration, production, tourism and study, is an essential feature of the new order; and national government is just one organization among many – albeit with the power to regulate the others.

All these processes give rise to mobile lifestyles – to individuals who spend a good deal of time working in countries other than the one where their household is based, and to others who move from one country to another, on short-term contracts. Since 1991, I have been one of these people. During the spring and summer, I have usually been based at home in Devon, living the life of a scholar (between about 4 a.m. and 7 a.m. each day, when I write, and sometimes again in the evening), and a smallholder (scything my orchard in the manner of Tolstoy, and digging my vegetable plot in the manner of the women in the first film described in chapter 1 – see pp. 13–15), as well as playing host to the visitors who come and stay in our converted farm building.

But in autumn and winter, I am often based in medium-sized European cities (where foreign visitors are treated as having novelty value, rather than as a form of pollution), living in small inner-city flats, and pretending to work in high-powered research centres. In the European Union, of course, it is now easy to pursue this lifestyle; but it is increasingly possible to do it on a global scale.

With my colleague, Franck Düvell, I decided to investigate how people choose to follow such transnational projects, which organizations have facilitated their strategies and how the immigration policies of states either hindered or promoted this mobility. We looked at both the recruitment of high-status and high-skilled workers, and the spontaneous movement across borders of people without proper migration status.[38] In this chapter, I shall look at nomads of the former kind; in chapter 8 I analyse the decisions and survival strategies of irregular migrants.

In our study of high-skilled work-permit-holders in the UK, we interviewed Indian and Polish information technology staff, financial experts, scientists and health professionals. They compared the advantages and drawbacks of Europe, the USA and East Asia, in terms of salaries, living conditions and access to work and residence permissions. They made a detailed assessment of the merits of each possible destination, as well as the costs and benefits of a nomadic lifestyle. They made it clear that it was their employers who arranged and provided for most of the infrastructure they needed for their lives. A Polish employee of a financial intermediary said, about the legal requirements for his migration,

> [T]hey did everything for me. I didn't deal with anything myself. A person who was the leader of the section I work for showed interest in the . . . knowledge and skills that I have. . . . Then I came for an interview with somebody higher up in this firm and then it all happened behind my back, you could say. They did it all. . . . I'm happy with this work with conditions of work, and I earn money. That's what I'm here for; I'm here for the money and for nothing else. Great Britain doesn't appeal to me. . . . I used to dream about work in the city. But now I'm here I have to tell you that working here is nothing special. Honestly. If it weren't for the money I wouldn't stay here for one more day.[39]

He added that his employer had also found accommodation for him, but he had since moved:

> When I came here I had a flat for two months, which my employer arranged. . . . and paid for it for two months . . . I found myself a studio flat . . . it's cheap and I'm happy with it. I just need a place to come back to from work; a place to sleep really.

A similar perspective was echoed by an Indian academic, also living alone. He chose not to live in an area with a concentration of fellow nationals, but to have a flat nearer the centre of the city: 'It's not very cheap, but that way I save my travelling expenses, which is very expensive in London, and hassle, and I'm independent. What more do you want in life?'[40]

These respondents found that the labour and accommodation markets met their needs as nomads, defined in terms of saving money and having personal freedom. Others mentioned that their firms provided recreational facilities that they valued. An Indian information technology development worker said:

> I played in the company's cricket team, and . . . Yeah, I'm a cricketer. I'm a little bit popular in terms of that, so a lot of people know me now. And I have a lot of other friends as well within the office.[41]

This man was married, with one child, and commented that Indians, unlike some of his fellow nomads from other countries (he had worked in the USA and Canada also, despite being only 27), tended to travel with family members, and to bring kin over to visit, and sometimes to stay: 'So it's me and my wife, it's my complete family and her complete family, formed into one long chain. . . . That's the way we are by tradition, tradition-wise we have grown up like that.'[42]

Other interviewees, both Polish and Indian, who travelled with partners and children, described choosing white English residential districts in which to live, and valuing the facilities provided by private clubs and commercial amenities in their areas. The only public services mentioned were the National Health Service and schools; as residents of these districts, they were by and large satisfied with these.

The accounts indicated how nomads were able to sustain their lifestyles within the frameworks provided by their employing companies and by private sector organizations, with those two exceptions. A Polish software developer, working on a three-month contract in the UK (arranged by his agent in Vienna), made this clear: 'Wherever you go their organizational structure and the way of your work is quite similar . . . it's a bit different, but it's not so much because of the country, it's more because of the type of company.'[43]

The nomads' accounts illustrate the inadequacy of social and political theory in relation to mobility. They barely engaged with the institutions of their host 'societies' or 'polities'. Although migrant workers pay income tax and social insurance contributions after three or six months in European countries, and some of them had to arrange for their families' visas and work permissions, these were about the only contacts they had with official agencies and government systems. Many appeared to interact only within the economic organizations which facilitated their migrations – their employers, and the private clubs they joined.

These economic organizations are in many ways ideally suited to sustaining the mobile lifestyles, which in turn fit the present-day projects of self on which intimate interactions are based. They regulate the workplace, they construct hierarchies of authority, and they demand adaptability, flexibility and self-improvement (see chapter 7). But – at the same time – their cultures are highly compatible with personal autonomy and self-development, promoting perpetual choices and changes, and a trajectory of realization of potentials. Some nomads consciously set themselves challenges, related to competition in a market environment. The Polish man first quoted said he originally came to London for 'the opportunity to . . . get to know how it is working in . . . the real capitalistic country where you have to work very hard and where you are judged by the results. . . . [I]f you survive here, then I . . . just think that I would survive everywhere.'[44]

The UK government sustains these forms of nomadism not only by its expansion of the work-permit scheme and by introducing new channels (such as the Highly Skilled Migrants' Scheme) and expanding others (like the Seasonal Agricultural Workers and Working Holidaymakers ones), but also by its promotion of the culture of mobility within public services and the commercialization of collective amenities and infrastructures.

In earlier times, nomadism was associated with movement of populations following their herds and flocks in search of pastures; or the wanderings of bands of entertainers, musicians and tinkers, like the Romanies. Such economic activities survived the division of the world's landmass into the territories of nation-states, and their practitioners became marginal groups, often with transnational lifestyles. Present-day global nomads are mainly young, in high-status occupations. They adapt their projects of self and their family relationships to a mobile lifestyle. Their migrations are facilitated by government systems and by economic organizations providing employment and collective goods.

Whereas past nomadic groups were regarded with suspicion by sedentary populations, or (as in the case of the Romanies) were actually persecuted, today's nomads blend into mainstream communities and their lifestyles are seen as enviable. Their mobility is interpreted as freedom, and the fact that their resources are portable is construed as widening their opportunities for self-development and self-fulfilment. Although sedentary people do not often aspire to be quite so footloose, they attempt to emulate some features of the nomadic lifestyle, such as spending time working abroad and having holiday homes in other countries.

It is easy to recognize in present-day nomadism some of the features of hunter-gatherer social relations that were defined as necessary and sufficient conditions for individual autonomy, weak leadership and lack of coercive authority structures (see pp. 103–5). Nomads' narratives of mobility contain many references to independence and self-direction. Many have made frequent changes of employers; others seek shifts of department and branch within the same organization. All are aware of the need to arrange their resource-holdings and lifestyle choices so as to allow movement and adaptation.

They speak very little of the consequences for others of their choices, mentioning only their immediate circles of family and friends. They do not seem to reflect on whether the opportunities open to them are denied others, or whether less mobile people, or less advantaged ones, bear some of the costs of their lifestyles. Although they do not seek power over others (in the sense of organizational or political authority), they certainly seek (in the manner of Hobbesian agents) the power to perpetuate the realization of their desires. Money supplies the main means to achieve this end.

In the next chapter, I shall start to analyse the consequences of the freedom and mobility of nomadic and mainstream Western lifestyles for those who lack the resources to pursue them. In particular, I shall address issues of membership of and exclusion from the economic organizations which now supply collective goods.

6

Keep Out: Organizations, Boundaries and Exclusions

My purpose in this book is to explain the joined-upness of individual experience, and the new forms taken by the collective landscape. But it is also to analyse which bits of our projects and lifestyles *do not* connect with those of others, and how particular others are *excluded* from the new infrastructures for belonging, sharing and ruling. In order to begin to understand how we link with some but not others, and how the majority of the world's population is excluded from the organizations which allow the minority to be autonomous, mobile and selective, I need to explain the nature of membership and interdependence in these new organizations and systems.

Our everyday experience tells us that groups, clubs and associations do not form randomly; they attract or recruit a specific mixture of members, or particular types with certain features in common. Even in the heyday of the welfare state, this was noticeable in the sports clubs to which I once belonged. Our own cricket club, representing a small industrial and market town, was fairly mixed in terms of the occupations of the leading players. We had lawyers, teachers, clerical workers, manual workers, a bookmaker and an apprentice signwriter (who went on to play for England). But when we played away, there were obvious differences in the class characteristics and the club facilities of our opponents. The top teams in the larger cities were made up of players in posh, professional and managerial jobs; they had well-appointed pavilions, and served bourgeois teas (scones, cakes, cucumber sandwiches). The lesser but aspiring clubs were far more proletarian; they sometimes rented council playing fields, and they produced proper working-class teas, with pork pies, pasties and salads.

In recent years, social scientists have claimed that the *social capital* generated by sports clubs and other civil society associations is a very important source of the interpersonal skills, the trust and reciprocity, the know-how and norms for a well-functioning democracy.[1] It is also a valuable basis for the expertise and enterprise which make a successful, dynamic, capitalist economy.[2] In his *Bowling Alone*, Robert Putnam traces the rise, decline and potential revitalization of such clubs and associations in the USA, and how they have not only formed bonds between citizens, but also built bridges between different parts of a diverse population.[3]

Although Putnam deliberately adopted the term 'social *capital*' (from James Coleman[4]) because of its links with economics, his analysis is not connected up in meaningful ways with the literature of fiscal federalism and public choice, reviewed in chapter 5. But it should be. The idea of 'bridging' social capital, in particular, implies that some social groupings generate cultures which span across divisions of class, ethnicity, faith and locality, and create strands in the web which serve to integrate the whole. If this is so, it is very important to understand the dynamics of this process, especially in economic terms, since this is the feature which is least developed in the literature of club formation and voting with the feet.

To return to my sporting example, it was not clear to me that the cricket clubs I came across generated such 'bridging social capital', though they did create strong bonds between members. But when (due to old shoulders, sore spinning fingers and a neck injury) I eventually changed to athletics (because my legs were still good), I could recognize the bridging phenomenon. This was the early 1980s, when the marathon craze was born. Clubs were truly democratic in their memberships, representing the whole social spectrum, and the big races attracted people from all over the country, of all ages and abilities, in a kind of celebration of cultural diversity and a mass orgy of masochism. (Marathon races are not for running, they are for practising dying.)

In such events, sharing an experience with others is not seen as a cost, but a benefit.[5] As in pop concerts and festivals, the fact that one is part of a big crowd is intrinsic to the whole thing, and adds to the thrill of it. In economic terms, this is a positive spillover or externality – the opposite of congestion and crowding. It is an example of the different kinds of interdependencies and external effects that stem from collective units.[6] The new economic organizations which supply collective goods to subscribers and affiliates create innovatory forms of memberships. Some of these are very complex; subscribers may be unaware of the nature of the interdependencies established, or the consequences for others who are excluded from them.

For example, a company called Holiday Property Bond owns up-market holiday complexes in the UK and several Continental European countries; its affiliates invest in the company through a substantial capital sum, which can be withdrawn if they decide to disaffiliate from it. This sum is in turn invested in the stock market, so the amount they receive on exit depends on share prices. Affiliation entitles them to a number of holiday points per year, and they can choose their country and complex of destination; but they must pay both a service charge and a specific rental fee, which varies from one venue to another. Affiliation also allows other family members to take holidays in these facilities, on payment of service charges and fees. Thus the organization has elements of an investment fund, a real-estate company and a time-share holiday scheme. I suspect that not many affiliates could list all the economic properties of their relationship with the company or their fellow members – how their individual interests are tied into common funds, facilities or income streams. For example, in what sense, if any, do they *own* the holiday complexes, and how is their entitlement to a capital sum on exit related to variations in the market values of these assets?

What's more, these organizations' physical assets and ongoing activities have an impact on the local economy where they are built – as do the small businesses set up by British people in European countries, such as those featured in the TV programme *No Going Back* (Channel 4). For instance, a friend who holds dual citizenship is converting an old farmhouse in a village in the Czech Republic to run as a residential facility for British and Czech people willing to subscribe to group courses and experiences. The groups will be recruited through the internet. But will she choose local builders for the work, and will they in turn employ local labour? And, when it opens, will she hire staff from the village? And will her residents drink in the local pub? Or will their presence stimulate new facilities (coffee bars, restaurants), run by locals or incomers? Here again, the potential interactions and spillovers are complex.

The common features of these two organizations, one large and complex, the other small and simple, might be summarized as follows:

1 They recruit and mobilize their members (subscribers, affiliates, participants) from very dispersed populations, by electronic means.
2 They allow them to travel in comfort and security, and to enjoy an experience which involves some sharing with others.
3 They give them easy access and exit, and allow limited and specific engagement with the organization.

Of course, these examples both concern leisurely or recreational breaks and could be taken as sophisticated developments of the idea of a package holiday. But they contain many of the features of other service organizations which are springing into existence and prospering. For instance, there are companies which assemble people from Northern Europe and fly them to Greece, Syria or South Africa for minor operations, or even for treatment of cancer and heart conditions. And there are all kinds of educational firms, which arrange short and long courses, from language schools to technical training, and which recruit and organize internationally. (Is it just my macabre imagination, or perhaps a latent entrepreneurial streak, which allows me to foresee a company that will transport groups of terminally ill people to Switzerland for euthanasia – Last Exit Tours?)

The point here is that the collective aspects of these services are strictly limited and camouflaged (in terms of the individual's subjective experience). The payment of a fee or subscription allows participation in precisely those aspects of the group's functions (travel, the specific service) which are purchased. The affiliate can choose exactly how long to participate, exactly which membership benefits to use and how much to engage with other subscribers or participants. All these aspects can be selected in advance of receiving the experience or service. And the affiliate can move about, in and between societies, with no outward and visible signs of membership of the organization.

All this is in stark contrast to the key problems of organization in early societies, and to the classic dilemmas of collective action in commercial economies. In the Dark Ages, after agriculture and a sedentary population had become established, the most difficult public good to supply was defence of property and infrastructure. Settlements were constantly under threat from bands of warlike raiders, and the role of leadership in such communities was, importantly, to mobilize peasants to defend their holdings and to negotiate coalitions with other leaders against predatory attacks. The technology of exclusive defence consisted of steep ditches and wooden walls, behind which mobilizations could take place; so both inclusion and exclusion were of this crude, physical kind, and membership was signified by a variety of hairstyles and warpaints. But defensive coalitions were extremely difficult to coordinate, which made such societies very vulnerable to raids, as the early history of Ireland and Scotland illustrates. My ancestor Brian Boru – a rough contemporary of the last Scottish king to achieve a similar feat, Macbeth – was the only Irish chieftain to pull off such a coalition.

These collective action problems of excluding enemies, mobilizing members and coordinating allied clans were all transformed through the emergence of commercial societies, with substantial cities, manufacturing and trade. Regular, employed forces in peacetime and compulsory conscription during wars supplied specialist troops to defend territory and trading fleets. Political authorities raised the taxes to fund these mobilizations, and to build deterrent fortifications and barriers around their borders. It is interesting to note that the organization of military services now relies very heavily on the private sector, and on transnational security firms, such as Global Risk Strategies and Rubicon International. The second-largest suppliers of personnel to the invasion and occupation forces in Iraq has been this sector, ahead of the UK's military;[7] it is a coalition of contracting companies, as much as a coalition of governments. In today's world, our interdependence in issues of security and the exclusion of external threats are represented through the coordination of a network of these commercially provided services.

Every system of exclusion and defence, of course, provokes a counter-organization of infiltration and subversion. Just as early peasant settlements called for the predatory raiders, so the electronically monitored and globally mobilized web of corporate security has given rise to networks of terrorist cells. For those who identify their exclusion and subordination with their ethnicity, faith and cultural tradition, the links in their different web of clan, community and worship provide opportunities for covert organization, and mobilization for Holy War or freedom struggle. They also channel money through the global financial web of electronic banking. Today's strategic conflict is not between rival forces on the open seas or plains, so much as the secret preparation for surprise ambush and stealthy attack on the enemy's heartland.

As in defence, so in the rest of the infrastructure of present-day societies. In the advanced economies, fewer resources are tied up in heavy plant and huge industrial buildings. This allows workforces to be more dispersed, in mobile and fluid units. The collective action problem for firms is no longer about assembling a mass workforce in a fortress-like factory, and dynamizing its productive energies under the surveillance of the overseers. Instead, it is increasingly about sustaining motivation and productivity through techniques of persuasive management and electronic communication, yielding self-sustaining, self-improving effort. The nature of present-day firms, and their methods of mobilization and exclusion, will be further discussed in chapter 7.

We have already seen how the organizations providing infrastructural services for the new economy encourage self-definitions in terms of choice, mobility and self-development, and how they themselves in turn, where they operate under contracts to governments, are set targets, quality-standards, performance measures and other incentives for improvement. In other words, they feed into the projects of self of autonomous, mobile individuals, which in turn affirm and support them.

As both employers and service providers, these new-style organizations work by confirming such identities. They try to promote the experience of free choice and user-friendliness, accessibility and momentum. They encourage staff and memberships to see them as enabling and empowering, allowing for self-development and the fulfilment of potentials. But although they are nominally open to all, on payment of a fee or subscription, or through recruitment and selection on merit, they filter out whole sections of the population[8] – those who cannot afford membership dues or who lack the necessary characteristics to join their staffs. Their modes of access, selection, inclusion, mobilization and exclusion use classifications, concepts and categories from the wider culture which are accepted as natural and rational, so the membership groups they create pass almost unnoticed as social phenomena, and the benefits and advantages they bestow can easily be justified by insiders.

All this can be illustrated from the debate about the Blair government's plan to introduce variable fees for entry to UK universities. This innovation is supposed to allow these institutions to raise or lower their charges in line with their position in the table of merit and the quality of the degree they offer, as well as the costs of providing it. It is also meant to make them adjust their aspirations, to be consistent with the fees they can get their students to accept. Those that are able to recruit only at a lower fee will be required to take more students, and to make corresponding sacrifices of staff members' time for research and publications.

I work at three universities in the UK: Exeter, Huddersfield and London Metropolitan. Each already enlists a very different profile of students, in terms of their class backgrounds. At Exeter, only 13 per cent of students are children of 'skilled manual', 'semi-skilled' or 'unskilled' workers. At North London, in the section of London Metropolitan where I am employed, this proportion is 42 per cent; at Huddersfield it is around 35 per cent. The latter two also have very high intakes of minority ethnic students from the UK, whereas at Exeter most such are from abroad.

The arrangements for students' repayment of tuition fees were considerably modified during debates on the issue in the House of Commons, to try to avoid deterring students from low-income backgrounds. However, the maximum fee will be almost three times its present level, and the whole point of variability seems to be to differentiate between the value of the degrees offered. In the medium term, it seems likely that universities that aim to attract target populations of disadvantaged students will face serious dilemmas over having to reduce their fees and increase their numbers in order to generate sufficient income.

The polarization which already excludes working-class children from would-be elite universities like Exeter (logo: 'Excellence at Exeter') is likely to be strongly reinforced by the measure. But the new processes of exclusion will quickly become routine, invisible and taken for granted. And, were Exeter ever to manage to make it into the top twenty group of research institutions, it will be easy for the Vice-Chancellor to justify this strategy – which has involved the transfer of smaller, more practical departments with strong community links to other, less elitist universities.

This example illustrates the fact that new organizations, using new technologies and generating new cultures of management and work ethics, can overcome Olson's problem of 'latent groups' in new ways. Collective action in post-war industrialized societies took two main forms. In the world of production and employment, it consisted in coalitions of companies to coordinate output and prices so as to create cartels and earn oligopolistic 'rents' (revenues which were higher than they could have got if there was perfect competition); and coalitions of workers, in trade unions, to present their employers with a united front in bargaining for wages and conditions, so these in turn could be higher than they would have been if they had all been in competition with each other for their jobs. In the sphere of government, it comprised coordinated strategies of politicians and bureaucrats[9] seeking to maximize their budgets; and social movements of citizens who, by their specific pressures and mass demonstrations, aimed at increasing the amount and quality of benefits and services they received.

As we have already seen (pp. 106–7), any other form of group or collective had to create its own special facilities and shared resources, and to mobilize around shared values, beliefs and practices among their members. But in today's context, made up of individuals pursuing autonomous, self-responsible projects of self, and choosing to make up their own highly selective infrastructures for mobile lifestyles, there is an open field for organizations supplying specialized collective goods. Each person, each partnership and each family is looking for groups, shared experiences and service providers which will confirm their sense of their own identities, both in the selected people with whom they will rub shoulders or chat over coffee, and in the kinds of milieu and culture they generate and sustain.

In this way, membership and participation constantly reinforce the sense of choice, self-responsibility and belonging to organizations which enable, empower and confirm. The 'selective incentives' which Olson identified in crudely materialistic terms (higher profits for capitalists, higher wages for workers) are not required. Instead, the subscribers or affiliates are prepared to pay for the more intangible collective goods of membership, the affirmation of their projects and commitments and the assurance of their identities, partnerships and careers.

So it is money, in the form of subscription charges and membership dues, which sorts populations into organized groups. And it is these invisibly exclusive groupings, segregated according to the collective goods they consume, which make up the new organizational landscape. The transformation of collective life has been accomplished, with little resistance, by the actions of millions of individuals, pursuing their projects of self and seeking satisfactory contexts and infrastructures for self-realization.

Far from strengthening a political culture of equality and democracy, as Giddens, Beck and others claim, what starts as the practice of intimacy and mutuality between autonomous selves, reinforced by sexual pleasure, becomes a commercial culture of social exclusion. Simply by choosing where to live, which schools and universities to attend, which kinds of health facility to use, and what recreational amenities to enjoy, these intimate citizens cluster into groups of similar incomes and tastes, and relegate others to inferior provision.[10]

So 'latent groups' are still latent in the sense that they are invisible, but the logic of their collective action is now clearer. They come together to share in certain experiences, advantages and services which are beneficial to them, and which these organizations can provide on favourable terms, because they select certain members. Welfare states, as systems of sharing between rich and poor citizens, had two great disadvantages. First, they required the averaging out process of supplying standardized, mediocre public goods to all. And second, they meant that the ablest, most ambitious and choosy had to subsidize the least able, least self-motivating and most needy. The rich had to share with the poor.

Neither of these is required by today's collective forms. Everyone can, in principle, choose their own quantity and quality of collective goods, to suit their incomes and preferences. And no one has to share them with others, whose needs are expensive, and whose presence is offensive to their susceptibilities and sensitivities.[11] Exclusion is automatic, and accomplished in tactfully low-key ways. The logic of variable university fees, foundation hospitals, league tables of schools and social care facilities, toll roads and private pension plans becomes the dominant dynamic of social organization.

There has, of course, always been fierce debate between economists about the ethical and political implications of their 'scientific laws'. As I shall show in the next chapter, political economists in the eighteenth and nineteenth centuries disagreed profoundly about whether the collective consequences of the commercialization of social relationships increased equality and freedom or allowed new forms of exploitation and domination by the rich and powerful. These new developments in collective life provoke fresh disputes about the transformation of societies and political structures.

In principle, claim the advocates of mobility and choice, there is no reason why the whole collective landscape should not be totally transformed, by allowing individuals and households to select which infrastructures and jurisdictions they wish to join. This could enhance both freedom and democracy, according to the following appealing formula:

1   A global democratic regime of localized self-governance through consensus will in principle come about if individuals are allowed to choose their suppliers of collective goods and to live where they please, so long as they have cost-free exit opportunities.
2   Such a regime is beneficial to all individuals in the world, because it releases them from the unnecessarily coercive regimes of state-imposed laws and penalties, for the sake of mediocre public goods, unchosen sharing, the self-aggrandize-

ment of politicians and bureaucrats, political corruption, high taxes and so on.

3   This happy consequence will occur without mobile and choosing individuals intending it.

4   It will happen spontaneously without them being aware they are doing it.

5   Free choices by mobile individuals will bring about true democracy and consensual self-government through a feedback loop passing through all the free and mobile individuals in the world.

The theoretical link between free movement and consensual self-governance was first made in the late nineteenth century by the political economist Knut Wicksell;[12] it has been explored and extended by libertarian political theorists ever since.[13] The argument goes like this. If people are free to select the collective goods they want, and to form themselves into residential groupings around their properties, then it is in their interests to organize themselves into committees or cooperatives to manage these facilities.[14] If any member does not agree with the rules made by the committee or cooperative, he or she is free to leave, so all have an equal right and power, based on exit opportunity.

In other words, the claim is that free movements and choice over these goods can in principle shift the collective landscape back into a version of the one created by our ancestors, the forest people.[15] We can establish social groupings which run on negotiations, with each holding the threat of exit over the collective. In this way, a global utopia[16] (based on ancient pre-political anarchy) can come about, through fluid and flexible interdependencies between property-holders with portable assets, which can be easily turned into cash. It is important to be aware, when politicians refer to the 'choice agenda' and argue for decentralization to local units of democratic governance (as in foundation hospitals and specialist schools), that they are referring to this tradition.

This was the connection made by Hirschman, from whom I quoted at the beginning of chapter 5. Although the principles are derived from an abstract economic model, they informed a global policy experiment in the final quarter of the twentieth century, and they still provide the logic for the programme of the WTO. But there are a number of serious problems in using this model in a context where none of its basic assumptions can actually apply.

For free movement to work in the way the model claims, people would have to start from a position of being completely able and ready to create any kinds of grouping they chose, around any form of collective good or residential jurisdiction. In other words, they would all have to be equally mobile on all dimensions, and not have their assets tied into any existing organization, social, economic or political. And to be equally mobile, they would, like the forest people, have to be more-or-less equally rich or poor. If anyone lacked a certain quota of portable assets, they would not be free to switch and shift; and so they would be excluded from the whole system of movement and choice.

This is roughly what has happened in the USA and UK; and the same patterns are beginning to appear globally, as the regime of the international organizations for finance and trade, the IMF, World Bank and WTO, takes shape. As Hirschman recognized in 1978, in the sentence which I omitted from my earlier quotation:

> Unfortunately, because of differences in income and wealth, the ability to vote with one's feet is unequally distributed in modern societies. In the United States, where the problem is compounded because of race discrimination, inequality in access to exit has had some appalling consequences, such as the 'ghettoization' and partial ruin of our big cities.[17]

Nowadays, as the new organizations for mobility and choice in collective goods have become global in their reach, this polarization is more massively structural. People whose assets are tied up in small land holdings, and who rely on family, kinship and communal systems of production (such as we imagined the people in the first film described in chapter 1 to be) are excluded from the regime of free movement – and they make up over half of the world's population. But so are urban populations who simply lack any productive assets, again the majority of the residents of the world's cities. All of these people rely increasingly on the archaic collective institutions of community, ethnicity and faith, as nation-states withdraw many of their public services, in favour of new economic systems.

It is often claimed that the technological basis for the transformation – the 'information revolution' – has brought about a fundamental shift in the global economy. The implication is that, under some kind of technological determinism, the old order of industrial, class-based economies, nation-states and territorially organized sharing was somehow suddenly rendered obsolete and inoperable. But the truth is that the new microelectronic technology simply provided a fresh impetus to the processes of commercialization and corporate consolidation which began at the end of the Middle Ages. The first period of globalization, and the first vision of a utopian system of a market-based spontaneous world order, were the results of that original 'Great Transformation'.[18] It consisted in the gradual overthrow of feudal forms of ownership, and monarchical regimes of government. But it ended with the First World War and the establishment of totalitarian regimes in Europe and the USSR. The era of welfare states and social democracy was a response to those developments.

Microelectronic technology is just the new means of transforming the collective world; but the drivers of change are still property and profit. That is why the Renaissance and Enlightenment philosophers' explanations of the origins of commercial society and political authority are still relevant. It is why the forms of analysis and argument they developed are still models of convincing accounts for us today. We still (as bourgeois property-holders and freedom-loving individuals) experience the everyday classifications, categories and concepts of capitalism, in these new forms, as natural and rational, and the social groupings which they create as corresponding to something in the physical world and in the ethical universe. And when we try to resist these forces, we still struggle to develop adequate alternative ideas, convincing counter-arguments and binding resistance coalitions.

Furthermore, the reach of these organizations is not only transnational, but also extends right down into the humblest local structures. It connects us up to the global model of the new world order, designed by the IMF, World Bank and WTO.[19] As governments come to adopt their blueprints for institutional reform and public-sector privatization (in the case of the UK, trying to get ahead of the game, so as to nurture corporations, experienced in public-private partnerships, to take over others' infrastructures and social services – to be predators to their prey), they redesign our civil societies so as to change even lowly clubs and associations into 'companies' and 'enterprises', all with 'business plans' (see pp. 112–13).

Not only is the cricket club I used to play for now such an organization; so too is the allotment association where I used to have a plot, and where (in 1972) the poor people's movement of our town established a notorious communal garden. As a founder member and treasurer of that movement, I wrote a book the following year, describing how a coalition of unemployed people, sick and disabled people, single parents and pensioners joined up to campaign together for reforms in the benefits system, to support each others' claims and to work on common projects. One was this collective allotment, whose produce was distributed free to members. It is a sign of the times that the plot's membership is now collectively described as a 'social enterprise', and – in order to draw up contracts with the local authority and apply for regional funds – must present itself as business-minded and display prospectuses and projections of its long-term plans.

These clubs and associations are, of course, still firmly rooted in their local communities, because their main asset is in land. The cricket team recruits a professional from Australia or India each year, and draws its other players from a far wider area than it did in my day. Yet it can scarcely be regarded as a global actor. But other social units, not traditionally perceived as being wired into the latest trends in global capitalist development, have also been shaped by the new technologies and organizational forms, and have responded to new opportunities for mobility.

For example, in 2003 the Anglican Communion was split asunder by the election of the openly gay priest, Gene Robinson, in the diocese of New Hampshire, USA (see pp. 75–6). Sex divided it into a liberal wing (mainly there and in the white Commonwealth) and an alliance between High Church traditionalists and radical evangelicals everywhere else in the world, and particularly in the numerically larger provinces of Africa and Asia. At a specially convened conference, the Archbishop of Canterbury was unable to broker a compromise between these factions, as the ordination of Bishop Robinson went ahead, to liberal celebration in the USA. But a very up-to-the minute solution was at hand. Through on-line links, conservatives of both kinds in the predominantly liberal dioceses in the affluent countries could affiliate to more traditional-minded provinces, such as the Church of Nigeria. In this way, 'virtual bishops' and 'virtual congregations' could join up worldwide, and the Anglican Communion could become a thoroughly modern, mobile, federal organization.[20]

But it was not so easy for gay Anglicans in India or the Caribbean, or poor liberals in Zimbabwe or Kenya, to make these switches and shifts. The creation of new groupings, based on electronic affiliations, assumes that members can afford the necessary technology. The federal structure, in which believers vote with their virtual and spiritual feet, also deepens the digital divide – between the rich who can choose and the poor who cannot. Some of the faithful are stuck with what they have got.

And this in turn reflects a wider reality. In the last resort, the microelectronic revolution does not alter the fundamentals of production and distribution in the global economy, except to deepen inequalities. The digital divide, in terms of access to the internet, is less important than what people bring, by way of assets, to the computer. When the post-Communist countries of Eastern Europe and the Balkans started to come on line in the early 1990s, they did not use the internet to start trading stocks and bonds. They used it to start pyramid 'clubs', and other mass confidence tricks. And when young people in Accra or Lagos go to internet cafés, it is often not to access information about movements in currencies, but to think up new scams, and try to reach subscribers in the affluent countries, to relieve them of their savings.[21]

Social exclusion is not, after all, a new and mysterious phenomenon; it is as old and familiar as poverty in affluent societies. In a Continental European context, it was meant to denote the 'new poor' – people of working age, who suffered from all kinds of disadvantage and problem, and who had dropped out of the social insurance system; and young people in depressed regions who had never gained entry to it.[22] They confronted societies (such as the newly formed market democracies of Central and Eastern Europe) with the fact that some citizens had lost membership of that primary system of solidarity, and hence were a reproach to the post-war social contract, in which all were supposed to look after the needs of each member. In the USA and UK, the same term came to be used as a more politically correct synonym for 'underclass', with the same implication that these groups were not only marginal, but also deviant (criminal, work-shy and irresponsible). So it deflected attention from their poverty and focused instead on their lack of participation, and often on their physical segregation from the mainstream.

But, despite the extensive search for explanations for exclusion, in terms of the characteristics of individuals and social policies, the theoretical work on the subject very seldom refers to the economic literature on the logic of collective action, the formation of 'economic clubs' or the dynamics of voting with the feet. If it did so, it would find that the most influential analyses of individual behaviour, group formation and collective goods all explain quite clearly why exclusion is beneficial for privileged and mainstream members, and why poor people get left out of such units, and hence confined to concentrations of disadvantage, deviance, conflict and disorder. It also explains how they come to get the worst and most coercive social services.

The other side of this analysis is then to show how those who are excluded from organizations which give collective benefits and services to those able to pay subscriptions, and districts which provide good amenities to residents who can afford to pay their house prices and local taxes, join together in different ways, to resist the damaging effects of this exclusion, and to support each other. In our study of a poor district in an English provincial city in 1991, with the highest indicators of both disadvantage and social deviance, we found that men and women pursued strategies of trying to cover household expenditures out of combinations of low-paid work, income supplements (the precursors of tax credits) and social assistance benefits.[23] They did so unorthodoxly, bending the rules of the tax and benefits systems, and justifying this in terms of the need to take responsibility for their families. And they did this as a community, with their own rules and norms for what was justifiable and fair by way of rule-bending, and what was damaging and exploitative. Mr Itchen, for example, said that his casual work for cash, while claiming social assistance, was in line with these cultural standards, and relied on contacts with others in the same situation, who did the same things.

> *Mr Itchen*: Yeah. Financially better off unemployed. 'Cause the £36 a . . . fortnight rent was paid and I get me £52 a fortnight supplementary plus the £25 FIS [Family Income Supplement], you know, so . . . I can, I can probably get ah . . . few decorating or building jobs like, you know. . . . As I say, I've done it all . . . you know . . . it's all word of mouth. . . . you know, boy down the road . . . might say, like 'oh my mate wants his house decorating'.
>
> *Mrs Itchen*: Because really part-time [employment] its just . . . a waste of time because they're just gonna . . . whatever I earn they'll take off, off Kevin's dole money, see. So really it won't be worth it in the long run.[24]

Another man, whose wife also did a good deal of undeclared cash work, explained how he hunted by night with his four dogs, and sold what he was able to kill – but that this could be interpreted as conforming to the benefit regulations.

> *Mr Bow*: Rabbits, hares, foxes, deer or you know that's . . . I get it all. . . . I sells 'em. . . . [I]f I go out rabbiting . . . it's me dogs do the work, see . . . And that money don't go into me wife's . . . or me. It goes back into food for the animals.[25]

So, although they were excluded from the new economic organizations which supply collective goods, and from insider positions in secure employment, they were able to compensate for this partly by rule-bending and partly by networks of local information, assistance and informal trade. One man, Mr Humber, had been building up his stock of fish and birds, kept in ponds and cages in his garden, while he was in work. He had also started to buy his council house. However, he had now been sacked (for 'going on a bender, alcohol-wise'), and was short on his mortgage payment. During the interview there was a knock on the door. When he came back from a brief conversation, he reported that his mate, Worzel, had made him an offer.

> *Mr Humber*: He suggested, he said, 'Now you ain't working, see, you have to ... flog off all your fish.' That's the thing. He said it'll pay half me mortgage. I said: 'I wish it would.'[26]

On the whole, most residents spoke of a strong sense of community and mutual help, despite the bad reputation of the district.

> *Mr Rother*: 'Cause most of the people are genuine people, around here. Salt of the earth. You get a lot of slagging off in the papers and things and that about [name] area, but it's only ... the minority spoiling it for the majority, around here, because a lot of people are salt of the earth, around here; I find 'em so. ...
>
> *Mrs Rother*: Mm.[27]

Many interviewees gave examples of assistance from kin and friends, especially over child-care.

> *Mr Cherwell*: I have got two friends that has done plumbing ... I can just say, can you do a job for me ... ?
>
> *Mrs Cherwell*: So my mother comes up Wednesdays and Fridays ... and ... sits with her [child]. ... And Saturdays and Sundays ... me mum comes up Saturdays, but a friend haves her Sundays so ... its not too bad.[28]

These networks of interdependence operate through kinship and neighbourhood friendship circuits. They run on a very different kind of social capital from the specific links in the new economic organizations supplying collective goods. Exclusion from the latter strengthens the bonds of the former; but there are few bridges between the two kinds of connectedness.

In the deprived inner- and outer-city communities of the UK and USA, and increasingly of both Western and Central-Eastern Europe, these networks take two main forms. On the one hand, there are overt but informal systems of mutual support, mainly among women. They provide each other with resources for such tasks as child-care and care of elderly and disabled relatives; they also lend and borrow money and household items from time to time.[29] On the other hand, there are networks, mainly of men, doing informal economic activities, some legal – such as helping each other repair and renovate their houses – and others not (petty crime, dealing and undeclared cash work).

In some situations, these systems and networks can develop into full-blown alternatives to the mainstream social services and formal economy. For example, in deprived Catholic districts of West Belfast during 'the Troubles', these interdependencies among community members were integrated and promoted by paramilitary leaderships.[30] They became part of a systematic strategy of resistance. Much the same thing happens in many third world countries, under the aegis of armed rebel groups, religious minority militia, warlord factions or organized criminal gangs. These forms of enforced loyalty, as bases for communal resistance and survival, will be further analysed in chapter 9.

Our own poor people's movement in the early 1970s drew on a rhetoric of resistance, and of alternative, informal economic activity and support, but tried to link it with an ideology of equality, freedom and voluntary cooperation.[31] This chapter has shown how commercial organizations have been far more successful in mobilizing individuals into groups in the name of these values, while excluding those who lack the resources for the lifestyles they promote, and the advantages they bestow.

In the next chapter, I shall turn to the economic basis for these transformations of collective life, and the political developments which sustain it. Power is opaque and covert in the new social landscape, but it can be identified and explained, despite its many disguises.

7

Organizations and Power

The transformation of collective life, which is happening through the process described so far in this book, is claimed (and experienced by some) as an expansion of choice and a minimization of coercion. Individuals are said to be gaining autonomy, opportunity and scope for exploring their worlds. The widening of exit options in social and economic groupings is supposed to give rise to greater possibilities of individual self-improvement, partly because it strengthens collective self-governance – spontaneous group formation and consensual cooperation.

This chapter turns to power in relationships. Power is the capacity to get others to do what we want them to do; some kinds of power allow us to achieve this even if it is against their interests. One sort of power is purely personal – the ability to subordinate others' ideas, feelings and purposes to one's own, simply by the exercise of physical, emotional and persuasive domination over them.[1] This kind of power will be analysed in chapter 9. But most power is exercized through organizations. It rests on people's position in a structure of authority, or a process of production and exchange.

My whole life story is one of resistance to organizational power. I am now in a position where I have traded everything – status, position, salary, dignity and comfort – for freedom and mobility. My situation of scholar-gypsy, wandering about with a ruck-sack full of books and a plastic bag full of running gear, is a consequence of this process. In most of the places where I work, I don't even have a place to put these encumbrances down. But I can choose how much time I spend visiting them. Much of the week I stay at home and write, tend the trees, or scythe the grass.

This degree of autonomy (if that is really what it is) has been achieved partly by working *between* organizations, rather than in and for them. I've always had more than one job, and played my employers off against each other. If I'm not at one workplace, they assume I'm at another. Usually I'm somewhere else. They can't presume that they own me, and I don't have to be accountable for *how* I do my work, as long as I do it.

I've also devoted a lot of energy to resisting abuses of power by organizational authorities against their subordinates or their customers, clients or service users. In my experience, such abuse is seldom based on malign intentions towards specific individuals or groups. Far more often, it is just the routine exercise of certain kinds of power, which are characteristic of the culture of the organization. This is why such power-holders always seem stunned by the accusation of abuse, and then try to cover up the means they used to do whatever they have done. They cannot recognize that anything unusual has happened, and similar successful cover-ups in the past have always seemed to confirm that their actions were perfectly legitimate.

The only organization which gained my complete loyalty was our branch of the poor people's movement in which I was active in the early 1970s. This operated as a radical democracy, which mobilized members to cooperate and show solidarity with each other.[2] In every other association or group I have always been a rebel. I even walked out of a county cricket tour in solidarity with a fellow player I felt had been unfairly treated. But I am increasingly aware that the kind of autonomy I now enjoy, based as it is on exit options of this kind, is not available to most others. This chapter investigates how the opportunity for exit modifies the exercise of power, and how this in turn affects the situation of those who do not have exit options.

Organizations of all kinds, including states, function best when members willingly comply with their rules and regulations. The dream of all authorities, from governments to the managers of small enterprises, is to create an order which is *self-enforcing*. This does not necessarily mean that every individual subscribes to the values and principles of the organization, or shares its purposes. It just implies that members act, of their own accord, in ways that reinforce the configuration of relationships, roles and tasks which make up the organization's structure and functions. This dispenses with the need for overt hierarchy and authority; people don't have to be made to do what they do not want to do, because, by following their own reasons, purposes and interests, they do what the organization wants anyway.

Here I have again, of course, simply restated the functionalist formula. From the standpoint of governments and managers, the ideal situation is one in which:

(1) an organizational (or political) culture of dynamic co-operation is the result of the configuration of roles, tasks and functions;
(2) all members benefit from an organizational (or political) culture of dynamic co-operation;
(3) individual members do not intend to create such a culture; they are just getting on with their jobs and their lives – earning a living and interacting with others;
(4) individual members are not aware that these actions create a culture of dynamic cooperation;
(5) the particular configuration of roles, tasks and functions which gives rise to this culture is sustained and affirmed by the actions of individual members.

But there is a paradox here. This particular functionalist formula is clearly intended to justify a regime of power. The background to the configuration of roles, tasks and functions is not the rain forest of the Amazon or the Congo; it is a firm producing commodities, or a state allocating resources. Even if company rules and government laws do succeed in producing or self-enforcing order, there are still questions about the equity of this order. Are members really consenting to the rules and distributions (of roles and resources) by their participation in the regime? Or might they arrange things quite differently, if they had the option to pull out, with their full stake in the whole collective system, and start again, perhaps with a completely different set of others (see pp. 157–8)?

These questions quite clearly arise from the analysis of the collective units formed by subscribers and affiliates, around particular services and amenities, which were set out in the last two chapters. These were claimed to be self-selecting, and their memberships to come about spontaneously. In principle, subscribers and affiliates could turn themselves into a ruling committee, or cooperative, and choose their own entry fees, service charges and other terms and conditions. This, of course, would be a regime of a kind, but one based on consensus, because all would enjoy an equal right and opportunity to move elsewhere, taking all their assets with them.

The justification of the power-based regime is rather different. It starts from an assumption that the collective landscape must be *designed*, so as to ensure that individual members are confronted with choices about their behaviour, and inducements to make these in a way which is socially desirable.[3] People may act in their individual interests, but the collective outcome should be in the interests of *all*. It implies an external standard of equity, to which power-holders can appeal, to legitimate that regime. Power is necessary to produce just outcomes, balanced communities or common interests.[4]

It also raises the question about whose interests should count in the assessment of the equity of organizational arrangements. Whereas the spontaneous order of choices over groupings, by mobile individuals with free exit, assumes there are no fixed boundaries (an infinite number of units is possible), the power-based model assumes that boundaries, like rules, can be altered by design. So boundaries too have to be justified, applying external ethical standards, to show that they are in the interests of all – all the world's population or all citizens, or whatever. Collective power, endorsed by all, is only possible in units where common interests are identifiable.

So these organizations allocate power, ownership and control of resources among their members; and they determine their boundaries of inclusion and exclusion according to the pattern of interests created by these allocations. Even if the order is self-enforcing, in the sense that subordinates (who own and control none of the resources) willingly carry out their tasks, we can question whether they receive the full and fair benefits due to them as participants. And we can also ask whether non-members' (outsiders') interests are considered at all, and what difference it might make if they were taken into account.

Here again we are confronted with the question of how political institutions are related to property ownership and commercial relations – the one which was addressed by all the Enlightenment philosophers discussed so far. Are the private ownership of resources and production for profit compatible with standards of equity which all can endorse? Can the use of collective power shape the organizational landscape in such a way that equity is achieved? What size and composition of social units is best, with this goal in mind?

Three interlocking problems confront any social scientist rash enough to tackle these questions:

1   *Technology matters*. No abstract account of a system of social relations will be convincing. We will only be persuaded by an analysis which explains how existing (or conceivable) ways of producing goods and securing boundaries can be reconciled with the patterns of roles, responsibilities and resource-ownerships recommended.
2   *History matters*. Existing allocations of power and resource-ownership are relevant; they bestow a form of entitlement which cannot be wholly discounted. This is partly because they relate to loyalties of blood, guts, faith and soil (see pp. 26–7). Power and possession derive in part from family, clan, ethnic and religious factors. What is justifiable rests to some extent on what happened before.
3   *Size matters*. What convinces us as being equitable depends on the definition of *us*. We recognize that there are different standards of efficiency and justice, depending on the size of the collective unit. What's fair for family members may have to be modified in the light of a view from the standpoint of community, country or world population.

One of the most appealing aspects of the functionalist formula, as developed by the Enlightenment philosophers and their successors, was that it seemed to deal with all these elements. They claimed to explain how historical patterns of power relations and property ownership were modified by new technologies, and how commerce and capitalist production might in turn transform them further. They all showed that technological innovations – such as the invention of money in Locke or the division of labour in Adam Smith – had unforeseen and dramatic consequences, which changed the ethical quality of relations between people, without them intending this.

Of course, they varied greatly in how they considered that power should be used to enhance or channel these transformations. Locke's theory of property justified revolution, when rulers refused to recognize the ethical implications of individual freedom and private possession. Rousseau's put forward a new version of legitimate government, with radical implications.[5] All of them tended to deal in societies more than in smaller or larger units, but Hume distinguished clearly between face-to-face groups and huge anonymous populations,[6] and Smith claimed that his model of limited government intervention and free trade could give prosperity to the whole world, as even underdeveloped countries came to benefit from investment and markets.[7]

What is really fresh about the present theoretical debate, and the connections between property, production and political authority which it postulates, is the new prominence given to *boundaries*, and hence also to *size*. During the Enlightenment, as I shall show, the important new connections in the collective life of societies (what joined up their vision of a new order) were commerce, peace and prosperity. Producing and trading in markets were supposed to make people less rivalrous and quarrelsome, and to give rulers a greater stake in harmony and economic development, both at home and abroad. So boundaries would become less about aggrandisement and defence, and more about providing the public goods required for trade and industry. Kings and emperors should tax and spend for the wealth of nations, not for war.

In the nineteenth and early twentieth centuries the focus shifted to the relations of production, and to whether new industrial technologies (steam power, electricity and the internal combustion engine) created conflicts of interests between classes (Marx), or the potential for free-market utopias (Spencer). Liberals like John Stuart Mill tried to explain how individual freedom and democratic government could be reconciled, and how great inequality of wealth might be made compatible with the moral equality of all human beings.

Liberals such as Herbert Spencer continued to develop explanations in the tradition of Adam Smith, later combining his functionalist formulae with those of Charles Darwin.[8] Socialists showed how these methods had consistently ignored the *organized* nature of capitalism, its use of *power*, and the *collective* consequences of individual actions. I shall consider the continuing relevance of their analyses.

But the central questions to be addressed in this chapter, and in the final three, concern the new claims made on behalf of autonomous, mobile individuals joining selective groupings. By my examination of the earlier arguments of Enlightenment philosophers, liberal political economists and socialist critics of capitalism, I aim to clarify the issues in this debate. Can these great disputes about property, profit and power really come down to a question of where to draw boundaries around collective goods and jurisdictions? And what kind of political authority is required, at which levels, in the newly reconstructed collective landscape? How, in other words, might power join up the world of global corporations and mobile individuals in ways which would be experienced as acceptable and fair by all?

The first clues to the unravelling of these puzzles lie in the origins of the functionalist formula. It emerged, as a convincing form of explanation for social phenomena, at exactly the moment when commerce and capitalism started to become the dominant economic relations of the major world powers. And its persuasiveness lay in the particular way it explained how new technologies of production and trade could transform old configurations of power, without the need for war and revolution. So it was able to account for new connections between individuals' inner worlds of experience and the collective life of societies – everything from tea and coffee houses, through stock exchanges and commodity markets, to debating clubs and radical newspapers – in an evolutionary way. It told bourgeois citizens (the earliest exemplars of the chattering classes) that their way of life was bringing about a spontaneous transformation of the 'old corruption' (absolute monarchy, arbitrary aristocratic rule, the dependence of clients on patrons, the serfdom of the peasantry) into a new order of equality and freedom.

These evolutionary arguments did not rely on the mobilization of reason, or the conversion of power-holders to new, enlightened ideas. The Enlightenment philosophers claimed that the process of social and political change would be driven by the 'passions' (emotions, desires and instincts, including the sexual impulse) and the 'interests' (the search for material and positional advantage, by individuals and groups). This was not to be a process of progressive pedagogy, but an invisible and gradual wearing down of archaic institutions and anachronistic attitudes. As Montesquieu, Steuart and Smith each explained:

> It is useless to attack politics directly by showing how much its practices are in conflict with morality and reason. This sort of discourse convinces everybody, but changes nobody. . . . I believe it is better to follow a roundabout road and try to convey to the great a distaste for certain political practices by showing how little they yield that is useful.[9]

> [A] modern oeconomy, therefore, is the most effective bridle ever was invented against the folly of despots.[10]

> Without any intervention of law, therefore, the private interests and passions of men naturally lead them to divide and distribute the stock of every society, among all the different employments carried on in it, as nearly as possible in the proportion which is most agreeable to the interest of the whole society.[11]

Of course, not all the Enlightenment thinkers took this line. In their very different ways, Jefferson and Rousseau adopted arguments about the distribution of property, and especially of productive assets, which pointed towards revolution rather than evolution.[12] If the corruption of political power and social relations stemmed from inequality and unaccountable authority, then collective action (as in the American and French Revolutions) to accomplish transformation was needed. But here again, the implication was that once this had been achieved, commercial and capitalist relations would supply a self-enforcing order of harmonious progress.

The common feature of all these arguments was that they failed to register the organized nature of commerce and capitalism, or the kinds of power this generated. They wrote as if the new kinds of economic relations released individuals from bondage to traditional authority, and left them free to contract with each other for mutual advantage. The microeconomics of student textbooks still perpetuates this view of the world; firms are treated as if they are individual agents, not organizations.[13] Power is not mentioned.

Of course, between then and now, a theoretical explanation of capitalism, which became the ideology of state socialism, insisted that the organized nature of productive relations, and the power this generated, were the very stuff of collective life. Marx and his followers claimed to explain exactly how firms exploited and dominated workers and consumers, and how states regulated and coerced citizens in their interests. They even offered explanations of how capitalists found it advantageous to include workers' organizations in the machinery of the state, in order to legitimate their ideas and methods, and brainwash the masses. This version of the functionalist formula went as follows:

1 The liberal state (and its legitimating ideology) are the creations of the capitalist mode of production.
2 The liberal state is beneficial for capitalists.
3 Capitalists do not plan the liberal state; it comes about as a result of all their activities, in pursuit of profit.
4 Capitalists are not aware that the liberal state is a creation of their mode of production; they believe it is the most ethical and efficient form of government.
5 The capitalist mode of production is maintained by the liberal state, through the activities of individual capitalists.

Why did this explanation convince hundreds of millions of people all over the world for more than a century? And why does it fail to make the connections between people's inner worlds and their experiences of work and society today? (If the notion of a 'global order presided over by the USA' is substituted for 'the liberal state', it does still persuade many. But these many are mainly young, or from countries with very little influence on world affairs. And one reason why they in turn have little influence is their difficulty in connecting the formula with mainstream experiences of autonomy, mobility and self-development among mainstream citizens of affluent countries – see pp. 50–1.)

In recent years, several leading thinkers sympathetic to Marx's project have suggested that this loss of credibility relates to his insistence on dealing in the interactions between collective actors, especially classes. He often wrote as if the desires and beliefs of individuals could be explained in terms of the (often hidden) purposes of those aggregate entities. Present-day 'analytical Marxists' argue that Marx himself at times, and his followers frequently, weakened their analyses, and invented unconvincing concepts, because they adopted this approach – 'methodological collectivism':

> Explanation proceeds from laws either of self-regulation or of development of these larger entities, while individual actions are derived from the aggregate pattern. This frequently takes the form of functional explanation, if one argues that objective benefits provide a sufficient explanation for actions that, collectively, generate them.[14]

Here, Elster is saying that Marx and his followers fail to meet his (and our) criteria for a successful functionalist formula,[15] because they dealt in collectives, not individuals. Elster is quite right to argue that any convincing social scientific explanation must be able to show how collective action *gets started* (see pp. 22–3) – how individuals come to adopt a set of institutions and practices, or to form a particular kind of association, with its characteristic culture.[16] But there is quite another phenomenon to be explained also – how the unintended products of these institutional creations and organizational cultures then influence the way they subsequently behave. Once a group, coalition or society forms, all that we need to assume is that members have some interest in its survival,[17] in order to include its collective thought patterns, or collective power, in an explanation of individual actions. And these may be actions occurring much later, or as a result of long causal chains.

Let me give an example from my own experience. The poor people's movement of which I was an active member in the early 1970s was committed to the proposal that the tax-benefit system should be wholly recast, to give each individual citizen a guaranteed sum (or basic income), sufficient for their subsistence. This should, we argued, be totally unconditional (like child benefit, or the National Health Service). Those receiving it should not be required to work to earn it; nor should those living in partnership have it reduced on account of sharing their living expenses with another citizen. This proposal was adopted as a defining demand of the movement, and advocated in my book about our local branch, written at the time.[18]

There are two obvious questions which a social scientist might ask about this. First, why did a group of poor people, claiming social assistance, come up with this utopian proposal at this particular time? A young Japanese scholar, Dr Toru Yamamori, is currently conducting research into exactly this question – going round interviewing ageing participants, such as myself, about where the idea came from and why we adopted it as the main item of our constitution.[19] The answer is quite complex. The idea can be traced to various radical thinkers – Tom Paine, Saint-Simon and Fourier, Bertrand and Dora Russell, G. D. H. Cole, James Meade and even Milton Friedman, amongst others[20] – and it came from the USA in the late 1960s, as part of the libertarian and emancipatory activism of the time. But it took a particular coalition of diverse individuals to turn it into the central organizing principle of that movement in that particular context.

The second question, though, is quite different. How did it come about that I have included this proposal in every other book I have written since then, and go on doing so now, despite the fact that our organization more or less disbanded in 1975? Why persist in this, in the face of ridicule and (initially) damage to my academic career? How did this idea continue to motivate and inspire me (and many other members) years after the organization collapsed? (Small groups in a number of cities do still exist today, and a few activists have kept going these past 30 or 40 years.)

The answers to these questions must be framed in terms of the central explanations developed in this book. What connected my personal experiences (as someone whose family was poor during my adolescence, when my parents divorced, and who worked with poor people as a social worker) with the principles and cultural practices of this organization continued to influence my thinking and behaviour ever afterwards. When the Newton Abbot Claimants' Union disbanded, I remained a member for life, and went on interpreting the world through the thought-styles developed with my colleagues all those years ago.

Exactly the same phenomenon was discovered by Mark Drakeford when he researched the Greenshirt Movement (formerly known as the Kindred of the Kibbo Kift), a paramilitary wing of the Social Credit Party of Great Britain, which was active in the 1930s. In his book, *Social Movements and their Followers*,[21] Drakeford interviewed members of the Kibbo Kift from the 1920s (some of whom had left after their radical scouting activities became overtly political) and some Greenshirts of the following decade. All of them spoke of their continued commitment to the movement's principles, which included the advocacy of a National Dividend (the predecessor of the basic income proposal).

Institutions and collective units organize their members' perceptions and actions.[22] They mould them into forms that are compatible with the social relations of the association, they provide settled ways of doing things and a subtle form of patterning their thought processes. We need something like 'methodological collectivism' to explain the transformation of economy and society worldwide if we are to capture these processes. Marx's formulae will not do, not because of methodological flaws, but because his categories and classifications – the rentiers, bourgeoisie and proletariat – no longer fit our collective forms in today's world.

The global capitalism which is so reviled by the young protesters who disrupt its summit conferences, and the global order against which millions marched before the invasion of Iraq, are not organized around the visible symbols of banks, factories and government offices. (More accurately, they are no longer organized in these massive, apparently permanent structures in the affluent, developed countries, though they still are in the developing and post-Communist ones). The most striking feature of the new form of global organization is how quickly it can move and change its shape. Its power lies in its capacity to shift and switch its resources – to move money, buy buildings, hire machines and staff. This form of organization is like an organism capable of splitting itself into very small and widely scattered segments, or of coalescing into an enormous whole, at bewildering speed.

As in the global economy, so in the polity too – though in more cumbersome ways. The wars in Afghanistan and Iraq have demonstrated how huge military force can be mobilized and brought to bear very quickly, for the sake of 'regime change', under US leadership. But this warlike action is then quickly followed up by 'reconstruction', which is actually the substitution of a privatized, business-based infrastructure for the former theocratic or state-dominated one.

The idea of an ad hoc coalition for war captures the flexibility and fluidity of the new form of power. While nation-states are rooted to their territory, and to strategies for defending their settled populations and excluding foreign armies, these coalitions take shape and propel themselves across the world with startling suddenness. Like the business corporations for which they prepare the way, they respond to particular situations, and to changes in the geopolitical configurations or threats to their overall dominance.

Recent innovations in the economic theory of organizations go some way towards explaining these phenomena. Power is the way that resourceful people choose to get things done when they are unable to achieve their purposes through some kind of self-enforcing agreement. A contract between individuals is based on agreed mutual advantages and equal opportunity for exit (if necessary, compensated by the one who terminates the relationship). Organizations (and coalitions), using hierarchies of power, use their control of resources and the authority of their agents to make sure that everything is done their way. The size and structure of business corporations is a direct reflection of the kind of power which is needed to get their owners' strategies implemented in the most profitable way. They will shift their operations, merge with others or take over suppliers and rivals to exactly the extent that this is advantageous in these terms.

The foremost theorist of this new analysis of the firm, Oliver Hart, acknowledges the similarity between his explanation of the size and shape of these organizations and the account of power in Marx's theory:

> Given its concern with power, the approach proposed . . . has something in common with Marxian theories of capitalist–worker

relationships, in particular the idea that an employer has power over a worker because he owns the physical capital the worker uses (and therefore can appropriate the worker's surplus).[23]

Hart shows exactly the kind of puzzle for which methodological collectivism supplies the only possible explanatory tools. In decisions about whether one organization should sign a contract with another (for instance, to supply components for a large engineering project), the question to be decided is whether one party might be able to frustrate the other's goals, or inhibit the most efficient productive processes, by withdrawing without completing the deal or simply delaying its part in completion. If there is a risk of these frustrations, neither will invest in the technology needed to do the job in the most cost-effective way. In these circumstances, it is probably most profitable for one firm to buy the other, or to employ its staff.

Such decisions are not like the ones which face individuals trying to decide which jobs to take, where to live or what products to buy. They are not even like decisions which firms make about whether to hire an extra worker. They concern choices by collectives over their organizational boundaries; and the criteria they use are about whether (as individual economic agents) to contract with other firms (as individual economic agents), or whether (as collective actors) to incorporate other collective actors and their assets, for the sake of the power they can exercise over the deployment of their resources and staff. If they choose to take over another organization, this decision is not about an exchange for mutual advantage. Instead, it follows a collective logic, which stems from the organization's power structure and its capacities to control material and human capital, not its production costs or demand indicators.

In economic theory, some of these differences are captured by the terms 'rent seeking' and 'entrepreneurialism'. In principle, rent seeking is when owners of property rights use them to raise their income, without improving productivity, whereas entrepreneurialism is the achievement of gains through greater efficiency and voluntary exchange.[24] What this does not entirely reflect is the fact that individuals are usually only able to be rent seekers in one-off opportunistic ways, whereas for organizations rent seeking can become a way of life (as in Enron, for example). This is because they are able to shift resources and exercise authority over people so as to gain a special position or extra power, to their own advantage. Creating and sustaining monopolies are examples of rent seeking activity.[25]

In the public sector, and especially in public-private partnerships, these distinctions are harder to define. For example, two of the universities that employ me have recently changed their boundaries in ways which affect my position. The University of North London merged with London Guildhall University, mainly as a defensive manoeuvre, it seems, to counter possible rent seeking by other institutions at its expense. Meanwhile, the University of Exeter decided to transfer our department to the University of Plymouth. This was a clear example of two organizations seeking to increase their income streams from public and commercial funds by improving their position in the different parts of the higher education market which they occupied.

This takes us straight back to the connections between autonomy and exit rights. Resistance to power relies to a great extent, in a commercial economy as well as an aboriginal society, on the capacity to walk away from attempts to coerce and control. It also consists in being able to hold up any coordinated action – to create space for renegotiation or to clarify the terms of this coordination. Sustaining autonomy rests on the threat of either of these actions. Hart's model of organizations uses terms which are uncommon in mainstream microeconomics, such as 'threat power'[26] – the ability to threaten withdrawal or renegotiation. Autonomy rests on threat power.

Hart also points out that his explanation of organizational boundaries and collective power is incomplete without an analysis of property rights. The reason why ownership of machines and buildings matters so much is that 'ownership is a source of power when contracts are incomplete'.[27] Since a contract cannot cover every possible eventuality which may arise, it is the owners of the physical assets of the organization (or the management appointed to look after the owners' interests) who decide: 'In fact, possession of residual control rights is taken virtually to be the definition of ownership, whereby the owner possesses the residual income from an asset rather than its residual control rights.'[28]

In other words, the capitalist has a key advantage in power relations with all other agents, in a capitalist system of production. It is the owner of the buildings and machines who decides on 'the optimal ownership structure'[29] – the size and shape of the organization, its configuration of resources and chain of command. And in decisions about whether one firm should take over another, it is the owners of the firm with the more extensive assets who are in positions of power.

Quite simply, what we mean by employment, as opposed to self-employment, is that someone can tell someone else what to do.[30] The reason why an employer has power is that he or she owns some *material* resources, even if these consist only in an office and its furniture. These assets 'glue' the firm together;[31] they join up the owners and employees, and create power relations between them. This is quite different from a situation in which self-employed individuals contract to work together, where each must 'bribe' the other to get their way: 'In the former case, if the relationship breaks down, the employer walks away with all the nonhuman assets, whereas in the latter case each independent contractor walks away with some nonhuman assets.'[32]

This was well recognized by the interviewees in our research on mainstream economic decisions over work and welfare. Several respondents spoke of the arrangements they were making to secure financial independence of their employers. They had worked to accumulate property rights, which they could translate into economic autonomy. Mr Spruce, a quantity surveyor, was about to become a partner in the firm which had employed him for several years. But in the longer term he planned to take early retirement and set up a gallery or bookshop in France:

> *Mr Spruce*: But what I want to do is set myself up financially, because I think I would want to get something out of what I've been doing for the last 20 odd years. And I think I would attempt to secure that over the next 10 years. . . . You attain sufficient equity to release an income. It's an annuity situation.[33]

Mr Spruce's long-term strategy reflected the desire to become an independent producer, and hence economically autonomous. This is often expressed in purely physical terms – employees leave the firm's offices, and go to work from home, as consultants. The opposite strategy was the one pursued by Mr Willow, who traded security and material advantage for freedom. He wryly and ruefully reviewed his long career as an insurance manager, referring to his firm's perks as 'golden handcuffs':

> *Mr Willow*: [T]he subsidized mortgage and non-contributory pension scheme, things like that tended to lock people into a situation of course, and therefore you become . . . your whole attitude of mind is against moving out of that comfortable situation.[34]

Mr Willow was self-critical about his lack of enterprise and initiative, and his willingness to take the easy option. The irony, of course, is that the rights accrued by employees like him, in the form of entitlements to retirement pensions, consist in ownership of shares in other companies. Over half of the shares traded on the UK stock exchange are owned by UK pension funds of this kind. Mr Willow, and millions like him, 'own' many of the firms based in the UK and abroad. But the ways in which these ownerships are dispersed among millions of rights-holders deny them any actual power or control over the collective decisions made by companies.

The obvious connections between ownership and exit rights (demonstrated when firms relocate to other countries or other regions of the world) have prompted theorists to redefine Marx's notions of exploitation and class in terms of opportunities of this kind. For Marx, exploitation lay in the actual physical process of employment, specifically factory work. The owners could get their employees to work for longer than it took to produce the goods sold to pay for their subsistence. These extra hours of work produced 'surplus value', the source of profit. This explanation is now discredited.[35] We simply cannot measure and compare the amounts of labour-time spent by a worker, and that which goes into the commodities bought for consumption, in any meaningful way. So one new approach is to imagine what might happen if any group could take their share of the goods they produce and the other assets used for production, along with their skills, and withdraw to find alternative collaborators.

This was the approach used by the analytical Marxist John Roemer in his *General Theory of Exploitation and Class*. He concluded that a coalition of individuals who were worse off as a result of this strategic withdrawal by another group could be defined as capitalistic exploiters, and a group who were better off could be defined as exploited in these terms.[36] This captures the idea that, although the employment contract is 'voluntary', those who own no means of production have no alternative, under the property laws which govern capitalist societies, but to accept terms of employment whereby owners can withdraw with all their non-human assets at any time, but workers can take nothing but their skills if they leave.

Under conditions of globalization, capitalists do in fact withdraw to relocate quite often; and public sector organizations are privatized, or merged with others. That is why Mr Spruce wanted to be a partner in his firm and take early retirement. It is also why I am glad that my converted cowshed is now worth a lot of money. Only ownership of property confers real autonomy.

Elster and others have criticized Roemer's formulation, on the grounds that it cannot be stated in terms of individual choices, concerning their skills, income-leisure preferences and use of time.[37] In other words, Elster rejects formulations of the concept of exploitation in terms of collectives, such as coalitions of owners of capital on the one hand, and employees on the other. But Hart's theory of the firm is just such a formulation.

Even orthodox microeconomic analysis recognizes that firms or cartels will aim to earn 'monopoly profits' or 'superprofits', or 'economic rents', under conditions of imperfect competition, if they can do so. And even conventional microeconomic theory concedes that there is no mechanism to ensure that such superprofits are distributed to workers, or to the general public, except in so far as they are members of pension funds and insurance schemes which invest in these firms, since the surplus goes to shareholders, not staff, under the usual assumptions.[38] Exploitation can therefore be defined in terms of how these 'rents' are distributed. Furthermore, Hart's model explains how the surplus earned by a firm *must* (under the logic of such organizations' collective actions) be maximized, by altering its boundaries. These changes in ownership structure are *intended* to increase the surplus earned, at least partly at the expense of the workers' share.

All this explains why it is such an obvious strategy for individuals to try to get together enough portable assets (knowledge and skills, rights, and material resources which can be moved around or exchanged) to evade the power of organizations. Not only does this fit with the idea of an autonomous project of the self, as a developmental, self-actualizing and self-fulfilling entity; it also represents the best way to combat exploitation and domination by the impersonal forces of collective power. Even someone like myself, who has always worked in the public sector, follows a strategy for protecting my own project of self from organizations which are pursuing their collective purposes, without reference to my interests or those of my colleagues and our students.

It also explains why so many small businesses have come into existence in the present era, especially in the USA and the UK; and why the IMF and World Bank emphasize that such businesses must provide the basis for growth in the post-Communist countries of Central and Eastern Europe. As huge global corporations spread across the world economy, following the collective logic of ever-larger ownership and control, and continually widening their boundaries, the logic of individual strategic self-protection is for former managers, professionals, technicians and skilled workers of the firms and organizations being taken over or closed, or going out of business, to turn themselves into consultants, freelance enterprises or suppliers of some kind. This increases their autonomy, without in any way reducing the power of global corporations.

But many individuals in affluent countries, and most in developing and post-Communist ones, do not have the option to pursue this strategy. Either they lack the skills and money, or they are too reliant on, and relied upon in, networks of family, kinship and community. For these individuals, resistance to organizational power must take other forms. This will be one of the issues examined in the next chapter.

I shall also seek to explain the emergence of new political ideologies and rhetorics around the power of the state to enforce work, and to require citizens to accept exploitative or powerless working situations. As mainstream individuals in affluent societies gain some strategic leverage, through mobility and personal asset portfolios, to evade the authority of organizations, so others who rely on state benefits and services become more vulnerable to these new forms of coercion.

Ideally, organizational power should be offset in two ways – the right of individuals to move elsewhere in search of fairer and less coercive rules, and the opportunity to influence collective decisions on both rules and outcomes. In most types of organization, the security and protection provided is not perfectly offset in these ways. As we have seen, ownership structures and inequalities in holdings of physical and human capital mean that certain individuals gain power over others in employment relations. Democracy is, of course, a less than perfect instrument of political authority, especially for minority groups; and it takes no account of the interests of non-citizens. Voluntary organizations focus on the needs of specific groups (often minorities), but are seldom able to meet general needs or cover whole populations, partly because they are limited in how they can raise money. Families provide care for children, disabled people and old people, but the very dependence of those members who need care makes for inequalities of power, sometimes leading to abuse (see chapter 9). So autonomous individuals do not readily put their trust in any organizations. They prefer to retain as much economic and moral sovereignty as possible.

States can and do regulate the other organizations which supply collective goods to members in their territories. But the adaptability of financial and business corporations in conditions of globalization has intensified their difficulties in regulating mobile, resourceful enterprises and families (gathering taxes and holding them accountable in various ways, as well as enforcing contract compliance). And government strategies and structures have in turn been transformed in response to these new issues.

> In processes of interaction across sectors the result is often that one or both of the organizations have to change their practices and routines. It often means different forms of mutual adaptation, which can be rather complicated when several kinds of organization are involved.[39]

This captures the transformation of collective life analysed in this book, in a very schematic way. However, it does less than justice to two fundamental issues of power. The first is how the basic units of societies, partnerships and families deal with dependence. Equal autonomy between self-developmental selves largely denies this phenomenon, and exit rights and opportunities are seldom available to children, disabled and elderly people. These questions will be discussed in chapter 9. The second is the problem of national borders, and the kinds of power exercised by governments in decisions about which non-nationals to admit, and on what terms. This will be another topic of the following chapter.

8

Power and World Poverty

In trying to explain the 'joined-upness' of seemingly incoherent experiences, I have also emphasized that the sense we make of them relies on the sensemaking repertoire of the organizations of which we are members. Autonomous, mobile, affluent selves make particular connections between their inner worlds of personal development and the collective forms of the global order. People who are rooted in land, localities and communities of fate make a different kind of sense, both of their own relatedness in their membership groups and of that other world of affluence, mobility and power.

Those, like myself, who travel a lot and work in other, poorer countries seldom ask ourselves whether we are adding to the disadvantages of the citizens of the lands we visit. When I was working in Slovakia, for instance, I tried to tell myself I was contributing to that country's transition to democracy. I was paid by the European Commission, as part of its attempt to get Slovakia up to speed for joining the EU in 2004. But although my teaching was offered, rather than imposed (and most of it was, I suspect, rejected by many students and almost all colleagues), the whole package of conditions for accession to the Union was scarcely optional. The EU was exerting power in shaping these societies; and it was doing so without a clear mandate or a clear perception of their citizens' interests.

Most of the world's population still live in traditional communities and rely on kinship systems and local networks. Partnership and family life still follow the principles and traditions of previous eras. This chapter investigates whether the sexual freedoms, personal development opportunities, resource holdings and mobility of the rich minority are gained at the expense of the world's poor. Do the former exploit the latter, and is power a disguised but prevalent feature of relations between the affluent and the indigent sections of the world's population?

Of the sum total of humankind (6 billion) 46 per cent (2,800 million) live below the World Bank's $2 per day poverty line, and 1,200 million on less than $1 per day.[1] This makes them extremely vulnerable to disease and adverse natural conditions, as well as to exploitation and abuse. Each year, around 18 million of them die prematurely of poverty-related causes, which represents one third of all human deaths in any year. Every day, there are 34,000 deaths of children under the age of five.[2]

Analyses of globalization reach starkly varying conclusions about the costs and benefits of the process. Even though the gung-ho spirit of the period of the Washington Consensus (1980–2000) has given way to the more qualified optimism of the World Bank *World Development Report 2002–2001*, distinguished economists still hold to the view that accelerated cross-border movements of money, technology, products and employees can benefit the vast majority of the world's population.[3]

The World Bank concedes that there has been 'a widening gap in average incomes between the richest and the poorest countries. In 1960 per capital GDP in the richest 20 countries was 18 times that in the poorest 20 countries. By 1995 this gap had widened to 37 times, a phenomenon often referred to as *divergence*.'[4] This is why critics in non-governmental organizations (NGOs), environmentalists and humanists often combine in a chorus of condemnation, both blaming the USA for its partisan promotion of national interests in the name of globalization, and damning the consequences of corporate greed.[5]

There can be little doubt that some form of power is used to bring about situations in which some populations become very affluent and others remain backward, or suffer catastrophic declines in living standards. Colonial and imperial political regimes were obvious targets of critical analyses of these processes; European states used their colonies as sources for cheap raw materials and semi-processed products, and as markets for mass-produced manufactures. However, in the postcolonial order of the period after the Second World War, interest in the power dynamics of world economic development grew, not least because state socialism represented an alternative model to capitalism, and because the Soviet Union claimed that 'forced industrialization' and the collectivization of agriculture had eliminated the injustice and exploitation in capitalist development.

Marxist critics explained 'uneven development' and the continuing poverty of postcolonial states as direct results of the logic of capitalism.[6] Goods manufactured in capital-rich countries contained less labour value than those goods produced by labour-intensive methods in poor ones, in exchange for which they were traded. But this explanation relied on the 'labour theory of value', which has since been rejected, for the reasons given in chapter 7 (see pp. 157–8). To be consistent with the approach adopted there, we need to explain how the collective action of some organized entities, following their own logic, allowed their members to gain unmerited and unjustifiable advantages over others.

In a world made up of states, each trying to gain maximum advantage for their citizens, we did not have to look far for the relevant collective entities. In the post-war era, governments used all means possible to channel national capital into national industries, to maximize employment and economic growth and to influence patterns of trade with other countries in order to improve the lot of their populations. Welfare states themselves were aimed at protecting national living standards, if necessary at the expense of those of non-nationals, and without reference to the effects on the global environment or the world's depletable resources.

Since the affluent countries of Western Europe and North America had a head-start, it is not surprising that their citizens continued to gain further advantages in this competitive process. Hence some would argue that the fundamental injustice between members of rich states and members of poor ones lies in the boundaries which governments draw around national economies, and not in the logic of capitalist development. It is restrictions on the mobility of labour and capital worldwide which mean that citizens of one country can expect their income to go up (or down) simply by moving from their own state to another.

Philippe Van Parijs calls this form of injustice 'citizenship exploitation',[7] and acknowledges that it may be quite common for the unequal distribution of global assets associated with national boundaries to be a more important element in exploitation than the distribution of physical or human capital. In other words, when I am working in Slovakia, I am perpetrating an injustice more as a result of my advantages as a British citizen (well, British *subject* actually, in my case) than as a member of a well-paid, global, professional elite.

Does this imply that free movement of everything would eventually lead to global justice? Yes and no, according to Van Parijs (following Roemer). When trade between rich and poor countries takes place, 'what occurs is the exchange of labor today for access to capital produced in the past'.[8] Differences in productivity between countries can be addressed *either* in terms of moving people (and their human assets) *or* by moving money. Roemer showed that, in principle, either form of free movement could produce a situation in which the rates of wages and of profits would be equal and in equilibrium all over the world – but only if borders were completely closed to movements of the other factor. So we can achieve global justice (in theory at least) by having open borders either for people, or for money, but not for both.[9]

Of course, this does not imply that all the unfairness in the distribution of assets worldwide, giving rise to variations in productivity and incomes, can be instantly rectified by inward movement of capital, and that this can come about just by abolishing these controls. There are also cultural factors (the work ethic and time preferences, and attachments to local customers and networks, of populations); and natural factors (such as differences in fertility, climate and mineral resources).[10] Van Parijs implies that the impact of cultural factors can be minimized through something like the World Bank's strategy for global development (see below, pp. 167–71). Above all, the free movement of money can avoid the painful process of mass migration under the pressure of poverty, because capital mobility provides 'a perfect substitute':

> This is not a massive altruistic transfer of resources in the form of 'development aid', but the unconstrained movement of money in search of higher profits. This sounds particularly good news today,

as we keep hearing that money is becoming increasingly slippery
and that its movements are ever harder to control . . . so that –
whether we like it or not – borders are more open than ever to the
flowing of money.[11]

The obstacles to the worldwide equalization of productivity
and wages which Van Parijs acknowledges are the 'political risks',
associated with instability and insecure property rights, which
cause investors to demand compensatory higher rates of profit.
Eventually, these would be reduced, because states would have
strong incentives to create stable environments for investment. Of
course, average incomes of citizens would still vary by states,
because those living in countries with earlier development histories would enjoy earnings from their larger holdings of wealth; and
there would still be significant differences in skills legacies. In view
of these obstacles, and the cultural resistance to change which is
embodied in local networks and customs, Van Parijs concedes that
the optimistic outlook for world development foreseen by his
model will be very slow in its realization.

Van Parijs's optimism takes no account of the transformation of
collective life which is analysed in this book. The nearest he comes
to addressing these (power) factors is in discussing the tension
between *internal* struggles over distribution within affluent states,
and *external* pressures for inward migration, by people from poorer
countries. He argues that, in order to achieve a system of income
distributions which is both equitable and unconditional (i.e., not
related to work status), major restrictions on immigration would
have to be put in place by governments of affluent states:

> There is no way in which such systems could survive if all the old,
> sick and lazy of the world came running to take advantage of them.
> The reduction of domestic wealth or job exploitation, it seems,
> clashes head on with the reduction of citizenship exploitation.[12]

Both Roemer's and Van Parijs's versions of global economic
justice suggest that the only relevant collective actors are states,
and the only relevant boundaries are state borders. Because they
assume perfect competition,[13] they can treat firms, including
global banks and transnational corporations, as individual economic agents, acting according to the laws of microeconomics.

But, as we saw in chapter 7 (pp. 153–4), both firms which provide goods for private consumption and organizations which supply collective goods to groups can follow a collective logic of their own, which is not the logic of markets. They can choose to adopt authority (collective power), rather than contract, as a way of achieving their purposes. So the assumptions are completely unrealistic, and the conclusions are misleading.

What's more, these economic entities have enough collective clout to make agreements with governments which consolidate their power. Such agreements were common in the era of welfare states, but they were between national governments and large national firms. In exchange for tax breaks, investment grants, and seats at the table of the various boards and committees which planned the national economy, these companies agreed to meet government targets on output, employment and salaries. The arrangements were called corporatism. They allowed 'the social partners' (firms and trade unions) to share gains from improved productivity, and states to manage income distribution. In other words, they reflected an institutionalized truce between the big collective actors, represented by governments, confederations of employers, and those of workers, for the sake of national economic advantage over foreigners.

Corporatism was rejected (in the USA, UK and the rest of the Anglo-Saxon world) or severely modified (in Japan, Continental Europe and Scandinavia) because transnational banks and businesses found new and more profitable ways of linking up worldwide, into global collective entities. In these larger, more fluid and mobile forms, they could confront governments with effective threat-power – that they should give them more advantages, or they would shift, in some new collective guise, elsewhere. At first, they were able to gain better terms from weaker governments in developing countries. Eventually they did so in the affluent states of the West, as well as bringing down the Soviet version of state socialism, whose system simply could not stand the competition.

The new forms of agreement look very different from the old corporatist institutions. There are no smoke-filled rooms, or negotiations between 'peak organizations'. Instead, governments are simply made accountable to the world's financial institutions. States' monetary and fiscal regimes are now subject to evaluation by international financial markets.[14] This means that governments must compete with each other to keep taxes, and especially taxes on business, as low as possible. They must demonstrate that they can control public spending, and especially transfers to poor people. They must show that their labour markets are 'flexible'. If they can do all this, then they will find favour with global financial institutions and – with suitable additional inducements – with transnational corporations also.

In affluent developed countries, these orthodoxies do not demand anything so demeaning as a signature on a piece of paper. Instead, all that is required is for presidents, prime ministers and ministers of finance to repeat these mantras of prudence, over and over again, on TV, at political meetings, at business dinners and whenever they are gathered together. If they form themselves into 'free trade areas' or other collective bodies, they must all swear allegiance to the same principles (as in the Stability Pact which underpins the European Monetary Union). Every programme and promise to citizens must be demonstrated to be financially sound and business-friendly. That is why all party manifestos everywhere look exactly the same.

For the developing and post-Communist countries, a far more explicit form of compliance is required. Their governments, in order to qualify for the loans from the International Monetary Fund and World Bank which they so desperately need, must demonstrate that they too have 'business plans' which conform to the prescribed model.[15] These must include evidence of 'integrity and transparency of public expenditure management and procurement systems', and an account of 'social, structural and key sectoral policies, which covers the policy reform and institutional development priorities' of the plan.[16] The central state continues to be responsible for the overall institutional framework, though its implementation is to be devolved to various local bodies and NGOs. But the long-term goal is still growth through 'market liberalization'.

What is new is the World Bank's emphasis on a 'social contract' between governments and their people, especially the poor. The key concepts are 'opportunity', 'empowerment' and 'security', and the aim is to help poor people develop their assets, and increase the reliable returns on these.[17] The framework for this is negotiation and agreement between civil-society associations and commercial companies, and through 'public-private partnerships', more at a local than a national level: 'Sound governance, competition and markets – and free entry for multiple agents, whether government, non-government or private – are essential for effective service delivery, especially for poor people.'[18]

At first glance, it might seem possible to recast the World Bank development model in a kind of functionalist formula for a self-enforcing order of progress towards global justice. Although purely aspirational at this stage, it could go like this:

1 Institutions for good governance, through fiscal prudence, flexible labour markets and balancing devolution of power, can result from a process of institutional reform and market liberalization.
2 All developing countries, and especially their poorest citizens, can benefit from these institutions.
3 Self-responsible and self-improving individuals and communities may not initially intend to consolidate or contribute to good governance by their actions – they simply participate in local projects, assisted by NGOs and commercial companies.
4 Self-responsible and self-improving individuals and communities may not be aware of the connections between institutional reforms, market liberalization, NGO projects and good governance – they may just be trying to improve their lot.
5 Institutional reform and market liberalization will lead to good governance by a feedback loop, passing through self-responsible and self-improving individuals and communities.

On closer inspection, however, this version does not link together in the required manner at all. What is missing are the 'invisible hand' or 'natural selection' elements of unintended patterning. What is substituted for these is wishful thinking.

The World Bank model gestures in the direction of all kinds of connection between these processes. From the side of central government, an array of regulatory, protective and redistributive measures are mentioned, but no guidelines as to their application are provided. From that of local communities, both traditional, communal systems and more radical ones, such as the redistribution of land, are endorsed, with no hints at how they fit together. What, for instance, is to persuade the rich to share with the poor? Above all, 'public-private partnerships' are supposed to arise spontaneously, from first principles, as if the governments of small, debt-laden states and municipalities could deal on equal terms with global corporations.

The fundamental reason why the World Bank model fails to provide a functionalist formula for development is that there is simply no economic theory of such partnerships and agreements and how they tie together in a coherent economic whole. Statements about how essential they are, for both efficiency and equity (whether by the World Bank, or by Third Way governments like Tony Blair's) are just declarations of faith.

If there were any theoretical basis for these declarations in terms of efficiency, we would expect to find them in the work of Joseph Stiglitz, a Nobel laureate in economics and an apologist for the World Bank model.[19] In fact, all we find is a mishmash of ad hoc nostrums, which purport to show how central and local governments can regulate the 'pacing and sequencing' of reforms and restructurings, so that these economies are not overwhelmed by global forces. He holds up China as a successful example of this approach, citing its two-tier price system and communal enterprise funds as indigenous mechanisms for slowing down the transition from a state-controlled to a market economy.[20]

The choice of China is revealing. Having no democratic accountability, the Communist Party leadership has been able to use the World Bank model in an entirely different way from the one which other small, poor states have been forced to accept. It can, for example, control flows of population from one region to another. It can make quite different rules for the administration of its effective financial capital city, Hong Kong, from those which apply to the rest of the country. And it can designate Special Zones for rapid industrialization and urbanization, allowing access to foreign investment on its own terms.[21]

The reason why there can be no convincing economic explanation of the relationship between governments, firms and NGOs is that each has its own collective logic, and they are all quite different. As collective actors, states are territorial and have relatively fixed boundaries and memberships; they must at least pretend to meet the needs of all their regions and populations. Firms are mobile and have extremely fluid boundaries; they serve the interests first of their owners, next of their customers and (to a limited extent) their staff, all of whom are changing all the time. NGOs are either local or international; their subscribers, staff and clients are all recruited from quite separate constituencies, and they are coalitions of values and goals, which respond partly to economic and political, but mainly to ethical, signals and incentives.

All this means that 'partnerships' and 'agreements' between such organizations are inevitably messy, mixed and uncertain. Economics, as a social science, was able to develop explanations of decisions over public goods by endowing governments with preferences and utility functions, and creating a special subject of 'public' or 'welfare' economics. Where collective actors interact within the same sector – states with states, enterprises with enterprises, NGOs with NGOs – they use the same kinds of power resource and set the same kinds of goal.[22] All states are, after all, no more than systems of collective authority; all firms just concentrations of physical and human capital under a single agency and control; and all NGOs simply organized deployments of charitable or communal effort. But when they interact across sectors, the outcomes are often contested. Ahrne quotes the examples of nepotism, corporatism, tariffs, taxation, strikes and social work as cross-sector activities whose legitimacy is often challenged: 'The outcome of this kind of interaction is often inconclusive. There are rarely any obvious winners or losers. Rules are mostly unclear or non-existent. The interaction between organizations from different sectors is unorganized and unsettled.'[23]

The reasons for this ambiguity, messiness and controversial ethical quality is that forms of power, which are seen as legitimate in one sector, are used in others where rights and resources to limit or resist this type of power are absent or inoperable. So, for instance, democratic controls over government decisions cannot extend to firms to whom military, policing or social service functions are contracted out. Companies, in turn, cannot get certain citizens to comply with their rules, or respond to their incentives, for utilitarian motives. Hence they must rely on state coercion (for example, benefits officials forcing claimants to take employment under threat of removing their income support) to recruit and achieve compliance. And NGOs, which depend on moral persuasion, find themselves mixing this with traditional patriarchal and aristocratic power in local, communal projects.

In this way, power becomes contested at every intersection in the joins which link up the World Bank model. Nothing about its connectedness is uncontroversial; its bonds are manifestly artificial and contrived. They are not experienced as either natural or rational by participants.

Of course, attempts have been made to invent a kind of legitimacy for these processes. The aim of these is to explain how, for example, local initiatives for self-help, supported by international NGOs, might come to be linked into the wider national and international economies, so that the 'empowerment' of the participants could spill over into their 'inclusion' in the global market. But by definition these communities are peripheral, and organize their lives in ways which fall outside both the formal polity (since they supply their own collective goods) and the formal economy (since they market few, if any, of their products).

For instance, when I was working in Hungary, I visited a project which was supported by an NGO, the Autonomia Foundation, in the village of Szentrolád, in a mountainous area on the northern border, known for iron-mining and (under communism) steel-making.[24] The small community comprised about 40 per cent Roma (gypsy) people, a group which had suffered racial discrimination since 1989 all over Central Europe, and was housed in accommodation separate from that of ethnic Hungarians throughout that region. With the unemployment rate at around 30 to 50 per cent for ethnic Hungarians since the local industries had closed down, that for Roma was almost 100 per cent; in many villages almost no economic activity was taking place, and the shops were empty of everything but the barest essentials. Migration to Budapest, or abroad, was high.

In Szentrolád, a village association had been started by a Hungarian steel worker, without any relevant education or training. They decided to try to rent *all* of the surrounding land from the cooperative, which was no longer farming it, and to recruit as many villagers as possible, in order to create conditions for equal cooperation (between Hungarians and Roma alike), and to eliminate speculation, exploitation and defection. They divided

the land into two halves, one for large, subsistence-orientated
family vegetable plots; and the other to grow vegetables to market
(using huge, redundant socialist tractors). Without any agricultural
or marketing expertise, the latter had hitherto barely broken even,
but the family plots were flourishing. Once again, people were
active in shaping their own destiny.

The leading members of the association explained that they
originally saw the project as a temporary measure, to tide them
over the transition to capitalism in their region. Now they recognized no signs of an external 'solution' to the problems, which had
become structural. They simply had to give up hopes of being
miners and factory workers again, and turn themselves into peasants. What was set up as a system of primitive communism would
evolve, they supposed, so that there would eventually be a market
in land, some would acquire more, and employ others, and so on.
At least the benefit authorities had allowed them to go on drawing
social assistance while they worked for the association.

It was like starting again, from the situation of the Middle Ages,
but without the feudal landlords, and without the iron ore. Their
project, and the economic relationships they created, reminded
me of the thought experiments in philosophical texts, like those
of Rawls,[25] Dworkin,[26] Roemer and Van Parijs. They had been
forced to redefine property, power and justice among their membership group. They had also been required to establish their own
system of governance – their rules and authority structures.

Admirable as this initiative was, it lacked any meaningful links
to the central authorities in Budapest, or to the national and global
economies. It is pure wishful thinking for the World Bank to
imagine that these subsistence activities create bridges with wider
networks of government or commerce. NGOs are supposed to
develop such projects, so as to 'enhance their potential by linking
them to intermediary organizations, broader markets, and public
institutions'.[27] The ultimate goal is 'increasing the capacity of poor
people and the socially disadvantaged to engage society's power
structure and articulate their interests and aspirations'.[28]

If there was any convincing ethical, as well as economic, explanation of how such connections might be made, we might have
expected to find it in the writings of Amartya Sen, acknowledged
by Stiglitz as the leading influence on the World Bank's develop-

ment model.[29] Sen is, after all, both a leading world thinker on poverty, famine and other aspects of 'underdevelopment', and on their relationship to wealth and power in the Western countries.

Yet in his book *Development as Freedom* (based on lectures he gave at the World Bank) Sen provides no such theoretical account. Instead he relies on a kind of dialogue between capitalism and the state, in which progressive values and enlightened public policies emerge through democratic processes.

> The emergence of social norms can be facilitated both by communicative reasoning and by evolutionary selection of behavioural modes. . . . The use of socially responsible reasoning and of ideas of justice relates closely to the centrality of individual freedom. But a sense of justice is among the concerns that *can* move people and often *do*. Social values can play – and have played – an important part in the success of various forms of social organization, including the market mechanism, democratic politics, elementary civil and political rights, provision of basic public goods, and institutions for public action and protest.[30]

What Sen is advocating in his book is highly relevant for the transformation of collective life, which is the subject of this one. He too sees individual freedom as the fundamental building block for equitable social arrangements, and holds that collective authority must supply certain basic goods necessary for freedom, especially the education and healthcare that allow individuals to acquire 'capabilities' for choice within personal projects. He also insists that freedoms can be meaningfully analysed only within a framework of institutions, which define the scope for individual and collective action.[31] He distinguishes between poor states which have achieved 'support-led' development based on advances in health, education and life expectancy (such as Kerala in India, Sri Lanka and pre-reform China), and those which have been able to capture the investment for economic growth (such as South Korea, Taiwan and post-reform China). He seeks institutions to balance these two kinds of development, under democratic political rules.

However, as the long quotation above suggests, Sen's recommendations are vague and rely little on convincing economic arguments. Simply finding instances of how capitalism has generated freedoms in some countries, and state policies have supplied greatly improved well-being in others, does not explain away the many cases where capitalist economies or socialist regimes have achieved neither. Hence pleas for 'a balanced approach', for compromise and 'partial agreements' sound somewhat hollow.[32]

Above all, Sen's book (and the World Bank's *Report*) do not explain what is to prevent special interest groups (business coalitions, financial groupings or professional interests on the one hand, and nationalist or religious movements on the other) from successfully persuading the majority of a society that their particular interests represent the general interest. If this happens, the common interests of the great majority in a society may remain invisible because there will be a lack of clear issues around which people can be mobilized in pursuit of them. At a time when the collective boundaries within and between all the world's societies are being redrawn, and new organizations are supplying new forms of membership and collective goods, these dangers are all the greater. The only consistent success story that can be claimed by Sen and the World Bank – China – was a dictatorship throughout the period in question, hardly raising hopes for reconciling development with democracy.

The main problem seems to be that both Sen and the World Bank implicitly adopt a model of development which accepts the principles of fiscal federalism and 'voting with the feet', outlined in chapters 5 and 6; but they do not acknowledge the implications of this for power and exclusion, explained in chapter 7. Hence they cannot provide convincing accounts of institutional arrangements to address these issues. While ideally political authority should regulate and restrain economic agents, so as to balance exit and voice rights, create heterogeneous communities and build bridges between organizations, the incentives for governments to reinforce social polarization and exclusion, and to increase inequalities of wealth and power, are often strong, especially where democratic cultures are still fragile.

So who or what is to blame for the injustices and abuses of power of the new world order under globalization? I have argued throughout this book that the problem lies in the way in which sex, money and power join up certain aspects of some (more able and resourceful) individuals' inner worlds with the public life of organizations, and exclude others, whose personal experiences are linked with quite different collectives by another set of connections. Increasingly, these two webs of relationships and cultures are set in opposition to each other, leading to conflict, violence and war. Sex, money and power, which glue the links in the web of affluence and autonomy that spans the globe, create a barrier against which the rest resist and struggle.

But it is important to be clear that no single one of these linking media in the First World web can be held responsible for these divisions, exclusions and antagonisms. Although the globe is often divided over issues of sexual morality, with rich countries favouring individual autonomy and diversity of orientations and partnerships, and poor ones condemning all manifestations of liberated female and gay sexuality, moral traditions alone cannot explain the present global clash of cultures.

Nor, I shall argue, can this cosmic struggle be reduced to a simple equation of advantage measured in money, or to the commercialization of all human relationships. It is only when money and power combine in particular configurations that injustices are done. So it is not *markets* which should be blamed for the endemic inequity of our lives together on this earth, but the collective forms of life which take shape in commercial societies, and now across the world.

It is fashionable (and appealing) in oppositional and resistance circles to make the contrast between the soulless individualism of markets and consumption on the one hand, and the warm, human sharing of collectives on the other.[33] Campaigners for global justice advance the claims of collectives of all kinds, from socialist states, through producer cooperatives and trade unions, to rural communities and eco-communes, as being the only ways to offset the destructive power of 'global market forces'. These very different kinds of collective are grouped together, as providers of the 'life goods' of 'the civil commons and the life-ground underneath';[34] or as upholders of '*communitas*' and the 'moral economy'.[35]

But this kind of elision obscures the unpalatable truth that the only thing which all these collectives have in common is that they are systems of authority and exclusion. Even the most democratic, egalitarian and eco-friendly communal unit (such as the Szentrolád village association) necessarily involves rules of ownership, cooperation, restraint of conflict and – above all – exclusion. Only 70 per cent of the population of Szentrolád were in fact members of the association. The rest got no family plots, no produce and no influence on the group's decisions. They had the option to join at the beginning, but not any more – all the land is gone.

It is true that collectives are the alternative institutional forms to markets, and that they offer ways of doing things which offset the effects of market allocations. Anything that can be done by dividing the world up into private pieces, and selling it for a price, can also be done by keeping it all in one piece, and sharing it. Each way of doing things has its characteristic strengths and weaknesses, costs and benefits.[36] Locke offered his contemporaries an optimistic account of how the invention of money transformed a totally collective world of shared poverty into a potentially harmonious and prosperous one of property, order and moral (but not material) equality. Yes, it was a con-trick, but the issues were well stated.

The question is not whether to opt for a world entirely dominated by markets, or one made up entirely of collective units. It is which combination of markets with collectives, of what size, quality and distribution of resources, can balance freedom and equality, individual and popular sovereignty. Another way of putting this is to ask what kinds of collective power can best offset the inequities of market outcomes, and which kinds of market freedom can best balance the oppressions of collective power.

In the present world order, injustice and abuse of power lies mainly in the enormous concentration of wealth in the hands of global corporations, and in their capacity to persuade weak governments and greedy officials to let them exploit the poor. Journalists like John Pilger and George Monbiot have documented the extent of human suffering through these collusive arrangements.[37] The new threat to any moral basis for international governance comes from the use of the military power of the richest and strongest nations as an instrument of spreading these systematic injustices and abuses over new territories, and provoking yet more conservative, theocratic, fanatical or fundamentalist resistance to them.

The real dilemma for those trying to formulate convincing alternatives to this international regime of power, both economic and political, is of linking up feasible collective ideals of sharing and cooperation with the equal autonomy of individuals which is so cherished in the affluent West. This was the problem which confronted George Monbiot at the Paris conference on the Social Economy (see p. 16). The reconciliation of accountable collective power with legitimate forms of individual freedom will be the topic of the remainder of this book.

Meanwhile, it is not only in the developing countries of Africa, Asia and Latin America that whole populations are experiencing the impact of the combined power of large commercial organizations and political authorities. Two groups are especially vulnerable to coercion by the joint forces of these different kinds of organization – the sedentary inhabitants of the most deprived districts, which have been deserted by their abler and more resourceful former co-residents;[38] and migrants from abroad, who have arrived in affluent countries without the proper immigration status.

This is because the increased international mobility of money and investment goods has not, as Roemer's and Van Parijs's abstract models suggested, led to *either* redistribution of resources for the sake of justice, behind national immigration control systems, *or* free movement for all worldwide. Instead, it has resulted in various kinds of compromise and collusion between the collective strategies of global corporations and those of governments representing mainstream individuals, with portable skills and material assets.[39]

Under these new arrangements, those citizens with few skills, no savings and strong interdependencies in local communities (who therefore are not autonomous and mobile) become defined as a 'surplus population'.[40] They must be coerced into employment and training, under 'workfare' or 'welfare-to-work' systems. Officials require them to take low-paid, casual or part-time jobs, and firms are subsidized to employ them at below-subsistence wages, through tax credit arrangements.[41] The politics of these developments will be analysed in chapter 9.

On the other hand, the mobility of skilled staff and the 'flexibility' of labour markets are increasingly enhanced by arrangements for recruiting workers from abroad. States cooperate with companies which need such workers, under schemes for 'managed migration', such as the ones which allow global nomads, interviewed in chapter 5 (see pp. 118–20). But the freedom of movement granted to those recruits does not extend to individuals who want to enter affluent states, either in search of political freedom, or to look for better opportunities of employment.[42]

Policy in the EU member states focused, in the 1990s, on restricting entry through the asylum channel, by making conditions less advantageous for those claiming humanitarian protection on the grounds of political persecution. Reductions in benefits, dispersal into remote districts or camp-style accommodation and rapid processing of claims all aim to cut numbers, both for the sake of saving government expenditure and to dampen nationalist and populist campaigns, based on protectionist or racist rhetoric.[43]

All this helps explain why large numbers of individuals choose instead to enter affluent Western countries as irregular workers in the shadow economy, without proper immigration status. In highly regulated economies such as Germany, their opportunities are restricted to 'invisible' roles, such as domestic cleaners in private households, or carers for infirm elderly people.[44] In order to get other kinds of work, they need to cultivate network relationships with citizens or settled migrants, on whom they rely for contacts and for protection. Brazilians in Berlin (both men and women) were able to get work in nightclubs, for example, through such patronage. They also relied on marriage to EU citizens as a strategy for regularization of their status; even gay men adopted this strategy for settlement.[45]

In the UK, by contrast, it was far easier for those entering as tourists, once they had convinced the port authorities of their status, then immediately to find accommodation and take work, with the short-term help of one or two friends. Our studies of people from Brazil, Turkey and Poland who were working without proper status in London showed that they all found a wider range of opportunities than their counterparts in Germany – for instance, in textile factories, bars, cafés, hotels and restaurants and in commercial as well as domestic cleaning and construction.[46] They were mostly well educated, and some had professional experience. They were proud of being skilled and hard-working, and claimed that they were enduring worse conditions than they had experienced in their home countries, and that they were contributing positively to the UK economy.

It is difficult to locate these people in the analysis of how power is deployed and abused in the new world order. On the one hand, those from Brazil and Poland say that they enter the UK voluntarily, and see their opportunities for earning as superior to those in their home countries. Brazilians, who have to pay much more for their passage, often get trapped in a situation where they cannot save enough to return; Poles, by contrast, are mostly able to accumulate enough to reach their targets, or come and go on a number of visits.[47] Migrants from Turkey explained that they had come in search of political freedom, though not all had applied for asylum. Their shadow work was simply a strategy for survival, as they argued that advantageous employment in the formal economy was not open to them in their area of north-east London.[48]

As a resistance strategy, their use of the exit option in relation to their home economy and polity was therefore a protest against lack of economic opportunity, or lack of political liberty. In the case of Brazilians and Poles, they were unspecific about who they blamed for the economic 'disaster' at home; Turks and Kurds seemed to attribute their lack of freedom as much to capitalism and the new world order as to the Turkish government. Many of them adopted a socialist critique, in which the UK government, as much as theirs in Turkey, colluded in their exploitation and oppression.[49]

However, in the face of their living and working conditions as irregular migrants in the UK, the Brazilians and Poles, on the one hand, and the Turks and Kurds, on the other, adopted entirely different strategies. The former were highly individualistic, and showed marked mistrust in their fellow nationals. They competed for work and accommodation, and reported numerous incidents of betrayal, even by relatives, who 'grassed' them to the immigration authorities, either to get their jobs, or to settle quarrels. These denunciations often led to removals by the authorities.[50]

> The Brazilian community here is very messed up. . . . One of my friends here was denounced by a Brazilian as well, because of gossip and arguments. (Carmen, p. 3)

> People in the 'black' are highly competitive. . . . I started to hear about people being caught and sent back because of betrayal and accusation. (Farina, p. 16)

> There is a lot of grassing around. People do grass! . . . Brazilians betray others. (Cris, p. 4)

> I am lucky because at the hotel I used to work at the Home Office turned up because of someone grassing. They caught a Brazilian who was deported after. . . . That was because they had a fight at the hotel and someone called the Home Office. (Rosa, p. 5)

> Poles envy you for having something, for having a good job and so on. (Jerzy, p. 11)

> My friend's brother was deported. Someone grassed on him. (Ivona, p. 8)

> In the beginning we lived with my uncle. The one who eventually called the police on us. (Tomasz, p. 1)

For Polish irregular workers in particular, there were markets for National Insurance numbers, for job information and even for jobs themselves.

> These Polish guys . . . said they know a guy who was selling National Insurance numbers. . . . I met him and I bought it. I paid £260 for it. (Jerzy, p. 9)

> I bought the job from some bloke. He had to pay £50 for it. There is a trade like this, and it still exists – selling jobs. (Dariusz, p. 2)

Such unrestrained competition leaves new entrants to shadow labour markets especially vulnerable. They have to pay 'entry fees' for multioccupation houses, for job information and for false papers. Some longer-stay irregulars are able to establish roles as brokers, to live by buying and selling these 'goods'.

Other Poles had developed a strategy for regularizing their stays, by applying for 'business visas' from the Home Office. They would submit a 'business plan' to an accountant and a solicitor, who then sent it to the Home Office. Several said that they based it on their contacts through shadow work, but it was then creatively developed. 'It's all fiction. I have never seen the business plan myself. I don't even know what's written there' (Pawel, p. 10).

If these migrants are being exploited, it is partly by each other – for instance by subcontractors who have failed to pay them for work done[51] – and partly by employers, who were frequently minority ethnic entrepreneurs. Turkish and Kurdish migrants, many of whom were claiming benefits because they gained entitlements as asylum seekers before the 1996 legislation, were far more explicit about the sources of power in their exploitation and oppression. They identified the form of collusion between Turkish entrepreneurs and the state which operated in their communities.

The Turkish garment industry, in particular, is highly mobile, constantly relocating in European cities, such as Amsterdam or London, and back to Turkey. It also recruits among migrants and asylum seekers, as well as back in the home country. One interviewee, Kadir, explained why workers in London are compliant, and lack a trade union perspective:

> For example, you come from Turkey, and you own a factory . . . and you have a contact with the mafia, and for example you need a workforce, and you send a message to the village that you need new people to work there, and they bring you these new people, and they start to work there, and instead of receiving maybe £30 they receive say £15 . . . and they are grateful, and they cannot complain about this. Maybe later, when they realize how their situation really is . . . but then their relatives [back home] will think they are disloyal, so although they earn [so little] they have to be thankful for that, so that's the way the system works. . . . So we are really exploited, and there are really bad conditions. . . . And when they want to complain about the situation . . . because the owner of the factory comes from their village, he is in fact their relative . . . that's why in the end people do nothing about it. (Kadir, p. 12)

Kadir and others saw the British government as complicit in these abuses:

> Illegal work is organized by the British government. . . . And there is something in it, since students are clearly a cheap labour force. (Kerim, p. 5)

It's not right for the state to criminalize people. These
people work, and the state needs them as cheap labour.
These people give their labour power and the state needs
them just . . . they're really cheap. . . . These people have
done the country big favours. (Aysen, p. 24)

The transformation of collective life, in which globalization has
played such an important part, has led to new combinations of
exploitation and domination, as political authorities strike deals
with transnational enterprises, and contract for previously public
services. These new arrangements follow the prescriptions of the
World Bank, but these 'public-private partnerships' generally do
not, despite the Bank's rhetoric, 'empower' poor people. They
make the use of power more opaque, powerholders less accountable, and large populations more vulnerable.

In response, marginal groups and whole poor countries have
adopted new and complex strategies of resistance. Most of these
have relied on exit options, including irregular migration. Some,
like the Brazilians and Poles in our research study in London, use
highly individualized methods, and rely on shadow markets for
almost all their needs, illustrating the perils of unrestrained competition. Others, like the Turks and Kurds in the same study, are
much more interdependent, in kinship systems, in political and
cultural associations and in communities. In the next chapter, I
shall return to the family, kinship and community as interdependencies, and analyse power relations in these units.

9

Power, Passion and Loyalty

The previous chapter reached the cold-eyed conclusion that, from an economic perspective, all human collectives are simply alternative ways of getting things done. Each can be used to do anything, and all have their own costs and benefits.[1] It may be possible, for instance, to decide that families are the most efficient units in which to raise children, global commercial organizations are the optimum forms of healthcare, and nation-states the most cost-effective suppliers of railroad tracks. There is no God-given way of dividing up populations into social units, just a large number of possible divisions that overlap with each other,[2] and all with a price tag and a consumer satisfaction guarantee for the collective goods they produce and distribute.

Of course, these same arrangements must also be evaluated for the ethical implications of their outcomes. We can always assess the benefits gained by members of any collective unit, both internally and externally. The terms of membership of an association may be discriminatory – some may gain more advantages than others. And there will be effects on outsiders, who might demand compensation or the right to enter under different rules or qualifications.[3] Injustice may stem from the way the organization is run, or the way it excludes and dumps on those outside it.

So nothing is sacred in the world of collective units. And this comes as a shock. Anthropologists have shown that human beings always endowed their membership systems with mysterious powers, and attributed magical properties to their ritual leaders.[4] The very idea of the spiritual, religious and supernatural qualities of the world is, they say, derived from the projection of such qualities onto the collective.[5] Because our societies give us our cultural concepts, classifications and categories, we take these to be derived from the divine order, as well as from nature and reason.[6] That is why we deal in bodies such as secret societies with mystical symbols and oaths of allegiance for office-holders, or with the Holy Roman Empire and the Divine Right of Kings.

It is a mistake to suppose that this tendency to attribute sacred qualities has vanished with the age of commercialism, bureaucracy and risk analysis. As I argued in the Introduction, even the most determined follower of an ethic of autonomy and self-development is prone to a belief in the existence (somewhere) of a soulmate, in whose partnership can be achieved the highest form of self-fulfilment. We are still moved to enthusiastic support of our favourite football teams or national athletes, and to endow their actions with heroic status. And we still urge our armies on in war with enemies, given the monstrous guise of evil, and celebrate inordinately in the capture of their vicious leaders.

This means that our inner worlds continue to link with the public realms of collective life in ways that are fundamentally emotional – in terms of love and loyalty, rather than pure calculation. It also means that we are willing to accept some forms of power (at least for a time) which owe little to the measurable benefits they bestow upon us, and much to these sacred and supernatural attributions. We give our hearts to partners, even when our heads know better; we revere deeply flawed leaders, and uphold ideas with dubious moral credentials; and we are willing to die for causes which turn out to be anything but noble.

This chapter is about the kinds of power which link the inner worlds of our fantasies and feelings with the public sphere of relationships and belonging. It tries to explain how the various discourses and organizations which connect up our experiences, and allow us to make sense of them, encompass these emotional elements. So it seeks to analyse power in sexual partnerships, in the family, community and nation – the power associated with lust and longing, with blood, guts, faith, soil and violent conflict.

If sex joins up the personal and the public in the most fundamental way, in what kinds of power does it deal? We are all indebted to feminist scholars for their analyses of the links between sexual power, including the use of violence and coercion, and the forms of the patriarchal family. Traditional morality gave a veneer of civilization to relationships of dominance and dependence, founded on property and physical subordination.

But are the optimists (like Giddens, Beck and Plummer – see pp. 26–7 and 46–7) right to conclude that sexual partnership has been transformed, with the new diversity in the expression of sexual orientations, and a new equality between the partners? Or are the pessimists, like Bauman and Fevre, justified in their condemnation of the egoism and exploitation of consumerist recreational sex and throw-away relationships?

Implicit in the notion of 'negotiated intimacy' is a minimization of traditional power. Equal and autonomous selves, each with a project for self-realization, meet on terms which allow no domination and submission. Where there is a balance of exit threat, and each holds portable material assets, both must agree the extent of their mutual commitment, and create a discursive democratic order.

But the central issue of personal relationships, identified by Scheff (p. 25), is exactly what needs to be negotiated in these conversations. He argues that, in a loving relationship, individuals forge secure bonds when they understand each other's thoughts, beliefs and feelings, accept what it is they understand, and engage in 'mutual sharing'.[7] This is in contrast with 'isolated bonds', where each constantly emphasizes their own point of view, and 'engulfed bonds', where each emphasizes the other's point of view at the expense of their own. The former tend to end up in mutual rejection; the latter in the subordination of one (or both) to the other, and hence the loss of personal identity and autonomy.[8] The ideal is therefore a balance between 'I' and 'we' (independence and interdependence).[9]

Sex, as the physical fusion of two bodies, tests out this balance to destruction. It challenges emotional autonomy by requiring each partner to hold on to their identity at the moment of surrendering it. And it demands that the violence of desire for bodily union and the release of pent-up tension coexist with awareness of the other's emotional state by staying tuned in to tiny manifestations of inner feelings. These are both the clearest expressions of the mutual sharing which is required for loving partnership and the most risky tests of it.

In so far as present-day partnership aspires to these standards of ecstatic pleasure in each other as whole beings, it therefore treads a tightrope, across a chasm between isolation and engulfment. To surrender too little is to spiral into the void of demanding and accusing claims – a cycle of recrimination, taking turns to give resentfully or withhold in vengeance, alternating between hot shame and angry rage.[10] To surrender too much is to lose one's bearings and eventually oneself – to be reduced to a puppet, a victim or a slave.

But to make this balancing act more complex, at least two quite different dimensions of dominance and submission are involved. One source of both communication and power is purely physical. Sex sends messages through the body, and they are messages of both mutuality and subjugation. Even someone who started his adult life as sexually inept as I was can learn, with the help of a generous and loving partner, the physical repertoire that may be translated into sexual power. Men seem to be biologically programmed to pick up this form of power quite easily, and to use it carelessly. Even exceptionally infantile, stupid and insensitive men are capable of acquiring the basic skills to exploit it.

Conversely, at the risk of gender stereotyping, women seem particularly adapted to the development of emotional power, which consists in communicating directly with their partners' inmost, hidden and protected feelings. They appear to possess antennae capable of sounding out the most vulnerable points in their partners' defences, and prising them open. Once this is achieved, they are then in a position to exploit this needy, helpless core being, by poking and pricking it at their leisure. Emotional power is both the more subtle and the more pervasive of two kinds of intimate dominion.

I suspect that many partnerships, even quite successful ones, deal in trade-offs between these two kinds of intimate power. Men, who are relatively disadvantaged in the emotional cut-and-thrust of partnership, compensate by using their sexual power to the full. At an unconscious level, they perhaps attribute to their partners the desire for such domination, and the need for physical dependence on them. Women in turn feel amply justified in using the weapons of emotional power to compensate for their physical disadvantages. They unconsciously endow men with childish qualities of emotional inadequacy, and project onto them their own deepest fears and fragilities.

Neither of the analyses of personal relationships reviewed in chapters 2 and 3 does justice to these issues. The more optimistic 'intimacy theorists' such as Giddens and Beck (pp. 26–7) elide sexual passion with negotiation over everyday practicalities. This conceals the real tensions between desire and emotion on the one side, and reliability and support on the other. The more pessimistic 'demoralization theorists', like Bauman and Fevre (pp. 46–7), see this problem through the lens of individualism and commercialization. But it is unclear how a stronger ethic of fidelity and commitment can be sustained within the wider context of the transformed collective environment.

Throughout this book I have tried to show how the forms taken by sexual desire and partnership are linked with the new culture of self-development, mobility and choice in public life. This means that partnership and family relations become focused on the realization of personal potentials and the management of risks and threats to these. It is not just that partners have higher expectations of each other; they also hold themselves and each other accountable for a far wider range of achievements, performances and responsibilities in the social world than under previous cultural conditions.

This is reflected in longitudinal surveys of satisfaction and dissatisfaction within relationships in the UK. The Institute of Education has conducted research on three cohorts, comprising 40,000 people, born in 1946, 1958 and 1970. The study found that, among first-married men and women in their early thirties, there had been an enormous rise in the proportions of those saying they were unhappy with their relationships. Among men and women born in 1958 and interviewed in 1991, this had been 3 and 2 per cent respectively. For those born in 1970 and surveyed in 2000, it was 22 per cent of men and 24 per cent of women. The rises in unhappiness with their current relationships among second-married, single and separated/divorced individuals were almost as large as these.[11]

It seems clear that such changes reflect something more than a decline in traditional morality, marriage and family values. In relation to qualifications, work careers, physical and mental health as well as sexual fulfilment, the new culture emphasizes personal choice and moral sovereignty. Individuals demand more control over all these aspects of their lives, and seek to wrest this from collectives. But this also implies a weakening of many forms of collective support, which previously shielded them from tensions and conflicts between these spheres of their development.

On the one hand, it exposes the potential rival pulls of individual self-realization and mutual support between the partners on a number of dimensions. On the other, it requires them to reconcile the economic logic of their decisions with the moral bases of their commitments in often painful ways. Because the sanctification of the sexual, mobile, choosing individual cannot entirely undermine belief in the sanctity of marriage and the family, or faith in the mass solidarities of the welfare state, this is a source of perplexity and potential unhappiness.

In their accounts of how they made decisions over work, pensions, schooling and child-care, we have seen how mainstream UK couples strove to combine 'quantity and quality reasoning' – economic with value rationality (see pp. 93–4). They also tried to explain how they resolved apparent conflicts of interest between them in terms of an ethic of partnership. Although they bargained in instrumental ways about issues such as where to live, what employment to take, and who did which household chores, they did so within an overall framework of shared commitment to the 'good of the family'.[12] This dealt with power differentials in any particular choice by putting them in a context of longer-term negotiations.

For example, Mrs Conifer, the wife of a scientist, had had a good job and a supportive network of friends when her two children were small. But her husband was then offered promotion and better pay at the other end of the country. As the partner with lower earnings, she felt 'in a weak bargaining position'.[13] But she hinted that her sacrifice of her short-term interests for the sake of her husband's career might be compensated later, because she would be allowed to choose where they should live in retirement.[14] It seemed as if they were 'taking turns' in giving priority to each one's preferences and interests in their decisions over the whole life cycle.[15]

Although women were generally at a disadvantage when they had young children, because they adopted 'supportive' roles, some wives did criticize husbands who failed to 'put the family first' – see for example Mrs Birch (p. 96). There was a 'partnership code' for making important choices and negotiating everyday activities, which tied individuals into the long-term common project, and limited their scope for selfish opportunism. This code regulated their relationships in terms of 'joint decisions' and 'agreements' that were flexible enough to deal with the unpredictable and messy nature of family life.[16] It seemed to be a third alternative to the precision of contracts regulating relations between market agents, and the hierarchies of power which operate in firms (see pp. 152–3), allowing them to respond reliably without prescribing in advance precisely who would do what.

Finally, the nature of commitment in present-day partnerships is further clarified by research on couples who choose not to marry, yet whose relationship endures over long periods. Jane Lewis conducted a study of such couples (twenty-four interviews with cohabitants who had been together for between six and twenty-five years, and aged between 28 and 49). Although most had 'drifted' into cohabitation, rather than choosing not to marry on principle, they had not responded to the birth of children by taking the step of marriage, as couples in another group of interviewees had done. They saw marriage as irrelevant to a commitment to each other which was 'private'; they wanted a relationship where, as one put it, 'I'm here because I want to be here and not because I'm feeling under a moral or legal obligation', or, as others said, 'We see our commitment as being a very personal one and nothing to do with signing a bit of paper or a service or anything like that', and 'I believe that my commitment to A is totally personal and I only want to make promises to him in private and I don't really want to make promises to him in public and stuff.'[17] It therefore seems that stable cohabitations reflect a version of partnership and family in which there is a conscious attempt to create bonds that do not rely on traditional or public morality. The element of choice and the voluntary nature of these bonds is stabilized and made reliable by 'private' commitment, but the sense of obligation is avoided. Equal autonomy is preserved within negotiated intimacy by the minimization of both personal and publicly sanctioned power.

However, the cultural standards of personal choice and moral sovereignty also enlarge the sphere of family responsibility, especially in relation to children. The cult of the individual demands that parents nurture their offspring in ways that promote a future project of self-development. This sets up an exacting version of the idea that all children should realize their full potential, and one that is reinforced by government policy on education and child protection, such as the Green Paper *Every Child Matters*.[18] Choices of schools and out-of-school activities become imbued with enormous significance, because they must reflect the developmental needs of each child, and make the best of each one's abilities.

Instead of providing social support for families, and integration into the local community, this implies that education is an extension of the responsibilities of parenthood. We saw in chapter 3 how parents perceived decisions over schooling as obliging them to move to another district, or switch to the fee-paying sector even when this was in conflict with their political principles. This indicated that choice in education was experienced by many as pulling away from community and collective solidarity, for the sake of the realization of individual potential.[19]

On the other side, those who argue for the progressive features of negotiated intimacy and equal autonomy in partnership detect a 'democratization' of family life, from which children are the beneficiaries. Giddens in particular has argued that the family as an intimate democracy allows 'in principle equality', on the basis that the child would agree with decisions and structural features if he or she had access to adult knowledge.[20] Furthermore, far from weakening bonds between parents and children, individualization and the decline in traditional morality may strengthen them; Beck and Beck-Gernsheim argue that the very frailty and insecurity of relationships between adults makes the parent–child tie all the more significant, and that it is now perceived as one 'which is more elemental, profound and durable than any other in this society'.[21]

Research suggests that this is in part wishful thinking. The high casualty rate of adult partnerships creates a new environment for children's development which is risky; there are real dangers, as well as some new opportunities. Feminists have pinpointed the weakness of the negotiated intimacy model of partnership identified in chapter 3 (see pp. 72–5) – its lack of connectedness to the wider public sphere of social relations. This is particularly relevant for the upbringing of children, both because public policy has an interest in these issues, through education, child protection and healthcare, and because families socialize children to be participants in society, economy and the polity. After all, the term 'democracy' is only loosely applicable to a family unit, because it really belongs in the sphere of political authority and its collective construction. Children are prepared for their roles as citizens in families; but this preparation is of limited value if families' internal dynamics and power structures are not related to the wider social world. In relation to 'democratization' of family life, Giddens's analysis fails to clarify this potential disconnectedness:

> [T]he effect of this may be to disguise and obscure the actual (institutionalized) positions in which children and parents are placed, in the process taking adult–adult relationships as the model of adult–child interactions in an abstract line of reasoning that seems to have little bearing on the lived experiences of parents and children in contemporary western societies.[22]

Ribbens McCarthy et al. reveal that the close bond between parents and children can construct exclusive and condemnatory practices as well as inclusive and tolerant ones. In their interviews with reconstructed families, they found that custodial parents and their new partners often dismissed the children's relationships with the absent partner (usually a defecting father), and justified this by referring to their commitment to, and sacrifice for, the children. This allowed them to prioritize step-parents' claims to full parental status, and there was little evidence of 'democratic' consultation about the exclusion of the absent natural parent.[23] Their discourse of exclusion was moralistic; defecting fathers forfeited the right to participate in their children's lives.

Carol Smart and her colleagues, building on previous interviews with post-divorce parents who had re-evaluated their marital experiences and who saw their relationships with their children as satisfying and enduring,[24] went on to examine how children handled post-divorce experiences of family relations. They conclude that these situations may offer children greater opportunities for participating in decisions about their relationship with their parents – that is, that divorce sometimes opens up a space for these relationships to be renegotiated, for the children to be more active in decision-making and to gain greater autonomy and respect. Some children conceptualized 'family' to include absent parents and step-parents, while others had 'closed boundaries' around biological or household units.[25]

Most children showed concern for their parents, and a sophisticated awareness of their needs, gained in part from the experience of living through divorce. Some described the post-divorce situation as an improvement: 'Mum and Dad used to really not get on and it used to be a really sort of tight-lipped situation and now, I don't know, just gradually. . . . But now it just feels as though, I mean it seems to be much easier and it's just so much better.'[26]

All this suggests that traditional moral notions and practices continue to hold sway, alongside the new norms identified by the negotiated intimacy and democratization theorists. These variations seem in large part to be class-related, with lower-middle-class and working-class families more likely to adhere to the older cultures. But that suggests, in line with the central argument of this book, that the model of equal autonomy, and the relationships it sustains, relies ultimately on adequate material resources for psychological and economic independence. It is rooted in secure property rights and an adequate and reliable income for individuals. So it is not surprising to find that, where members of a household with low earning power have strong economic interdependence, they demand a family code of moral obligation, with emotional exclusion and social condemnation for those who default on their duties. Here again, research evidence upholds the view that individualization, equality and post-traditional codes require a specific economic underpinning to get established as institutions.

These factors apply even more strongly to notions of 'community', as the ensemble of civil society and voluntary organizations and associations in any territory. In much of the world, communal methods still supply the basis of all economic activity, with shared material resources (tools, common land), and minimal private property. Capitalism has gradually stripped community of its economic role, so that, in affluent first world countries, voluntary associations provide the organizational framework for religious, recreational and cultural life, and little else. Hence the mobilization of voluntary effort and associative participation requires some kind of economic reinforcement in order to be sustainable, and organizations themselves must deliver tangible benefits, either intrinsic to shared activities, or as outputs for members.

However, this way of getting things done survives strongly in deprived communities, of the kind illustrated by the interviews in chapter 6. It is certainly not the case that their residents are incapable of collective action (any more than the disengagement of rich people from education systems illustrated in chapter 3 indicates that they cannot organize themselves). What both examples show is that people in certain circumstances and contexts adopt exit strategies – rich people exit from state systems, and poor people exit from the rules that govern the economy and the public services. Because neither the state nor the commercial sector provides them with the collective goods they need, they act together 'informally' to supply them for themselves.

As we saw (pp. 136–9), individuals and households in districts which have been deserted by productive industry and by other employers who went elsewhere, and also by more skilled and resourceful residents, tend to mobilize covertly around forms of resistance action, using what James C. Scott called 'the weapons of the weak' – informal economic activity, minor property crime, sabotage, absenteeism and malingering.[27] In an urban setting, these include various forms of mugging, hustling, begging, prostitution and drug-peddling. They see the efforts of the benefits authorities, schools, police, psychiatric and social services to engage them with the formal economy and the wider social organization of society as largely imposed against their interests, and act together to circumvent and evade them, or to turn them to their advantage by transforming their outcomes. The barriers and costs associated with any transition to official or commercial systems would be too high, especially for those who wield informal power in these communities.

This is because the social bonds which link members of these communities of fate are ones of loyalty. Lacking choice and mobility, but relying on each other for everyday survival, residents sustain these links through codes which often suppress individuality and difference, punish scapegoats and enforce orthodoxy. Of all the kinds of power considered in this chapter, this one is therefore least compatible with the mainstream cultural standard, and hardest to reconcile with its practices. Policies for combating social exclusion in the USA and UK have focused primarily on attitudes to training and employment. Welfare to work measures have aimed to inculcate projects of self-development and self-improvement among residents of these communities. But these initiatives have to draw members out of networks of interdependence and informal activity which reinforce the loyalty-based order.

Studies of informal activities show that these consist mostly of mutual assistance and support, rather than the generation of income through undeclared employment or through crime. A series of studies of deprived districts in the UK have found that 'most paid informal work is conducted on a voluntary basis for kin, neighbours and friends for social rather than economic reasons . . . under social relations akin to the unpaid community exchange that many [politicians and theorists] wish to nurture'.[28] Comparisons with higher income groups reveal that the more resources UK residents have, the more they are likely to do paid informal work on a contractual basis for strangers, whereas in poor areas it is likely to be done 'for reasons associated with redistribution and sociality' between kin and friends.[29]

The problem for governments of such communities is that they become 'locked into' informal and illegal activities, and require expensive schemes, of inducement and enforcement, to bring them into the mainstream. Because they lack the institutional structures of the wider society, they have come to rely on systems of loyalty and belonging which are difficult to undermine. In the social capital terms, they create strong bonds between members, but defy attempts to build bridges to the mainstream. Indeed, the history of the last twenty-five years of the twentieth century was the development of cultures of dissent, deviance and lawlessness in these districts, based on various ethnic solidarities and criminal loyalties, or on cultures of support between lone parents and survivors of various forms of domestic and communal abuse.

From the standpoint of political engagement and democratic citizenship, the fear is that informal activities and supportive networks flourish most where alienation from collective authority (police, social services and benefit authorities, as well as political institutions) is most pervasive. And they also mobilize ethnic and faith communities against each other. This is dramatically illustrated in Northern Ireland. Research by Madeleine Leonard[30] has shown that republican districts of West Belfast sustained a virtually autonomous set of institutions for informal economic activity, including both paid (mainly done by men, such as in construction) and unpaid self-provisioning exchange (mainly done by women). This 'alternative economy' had somewhat higher overall rates of male (36 per cent) and female (21 per cent) participation than did formal employment (25 and 22 per cent).[31] They also expressed a strong preference for informal work, and justified it in terms of their marginalization from the formal economy, which they blamed on the UK government. One respondent, a community activist, commented:

> We prefer the autonomy of doing our own thing without any formality or regularity. We are in control here and we like to keep it that way. If we started to formalize, you might say that that would be a good thing, it could lead to a few jobs being created. But who would those jobs go to? Certainly not any of us. We've no fancy qualifications. In fact, to be quite honest, we've got no qualifications. So how would any of us have a chance? Who would employ us? The only way we could do community work is to do it voluntarily.[32]

What gives politicians concern about these findings in West Belfast is that these extensive forms of reciprocity and cooperation were developed under conditions of extreme economic adversity and political conflict, but in the absence of public officials to enforce society's rules, for whom these were virtual no-go areas. These were hardly models for the benign by-products of community and social capital – engagement and democratic competence. They were governed by paramilitary groups, enforcing strict loyalty and ideological conformity, under cultural codes sustaining traditional gender relations; they upheld long-term continuous struggle (sometimes armed) against the British government. And they called forth similar mobilizations by Protestants in their deprived districts nearby. The same phenomenon has appeared in some northern English cities (Bradford, Burnley and Oldham) where Asian and white deprived communities have organized around rivalry and hostility, resulting in riots and violence. The crypto-fascist political party, the BNP, has been quick to capitalize on this situation, and has gained some local representation in Burnley. This has forced the UK government to seek new policies for 'social cohesion'.[33]

Even where these overt organizations of political resistance are absent, the cultural features of deprived districts evoke dismay among liberal democrats. Under the 'blood and guts codes' regulating social relations,[34] respondents in our study of the poor district of an English city expressed traditional views of gender role relationships:

> *Mr Ribble:* If . . . I was on the dole and Sheila [pregnant wife] had the chance of getting a job, I wouldn't let her do it. . . . I couldn't be kept like [laughs]. . . . No way. . . . I would have felt inadequate by not bringing in the money . . . a man should be the money bringer, you know.[35]

More disturbingly, such communities have been the sites for rioting and violence against suspected paedophiles, and for hate campaigns against families that become scapegoats for local problems. The 'blood and guts code' deals in tribal loyalty, and can be mobilized around issues of kinship, traditional morality and territorial control. Once such cultures become established, any process of change in their collective lives is costly for residents and government alike.

Hence, the evidence from deprived communities is ambiguous. It shows that collective political action and semi-organized or coordinated economic activity are feasible and sustainable, that these can be spontaneously generated among residents, but that they have sometimes been based on racist, xenophobic, sexist or homophobic ideas, and used bullying, shaming, excluding and punitive methods. The positive side of this evidence offers some hope for community development approaches to the regeneration of these areas; the negative side warns of the dangers of the isolation, exclusion and impoverishment which breeds resentment and violence.

But this problem for the UK government is just a microcosm of the situation worldwide. The configuration of institutions and interests represented by the leading affluent states links up global financial organizations, transnational business corporations and the governments of those regimes which keep their rules. It allows them to mobilize against 'rogue states', 'dictatorships' and 'global terrorist networks', under the military leadership of the USA. It lets them impose their terms, through the IMF and the World Bank, on governments which try to borrow against their political programmes. It also permits them to dictate the framework under which trade is carried out between rich and poor states, under the various WTO agreements.

All this drives the world's losers and outsiders, who are excluded by the connections in this tightly woven web, into a set of relationships which resembles the ones in deprived districts of affluent countries. In order to protect themselves against the damage done to their societies by their lack of access to the collective advantages of those systems, they form into self-protective units – statist regimes, traditional monarchies, concentrations of corrupt power, jurisdictions of faith and patriarchy, mobilizations for Holy War, suicide bomb squads, terrorist cells and so on.

For the great mass of the world's poor and excluded, they have little choice in their communities of fate but to put their trust in these organizations. When climate or soil deteriorate, the choices for many are stark. If they are unskilled, timid and immobile, they can wait for NGO food aid, grow drought-resistant drugs or starve. If they are more bold and violent, they can join a band of brigands, the army of a warlord or the forces of a resistance struggle. If they have some education and are mobile, they can try to reach an affluent state, as asylum seekers and economic migrants. And if they are both bold and mobile, they can become international drug smugglers, people-traffickers or terrorists.[36]

In the concluding chapter of this book, I shall address the central issues for politics in this global situation. If the transformation of collective life has clarified the question of how to supply the goods we need to share a peaceful and sustainable life together, what is the role (if any) of the various territorial jurisdictions in which political authority is mobilized? What do we need from local and central governments? Which regulatory and distributive roles are best left to international organizations? How is power in political units best balanced by popular sovereignty, by rights of entry and exit, and by informal community? Should political borders act as barriers, or should there be free movement across the globe?

I have traced the connections in the web of ideas and organizations that sustain the affluent parts of the world's population to sex, money and power, in particular configurations. Projects of self are based on portable assets, on mobility and on access to exclusive clubs for collective goods and to communities of choice. But the equal autonomy which sustains negotiated intimacy in partnerships lacks convincing links to the civic and political community, in the form of voluntary associations, generating democratic participation and civic engagement. Theories of social capital attempt to supply these links, by showing that localities and polities with high rates of membership and participation in civil society organizations also have high rates of trust, reciprocity and democratic political cultures. But the notion of 'bridging social capital' fails to supply the missing link between these elements.

Social capital may provide part of the explanation why people do *not* move from one district to another. Certainly, the bonding between members of deprived communities and the economic advantages they get from informal activities, as well as their interdependence in kinship and friendship networks, are aspects of their lack of mobility. But mobile affluent groups have 'portable' social capital as well as material resources; they can use their transnational networks to facilitate exit strategies. These bridging capacities add to their advantages over poor and sedentary populations worldwide. What, if anything, can politics do to address the injustices that are built into the new collective landscape?

10

Connections and Conclusions

In the affluent countries, one of the main casualties of the transformation of collective life has been political democracy. It is not
only that the old ideological strife between left and right, state
and market, has been rendered obsolete. Despite the optimistic
enthusiasm of theorists like Giddens and Beck, a new politics of
discursive negotiation has not engaged the majority. All over the
world, this is reflected in lower turnout at elections.[1] More sovereignty for individuals means less participation.

It is not surprising that people are apathetic and disillusioned
about politics. We have seen that, in principle, autonomous individuals, with self-developmental projects of self and portable
assets, can form themselves into communities of choice, and agree
about the price and quality of the collective goods they wish to
share. There is, in principle, no standard size of such units, and no
standard bundle of facilities which local jurisdictions should
supply, by way of infrastructural amenities. Any combination is
possible, and all kinds of possibility are desirable, so long as people
are free to move between them without hindrance. Each unit
should therefore exclude non-contributors, and should avoid
dumping pollution and such by-products on others. Apart from
that, they might as well just get on with it.

What's more, we have also seen that people have good reasons
to be wary of political authority. Power is still alive and well in
the world, and is being used to screw the unwary. Organizations
of all kinds are vehicles for collective action, through which those
who control their assets gain further advantages, without necessarily conferring any advantages on others and without making the
world in general better off by any measure. In technical terms,

organizations are very prone to act as 'rent seekers', opportunistically going for these gains, rather than as 'entrepreneurs', achieving greater productivity.[2] And politicians, along with their officials, are the most notorious rent seekers of them all.

The collapse of Soviet-style state socialism, and the disgrace of various one-party national leaderships and local mafias, has revealed the potential for corruption and embezzlement wherever governments control key resources. The alternative which we are now offered is that we should all aim to be both self-improving and self-sufficient, and to avoid being under the control of either bosses or politicians. My own life is a kind of case-study of this strategy. Although I can scarcely count my professional career as a successful one, my diligence as an unskilled builder and a more gifted grafter in the garden has produced windfall benefits. As property prices soared, I became one of the world's accidentally rich (a largely unintentional rent gainer).

My case also illustrates the decline in political activism, as the rewards for mass collective action shrank under transformed conditions. In my young adult life I was a model active citizen, with my participation in the social movement of the poor, and hence in many other local and national political fora. As a German colleague later commented, I was not so much the good burgher as the Burgher King. Now I spend my time toiling in my orchard, and trotting between countries, with little involvement in the political life of any of them.

Furthermore, the sons and daughters of the members of our movement have not joined similar groups and unions; they have, if they remained as poor as their parents, resorted to individual strategies of undeclared, informal work and mutual support within their communities, in the ways described in chapters 7 and 8, and illustrated in the interviews quoted (pp. 136–7 and 194–6). Collective action – and hence wider political involvement – has just not been worth the effort, since first Margaret Thatcher's governments, and now Tony Blair's, farmed out the public services to agencies with no direct political accountability. It pays more to do minor fiddles, bits of fraud, and to exchange favours with your friends.

In a global context, the end of the bipolar world has projected this local picture onto the transnational screen. Governments in poor countries can no longer play the big power blocs off against each other; so they must outwardly conform to the model prescribed by the IMF and the World Bank, while doing any deals they can with global corporations. Their citizens are stuck with living under the twin collusive power of rulers who gain personal advantages from such stitch-ups, and firms which profit from the licence given to exploit them. No wonder they resort to trafficking drugs and people, or to nomadic lifestyles overseas.

All this is clearest in the post-Communist countries of the former USSR and Central and Eastern Europe. The privatization of their industries and infrastructures was, almost without exception, a massive rip-off. Local party bosses and the 'presidents' of state enterprises grew immensely rich by flogging off these assets to their buddies, or to foreign companies, all at bargain prices. Schemes like 'voucher privatization' in the Czech Republic turned out to be fraudulent on an epic scale. What citizens got in return was, for the most part, poverty and insecurity. And, of course, they got democracy – just at the moment in their history when it became virtually worthless, because the people who now owned their national resources had escaped any political control.

This is particularly sad for those of my generation, who were children in the aftermath of the Second World War, at a time when there was, for a brief moment, a real possibility of freedom and democracy on a global scale. I somehow always contrived to be in the wrong place at the wrong time. My first political memories are of South Africa and the watershed election of 1947, when my other grandfather was a candidate for General Smuts's defeated party. The victorious Nationalists, under the exceptionally dour Dr D. F. Malan, proceeded to introduce apartheid, and to close down the racially integrated school where I had been a pupil. The Nationalist government next skilfully gerrymandered an electoral map which gave it virtually guaranteed power, taking its revenge for the rent-seeking behaviour of English-speaking white South Africans during the previous fifty years, by making sure that white Afrikaners got all the political pickings for the next forty.

So it was one of the most emotional moments of my life when I listened (in Europe) to reports from the South African elections of 1992, when black people for the first time had the chance to exercise their political rights as citizens of the Republic, and queued overnight at the polls to do so. But how frustrating it has turned out to be for them to discover that electing a government is not enough, under present global conditions, to ensure much improvement in their living standards. Income redistribution is largely blocked by the requirements of the world's financial institutions, so – for the time being – the ambitious and the desperate must rely on armed robbery and petty trading, respectively.

For politicians in the affluent countries, the new challenges of the transformed collective landscape have evoked some creative responses. Instead of relying on the largely covert manipulation of aggregates and averages under corporatist arrangements (see p. 166), they must instead try to mobilize as many of the population as possible to become autonomous and self-improving individuals, willing to switch and shift with the best, for the sake of marginal advantages. In order to legitimate these programmes, they must find symbolic icons and portentous phrases, around which new coalitions can sweep them to electoral victories.[3]

In the UK, of course, we have witnessed two such successful mass mobilizations, which broke up traditional solidarities and created new alliances. Margaret Thatcher's, in the name of freedom, choice and the property-owning democracy, eventually foundered on the manifest unfairness of taxing individuals rather than their resources (the poll tax), and on the sleaziness of her successors. Tony Blair's successful appeal to 'national renewal', through the work ethic, 'social inclusion' and 'responsible community', is, at the time of writing, in danger of stalling, because it is compromised by the dubious strategy of regime change on the global stage. What is evident is that, in the absence of the organized solidarities of the post-war welfare state, and of political alliances between parties and either organized capital or organized labour, political coalitions of these kinds have constantly to be recreated. In other words, because these connections are no longer made through organized interests and their institutions, they have to be joined up by energetic rhetorical innovations.

(What is worse by far, of course, for political leaders, is to be stuck with organized structures which glue people too well together, but which no longer deliver economic results to impress financial interests. German[4] and Japanese leaders have suffered this fate. German and Japanese citizens are still far too devoted to the post-war institutions, foisted on them by the conquering Allies, to venture forth as the autonomous, unprotected individuals of the Anglo-Saxon world. So their politicians are left to promise reforms in the name of flexibility and reduced taxation, which they are generally unable then to deliver.)

There is a formula under which political leaders now attempt to create electoral coalitions. In the USA and UK, it starts by taking up, as its background assumptions, something like the functionalist formula I set out in chapter 2 (see pp. 50–1). This explains the connections between a culture of mutuality in partnerships and families, personal autonomy, mobility and choice (projects of self, by financially independent individuals), and interactions within markets and chosen communities. It implicitly claims that these are the basic social institutions of a free and prosperous society – the discursive democracy of the domestic unit, the voluntary engagement between equal holders of 'portable property' and the self-selected collective units of a market order. So where is the space for politics?

This is how the rhetorical skill and charisma of political leaders comes in. Their task is to persuade us that they understand our collective identity. That they want to enable our chosen developmental path and that they can link both of these to the realities of the global economy. In this, they more or less reproduce my formula for the convincing version of myself, told to fellow-passengers on trains and planes (see pp. 19–21). They tell us the collective equivalent of this story – who we are, where we are choosing to go and what we are making of ourselves in the moving, changing, wider world of economic constraints and opportunities.

However, because this story is directed as much at the international financial community and at transnational business corporations as it is at the electorate, they are required to reverse the order of my informal, public transport version. Instead of starting with the historic origins, shared values and defining characteristics of the nation, they begin by explaining the laws of nature and reason to which human collective life must conform (a.k.a. the IMF/World Bank model). Only then do they go on to say how these require the adaptation of those same origins, values and characteristics to that natural and rational order.

So the story goes like this:

1   In the real world of today's global economy, every nation must compete for inward investment, and for the confidence of the international financial community, by demonstrating its fiscal prudence, innovative entrepreneurship, labour flexibility and modern, adaptive infrastructure.

2   In order to continue to prosper, our nation must show that it can meet these challenges, by adapting our cultural traditions, social institutions, collective values and public services in the ways required to make them relevant and modern.

3   We in the United Kingdom [amend as necessary, for each national tradition] have a long history of balancing freedom and solidarity; we believe in justice for all members of our society, based on respect for and tolerance of diversity, strong civil society, and equal access to certain key collective goods, concerned with the health and education of all citizens.

4   It is now necessary to modernize our social institutions in line with the realities of the global economy, in order to maintain the very traditions and values which constitute our national identity; to try to protect our old ways of doing things would put our children and grandchildren's prosperity at risk, and cause damaging divisions and conflicts among our people; it would also put at risk the very values we cherish.

5   In line with this updating of our values and social institutions, we therefore announce the following policy measures:
    (a)   public-private partnerships of one kind or another, together with various extra contributions by individual citizens, or opt-outs into commercial systems, for our health and education systems and any other remaining public services;
    (b)   'devolution' of more control over the local infrastructure to local authorities, or the boards of hospitals, schools, 'social enterprises', voluntary organizations and community groups;
    (c)   more 'targeted' benefits for poor people, and less reliance on social insurance; these new measures will take the form of means-tested benefits, tax credits for people with

low incomes from employment, rent subsidies or rebates of taxes and social insurance contributions;

(d) in exchange for all these benefits, credits and concessions, those who qualify will be expected to demonstrate their commitment to an ethic of autonomy, hard work and self-improvement; if they fail such tests, they will lose eligibility;

(e) to protect these systems of solidarity and support, only selected recruits will be allowed to enter the country as immigrants; other foreigners will be forcibly excluded.

The point about all these versions of the rhetorical formula is that they join up the public world of political regulation and resource distribution with the private world of projects and property in a way which makes the wider institutional order seem justifiable, because it is both natural and rational. Electorates are told that their national identities and cultural traditions are not put in jeopardy by globalization, and that their political values are simply being brought up to speed to match current global realities. There are no unlucky losers, just a few deviants, who must be brought into line, if necessary by compulsory (but caring) measures – tough love.

Furthermore, these rhetorical versions are in many ways consistent with the latest analyses of democratic theory. Under 'contractarian' accounts of political authority,[5] governments gained their legitimacy from the power vested in them by their citizens. In so far as there were conflicts of interest between groups within the population, the structural ones among these were dealt with by constitutional arrangements (minority rights, for example), while the processes of ongoing arbitration between interests were handed over to competent elected authorities, capable of reaching fair and balanced judgements, and mediating solutions. So governments were given power to 'do the right thing'[6] – to make decisions for the sake of political justice, giving all citizens their due, and establishing conditions for all to live the good life together.

The new model of democracy shifts from this delegation of power to leaderships to a more deliberative process, which relies on the responsible participation of citizens in improving their society.[7] When Tony Blair announces a 'Big Conversation' with the electorate over public sector reform (a term borrowed from the USA), or Peter Mandelson says that the Left all over Europe must create 'a new politics' (again?), to be relevant for mainstream lives, they are referring to these ideas. Justice is not the outcome of government arbitration, but of a process of deliberation, cooperation and finding solutions to collective problems by well-informed citizens, willing to negotiate in the public interest.

Public policy will have legitimacy because it is the product of interactions between responsible and autonomous agents, who (after all) have several options about shifting their assets between various collective units and residential infrastructures. Negotiation takes place between equals, under threat of exit, with the aim of achieving consensus among morally sovereign agents.[8]

In this way, the state is, so the argument goes, no longer the instrument of power and domination, but becomes instead the guardian of public reason. Gradually, all are brought into the circle of political discourse, and become able to act as competent members of the democratic community.[9] This process is helped by the devolution of decisions to the level of 'communities'. For instance, the running of hospitals and schools should be devolved to staff, service-users and local residents, who can make the best choices for their membership.[10]

This book has tried to explain both the peculiar appeal of such proposals and the residual unease they leave at the back of people's minds. As citizens who aspire to personal relationships of negotiated intimacy, to the autonomy which comes with owning enough assets to be beholden to neither boss nor government, and to the mobile, innovative lifestyles of transnational entrepreneurs or consultants, we welcome this political expression of confidence in our projects.

But as heirs to welfare state arrangements, as members of professions or trade unions, and as witnesses to past programmes of reform and modernization, we are not so easily convinced by the jaunty optimism of this prospectus. Above all, we are uncomfortable about the links, so confidently asserted by the US President and the UK Prime Minister, between this trajectory for reform of our social institutions and the global war against terrorism.

There is something odd about the juxtaposition of a radical, deliberative, discursive democracy, which devolves power to the local school, hospital, allotment association and parish council, and the military imposition of a market regime and a very attenuated, monitored and conditional form of 'democracy' on states which step out of line with the prescribed model. If democracy and individual freedom are such natural and rational bedfellows with commercial relations and global capitalist organizations, why is it necessary to be in a constant state of alert against an army of secret and invisible enemies; and why do those enemies seem to enjoy the tacit support of such a large proportion of the world's population? Are they so deluded by the obfuscations of their evil leaders, or mired down in the anachronisms of religious traditions and oppressive patriarchal systems? Or are they actually locked out of the benefits of an order which gives us more and more advantages?

It is not too difficult to spot two elements in the theory of deliberative democracy and in these political programmes which explain both their special appeal to those in the affluent mainstream, and their shortcomings in a diverse, global context. By assumption, the participants in the devolved governance of collective units are equal, autonomous and mobile. They are simply assumed to be capable of the style of public reason and negotiation between such individuals, who share a common interest in the good quality and value-for-money price of the collective goods at stake. Because they also have the exit rights and property holdings to shift to other providers if they cannot agree, there is no problem about abuse of power or exploitation under these conditions.

Second, the theory and the programme implicitly rely upon the model of 'voting with the feet' and fiscal federalism, under which all the world's population can sort itself into self-selecting clubs and communities of choice (see pp. 113–14). The idea that the discursive democratic governance of these units can achieve consensus assumes that every individual on the planet has a club to join and a community they can afford to live in. So the optimism about both democracy and markets rests on frictionless mobility across the globe, and on everyone (however poor or disabled) being able to find the means to enter a collective which can meet their needs.

This leaves nation-states, and international organizations like the United Nations, with the role of policing and regulating these arrangements. And it at once becomes clear that this is no small task, because the real world does not at all conform to these assumptions. Even in the affluent countries, there are millions who lack the skills and resources to negotiate on equal terms with autonomous, mobile property-holders, let alone with collective actors like large firms and professional organizations. Movement across borders is far from free for the mass of the world's population, and huge differences in national per capita incomes give unmerited advantages and distorted incentives. And, although the provision of collective goods in the advanced economies is beginning to resemble the model in the theory and the programme, that in the rest of the world is not. Post-Communist and developing world collectives still look much as they did before – like communities of fate, divided into genders, clans, castes, faiths, ethnicities and empires, on traditional lines of power and hierarchy.

So national governments are charged with getting their citizens up to speed with the transformation of collective life, by educating, training and cajoling them into being autonomous, mobile individuals. This is difficult enough in affluent countries, where so many are locked into the loyalties and reciprocities of communities of fate. It has so far proved too difficult for the UK government to achieve in Northern Ireland, for example (see pp. 195–6). But it is far harder to do it in Afghanistan or Iraq, where communities of choice exist only for elites, and where even educated property-holders rely on the protection of clan, mosque and warlord for their security.

For national governments to be in the situation to move from holding delegated powers of arbitration between competing rivalrous groups under a social contract to the more regulating role foreseen by the model would be another whole step. It has taken centuries in the affluent West, and is still far from being complete. In Afghanistan and Iraq, the first step, of creating a national government which is accepted by the rival ethnic and religious factions, is not yet accomplished. Yet the military occupying powers are simultaneously trying to bring about the second step, by privatizing most of the material infrastructure.

The post-Communist countries demonstrate the perils of trying to pull off this two-handed trick. In Russia, in particular, capitalism has made a few immensely rich, but democracy has scarcely captured the popular imagination. Because of the determined, armed resistance of the Chechen rebels and the recalcitrance of the other defensive communities into which the population has retreated, central government has slipped into more and more authoritarian methods. The elections of 2003 became little more than a plebiscite for President Putin's personal power – more Uncle Joe than Uncle Sam, in the democratic calculus.

Is there any way to square this circle – to connect across the gulfs between two separate webs, that of intimacy, cash and power, and that of blood, faith and soil? This book has set out to explain the existing bonds and connections inside these webs; it would take another to suggest ways to build reliable bridges between them. I have tried to account for some of the ironies in my personal life, and how these have related to the transformation of the collective life of the world around me. However – being a true grandson of my Neo-Hegelian grandparents, and a life member of the Newton Abbot Claimants' Union – I shall attempt a few suggestions about the way forward.

Let's go back to the two imaginary films, with which I introduced the issues for this book in chapter 1 (pp. 12–14). I have explained why there is *no* functionalist formula which can show how the actions of the man flying to a foreign city to meet his sexual partner in the second film benefit the two rural women in the first film. Because the ways in which resources are distributed worldwide through commercial transactions are mediated by the collective actions of international banks, business corporations and states, the money spent by the affluent couple and the deals they strike with their associates in the city will affect the poor women only in the most indirect ways, through the decisions by which those huge and resource-rich organizations choose to use their power.

Not only may none of the increased cash generated by the entrepreneurialism of the affluent couple reach the pockets of the poor women; but also any improvements in their collective infrastructure which those deals might enable are very uncertain to reach down right into the social amenities of the poor community. This is because the links between the two webs, the one of affluence and the other of poverty, do not rely on the unintended consequences of individual or collective decisions. They depend on the good intentions of the most powerful agencies in the world, and those good intentions are not reliable.

As moral and political beings, those of us lucky enough to be living in the affluent mainstream fervently wish that this was not the case. We want to believe, along with Hume, Adam Smith, John Stuart Mill and Maynard Keynes, that there is a formula to guarantee that our everyday activities and projects will benefit the world's poor, or at very least not damage them. But no such formula exists, as property and national borders are now disposed.

What's more, our desire to believe in such a formula makes us all too eager to trust those politicians and officials of international organizations who are keen to tell us that one exists. We are able to insulate ourselves against the guilt of recognizing that our advantages are gained at the expense of their sufferings, because we choose to put our faith in their false formulae. In fact, the only links between our web and their lives are moral ones.

The one thing that the people in the first film have in common with those in the second is their humanity. They all were born by the same biological processes, breathe the same air and will in time (though probably in a different span of time) eventually die. If we believe that all human beings are of equal moral worth, then this alone is sufficient to justify our equal concern for poor people in developing countries as for our affluent friends, and for their equal human rights.

They have as much right as we do to elect governments which will protect their interests, and to be able to veto arrangements between their rulers and the chief executives of transnational companies, under which they will be made worse off.[11] Their interests must be included in any attempt to spell out a global model of social institutions, and a collective infrastructure for all kinds of human flourishing. As Thomas Pogge puts it:

> We need, then, a holistic understanding of how the living conditions of persons are shaped through the interplay of various institutional regimes, which influence one another and mingle their effects. These interdependencies are of great significance – and are nonetheless frequently overlooked by moral philosophers, social scientists, politicians, and the educated public. . . . In the contemporary world, human lives are profoundly affected by non-

domestic institutions – by global rules of governance, trade, and diplomacy, for instance. . . . If it is possible to justify them to persons in all parts of the world and also to reach agreement on how they should be adjusted and reformed in the light of new experiences or changed circumstances, then we must aspire to a *single, universal* criterion of justice which all persons and peoples can accept.[12]

So it is appropriate that the IMF and World Bank, the most powerful of those global organizations, should at least be taking seriously this challenge, to set out principles for global justice, and the collective institutions most suitable to achieve it. And it must be recognized that the World Bank's development model, though still deficient in many respects, is an important step in the right direction, because it does attempt to specify *moral* links between global economic growth, trade, collective infrastructures and the well-being of the most vulnerable people. And finally, it is also an encouraging sign that the developing countries were able to come together to subvert the latest round in the WTO's rolling programme of global trade agreements, if only because it demonstrated that their interests must be fully taken into account.

But it is all the more important, once we recognize that these are moral and political connections and not links in a functionally integrated chain of unintended consequences, to see also just how fragile these bridges are. Since all forms of collective power are now accountable to international financial organizations, both commercial and global-public, we should be clear who in fact are 'the new rulers of the world'.[13] We need few reminders of how well linked these are to the White House, the US Treasury and the Pentagon.

This fragility does not stem solely from its dependence on the goodwill of US politicians and officials. It also arises from well-acknowledged features of the theoretical model driving the World Bank's development plan. The model promises to allow autonomous, mobile individuals to improve their personal capital holdings, and to switch and shift between collective infrastructures, to their advantage. It is day-by-day transforming human organizations and reconfiguring the collective landscape, with the avowed aim of making them more adaptable to this new order.

This whole dynamic is fuelled by the notion that people can select the 'clubs' which supply the best collective goods for their needs, and move to the most suitable communities of choice.

But even the most ardent advocates of the public choice theoretical model do not claim that it can achieve all these aims on its own. In particular, there is nothing in the explanation of how it works to show how the necessary boundaries between collectives should be drawn, which populations should be included in which clubs and jurisdictions, or which goods should be supplied by clubs, and which by local governments.[14] Since – in principle – any collective goods could be provided by any of these means, and the best combination will depend on the size and composition of the available populations, the problem of how to group them, and in what kinds of jurisdiction, is an infinite regress.

So the model cannot tell us how best to organize the social world, how to divide it up or how to regulate these collectivities once they have taken shape. But – more damaging still – it can tell us that certain vital goods will be undersupplied, whichever division is adopted. Strong advocates of fiscal federalism and voting with the feet admit that, if clubs and jurisdictions are allowed to compete with each other for memberships, it is not only 'inefficiencies' and 'rents' that will be competed away. Certain collective goods, essential for the overall justice and sustainability of human society, will also be among the casualties.

Critics of the model have always alleged that it could not provide these basic guarantees of human rights and viable resources for all. Now public choice theorists themselves have admitted that this is true, in relation to two crucial aspects. There need not be a 'race to the bottom' in competition between health-care providers, schools or residential homes, because the various jurisdictions in which they are located have an interest in sustaining standards consistent with high productivity and a cultural context for conviviality. But there are strong inducements for them to reduce both *income redistribution*[15] and *environmental protection*,[16] which do not directly lead to higher productivity or to greater comfort.

So, the economic model which claims to provide the explanation closest to a functionalist formula in the World Bank model –

the theory of how individuals who switch and shift in their decisions about collective goods bring better allocations – points to a constant erosion of those systems which protect the poor from starvation, and of those which protect the ecological infrastructure from depredation. These new collectives, therefore, will exclude the poor and exploit natural resources. The process of competition for members will require them to cut back further and further on redistribution schemes and conservation measures. The global justice movement is right to warn that this erosion is built into the globalization process, unless it is offset by vigorous measures.

The trouble is that the measures recommended by the World Bank model are not vigorous enough. The model does implicitly acknowledge that the whole justification of nation-states in today's new collective landscape rests on their claims to protect the poor and the natural environment. But the measures it recommends do not provide a convincing version of how to do this. They are hedged about with far too many caveats, insisting on the priority which should be given to liberalizing all transactions and to opening up all forms of activity and infrastructural provision to capitalist enterprise. For example: 'In today's globally-integrated world, intrusive state action can undercut the functioning of markets and the incentives for private investment, killing job opportunities, not creating them.'[17]

The model is especially hostile to income transfers, because it is so aware that these can trap poor people in poverty, rather than increase their capabilities and enhance the return on their skills and material assets. Some of this suspicion is entirely justified. In the developing world, social assistance schemes can indeed make idleness or inefficiency a better strategy than industry and innovation. Social insurance systems are generally the prerogative of the better off, so they are protections for privilege, rather than genuine redistributive measures. And in the affluent countries, social insurance benefits have been paid on conditions which keep millions in unemployment, while rising social insurance contributions have made it more and more expensive for employers to hire less skilled workers.

Yet the fact is that it is the *terms* on which such redistributions are carried out, and not the transfers themselves, which cause these problems. Giving more land to poor peasants does not make them idle, it stimulates them to greater efforts. Providing tools, or irrigation schemes or wells does not reduce the return on people's skills; it increases it. But the World Bank, while endorsing all these measures, does not explain how they can be reliably set in motion. Why should weak governments redistribute land to poor peasants when they are under strong pressure from international banks and corporations to increase the quantity of GM crops for world markets? And why should the NGOs, which the World Bank trusts to supply village infrastructural goods and to raise productivity, do so in a more universal, efficient and dependable way than governments would?

So as not to seem too pessimistic, let me give some examples of how all these things have been done successfully, in both the developing and the developed worlds. It is worth restating what the overall aim might be for such a programme. If, in the new transformed collective landscape, the goal is to make as many individuals as autonomous as possible, and their collective goods and infrastructures as convenient and acceptable as possible for their needs (expressed through exit and entry decisions, and through governance systems), then we could summarize the objectives as follows:

1 Resources are transferred from the rich and advantaged parts of the global economy to the poor ones, which are not connected up to circuits of money and power.
2 This enables individuals and/or communities to gain a degree of autonomy and improve their collective infrastructures.
3 This in turn allows them more scope for linking into the affluent world if they choose to do so.

My first example is the Meru Goat-Breeding Association in Kenya, a project which is supported by an Agricultural Research Foundation in the UK.[18] In that district, the problem for the local economy was not the usual one of a few large landowners, unwilling to share their resources. It was that all the people's landholdings were too small to produce a decent level of subsistence, and there was no spare land. The research team introduced a species of goat which produced plenty of milk, and persuaded local residents of the benefits of this product – especially that it improved children's immune systems. Subsequently, as well as giving a better subsistence, the goats allowed small farmers to sell their milk further afield, and there is a possibility of it now being marketed, at a considerable premium, in Nairobi. Although they are still limited by the size of their landholdings, farmers should in time build up a capital asset, as well as having acquired new and marketable knowledge and skills.

My second example is the movement called Habitats for Humanity – an international initiative, whose chairman is former US President Jimmy Carter. The purpose of this movement is to create communities in which the residents all become homeowners, in every kind of economic environment. A great deal of thought and planning has gone into the financial arrangements and the interdependencies created by them. Members are locked into the associations they create, so their exit rights are limited. This is to prevent members, on whose contributions the community relies, from simply selling up immediately and moving away with their capital gains. So the form of autonomy and mobility conferred by the scheme are partial ones, and the community created is partly one of choice, and partly one of fate (at least temporarily).

The third example is the Emmaus Movement, started in France, but now flourishing also in the UK and elsewhere.[19] Homeless people live together in communities as 'companions', and work on projects which in turn finance their common life (such as recycling scrapped household items for re-use). They are not allowed to drink, use drugs or take part in any activity for individual gain, so all their efforts are devoted to the benefit of their community, or of others needier than themselves outside it. They are free to leave at any time, taking with them none of the products of their joint labours. But they do take the skills and social capital they have generated during their stays. So they are fully mobile, but without accumulated property rights.

(There is an interesting difference between the Emmaus Movement in France and that in the UK. In the former, it defines itself *against* the state, which it holds responsible for the social exclusion of homeless companions and many others; it therefore refuses to accept any public benefits or services. In the UK, the Movement initially accepted housing benefit on behalf of companions, but then found that it had to do individual 'assessments' of them and to present itself as providing 'care' – both of which were inconsistent with its principles – in order to qualify under modified rules. All this has required renegotiation. Emmaus UK is listed as a model 'social enterprise' by the government.[20] This indicates that it prefers to emphasize its entrepreneurial role, rather than its insistence on a communal existence, without private property.)

All these are examples which would be cited with approval by the World Bank, because they involve action by NGOs, because they invest in human capital and in infrastructure and because they actually or potentially improve productivity. But these are not the only ways to improve the individual autonomy and collective goods of poor and excluded people. They could simply be given money, and left to decide how to spend it, either individually or collectively. That, after all, is what mainstream people in affluent countries expect, whether from work, from pensions or from other property rights. Their projects usually consist in building up their earning power, so that eventually they have both the skills and the material resources to become organizational powerholders (i.e., successful rent seekers), autonomous entrepreneurs, consultants or persons of leisure. And the organizations which they would subscribe to as affiliates or members would be expected to give them tangible advantages, over which they had control, exercised either by voting rights, or by exit threats.

The problem of how to accomplish transfers of this kind, between wealthy and powerful individuals and organizations, and poor and powerless ones, has always been the greatest challenge to liberal democracy as a political system. Because liberals consider that all human beings are of equal moral worth, they see the force of arguments for giving them a material basis for this equality – for the means of achieving autonomous use of choice and initiative, including moral judgement. But they also see private property as a kind of extension of the person, and hence part of what is inviolable about each individual's identity. So they are very resistant to ideas about *entitlements* to any share of the wealth created by individual effort.

If we see the resources accumulated by societies, like the affluent nations, as the sum of purely individual enterprise, then this principle is hard to challenge. But if we see it as also partly the product of collective power, including 'rent seeking' of a particularly ruthless kind – as in colonialism, slavery and the spoils of empire – then the moral basis of individual wealth is a good deal shakier.

People in affluent countries can now transfer quite considerable sums to their children on their deaths, or to their grandchildren in their lives, at modest rates of taxation. Inheritance and intra-family gifts are no longer controversial modes of transfer. But, conversely, social benefits systems have become more controversial since the heyday of welfare states. Citizens are expected to try to avoid falling as costs upon the earnings and property incomes of their fellow citizens.

In the USA and UK, ingenious systems have been devised to try to make such transfers more acceptable for taxpayers. Conditions surrounding benefits have been tightened, so that claimants must demonstrate either their zeal in seeking work, or their abject incapacities to do any. They must also exhibit an almost Stakhanovite eagerness to make themselves employable, or an insane optimism about their entrepreneurial prospects. If they take modest amounts of low-paid, insecure or part-time work, they are rewarded with relatively generous tax credits. If they really cannot do such jobs, or cannot find them, then they do get benefits.

This one-sided emphasis on paid work distorts both the economy and society. It means that people are drawn away from family, from voluntary association and from community, to do labour-intensive, menial work of dubious social value. The rewards for this, in terms of tax credits, keep rising, while the value of benefits declines, relative to earnings. So those who cannot work at all will eventually be paid less by the state than those who can and do. And those who can are made slightly better off, but also very exploitable by low-paying organizations. This cannot be justice.

Governments are already seeking ways to transfer money to communities, and to empower them to spend it on collectively improving their quality of life. They might also pay individuals to take part in such projects, as residents and citizens, rather than as employees; or to qualify for tax credits for supplying their part-time, voluntary labour.

Elsewhere I have argued that tax and benefits systems in the affluent countries may be stumbling backwards towards giving citizens unconditional rights to basic incomes, unconnected with their work status or family situation.[21] Even as today's politicians and officials make these rules more conditional on work, and more targeted on those without resources, they are creating anomalies which ultimately can only be resolved by universal, unconditional systems.[22]

There may be reasons to maintain, as Philippe Van Parijs does (see pp. 164–6) that these developments can only happen behind the protective walls of migration controls and 'entitlement cards' for citizens. But it is ironic that they are now under much more active discussion at a time when affluent countries are recruiting more and more labour power from the developing world, and especially in the form of public service professionals.[23] If young, skilled workers are needed, both to deal with these shortages in the supply of infrastructural services and to balance populations, immigration restrictions do not seem to be practical preconditions for the evolution of transfer systems aimed at guaranteeing autonomy and mobility.

Let me conclude with what is still a Utopian vision. If liberals and democrats are genuine in their desire to make the moral equality of all human beings into a material reality, they will want to look for ways that give all the people in the world the 'portable property', the exit rights and the access to communities of choice which they need for an autonomous existence. This could be done either through transfers within national systems of sharing (National or Citizens' Income Schemes), or through transnational transfers, in equal amounts for all the world's populations, administered by international agencies (Global Basic Incomes).[24]

The first approach would have the advantages of being simple, of replacing existing complex systems and of being linked to democratic political institutions, thus making net contributions and net beneficiaries readily accountable to each other. But it would perpetuate inequalities between nations. The second would be more remote, impersonal, administrative and unaccountable, especially if it was provided through the World Bank or some other financial organization. And it would be little more than a partial subsistence for citizens of the rich countries. But it would have the advantage of being rooted in human rights, and hence in universal principles of moral equality and global justice.

Perhaps some day in the future it may be possible to offer the following functionalist explanation of the world's social institutions, and the transformed collective life of humankind,

1 The current allocations of natural resources, property rights and territorial claims by jurisdictions are the results of agreed principles of environmentally sustainable social justice, embracing all individual and collective interests.
2 These allocations benefit all individuals, globally.
3 Within the institutions for taxation, income transfers and grants to collectives, individuals pursuing their autonomous, mobile, projects of self can interact with each other beneficially, without intending to uphold universal principles of justice.
4 They need not necessarily understand how their actions contribute to agreements and allocations in the name of justice.
5 Agreed principles of justice sustain current allocations and institutions, by feedback loops passing through interactions between autonomous, mobile individuals.

Now that really would be something!

Notes

Introduction

1 A. Bennett, *Telling Tales*, London: BBC, 2000, pp. 10–11.
2 M. Douglas, *How Institutions Think*, London: Routledge and Kegan Paul, 1987, p. 113.
3 Researchers have repeatedly found that women in particular subscribe to this view. In her study of women who had been teenage mothers, many of whom had had several sexual partners, Kate Milnes found that 'the sexual relationships described most positively . . . tended to be those . . . where sex took place in the context of a long-term, committed, monogamous relationship characterised by a high degree of love, romance, intimacy and trust' (K. Milnes, 'Young Women and the Romantic Narrative: A Story of Conformity, Resistance and Subversion', paper presented at a conference on Narrative, Memory and Identity, University of Huddersfield, 5 April 2003, p. 1). Similarly, two pieces of research into women's use of contraceptives noted that they were less likely to suggest that men use condoms when they saw the encounter as one which might develop into an emotionally significant relationship – as one said, 'condoms are very unromantic really, aren't they?' (N. Gavey and K. McPhillips, 'Subject to Romance: Heterosexual Passivity as an Obstacle to Women Initiating Condom Use', *Psychology of Women Quarterly*, 23, 1999, pp. 349–67, at p. 358). As a woman in another study put it: 'It's a bit awkward when you have to go up to somebody and say, excuse me, are you HIV positive, when you're in the middle of a romance. Kills the atmosphere a bit' (C. Willig, 'Constructions of Sexual Activity and their Implications for Sexual Practice: Lessons for Sex Education', *Journal of Health Psychology*, 3(3), 1998, pp. 383–92).

4 Z. Bauman, *Liquid Love: On the Frailty of Human Bonds*, Cambridge: Polity, 2003, pp. 21, 23.
5 E. Durkheim, 'Individualism and the Intellectuals', *Revue Bleu*, 4th series, 10, 1898, pp. 7–13.
6 See for example, Michael Howard's 'political credo' published in a two-page spread in UK newspapers on 2 January 2004, which started: 'I believe it is natural for men and women to want health, wealth and happiness for their families and themselves', and contained 15 other 'principles', such as, 'I believe that people are most likely to be happy when they are masters of their own lives, when they are not nannied or over-governed', and 'I believe there is no freedom without responsibility; it is our duty to look after those who cannot help themselves.'

Chapter 1   Inside the Web

1 T. J. Scheff, *Emotions, the Social Bond and Human Reality: Part/Whole Analysis*, Cambridge: Cambridge University Press, 1997, p. 68.
2 D. Hume, *A Treatise of Human Nature* (1739), ed. L. A. Selby-Bigge, Oxford: Clarendon Press, 1978.
3 M. Douglas, *How Institutions Think*, London: Routledge and Kegan Paul, 1987, ch. 4.
4 The case for demoralization through the commercialization of social bonds is argued by Z. Bauman, *Liquid Love: On the Frailty of Human Bonds*, Cambridge: Polity, 2003; see pp. 45–7 below.
5 G. Monbiot, 'Rattling the Bars', *Guardian*, 18 November 2003, p. 25.
6 A. Giddens, *Modernity and Self-Identity: Self and Society in the Late Modern Age*, Cambridge: Polity, 1991, pp. 75, 78–9, 89 and 97.
7 U. Beck, *The Reinvention of Politics: Rethinking Modernity in the Global Social Order*, Cambridge: Polity, 1994, pp. 46, 102.
8 A. Smith, 'The Theory of Moral Sentiments', in H. W. Schneider (ed.), *Adam Smith's Moral and Political Philosophy*, New York: Harper, 1948, part IV, ch. 1; *An Inquiry into the Nature and Causes of the Wealth of Nations* (1776), ed. R. H. Campbell and A. S. Skinner, Oxford: Clarendon Press, 1976, bk IV, pt VII, ch. 88.
9 T. Hobbes, *Leviathan* (1651), ed. J. Plamenatz, London: Collins Fontana, 1962, ch. 17; J. Locke, *Second Treatise of Government*, ed. P. Laslett, Cambridge: Cambridge University Press, 1967, section 50; see pp. 81–5 below; C. L. Montesquieu, 'On Politics' (1734), in *Oeuvres Complètes*, Paris: NFR Pléiade, 1949; Hume, *Treatise of*

Human Nature; see pp. 35–40 below; J. J. Rousseau, 'A Discourse on the Origin of Inequality Among Men', in *The Social Contract and Discourses*, London: Dent, 1952; see pp. 40–3 below.

10 R. Merton, 'The Self-Fulfilling Prophecy', in *Social Theory and Social Structure*, New York: Free Press, 1949, pp. 475–90; J. Elster, *Explaining Technical Change: A Case Study in the Philosophy of Science*, Cambridge: Cambridge University Press, 1983; *Making Sense of Marx*, Cambridge: Cambridge University Press, 1985, pp. 28–9; Douglas, *How Institutions Think*, ch. 3.

11 E. Goffman, *Interaction Ritual*, New York: Anchor Press, 1967.

12 E. Goffman, *Frame Analysis*, New York, Harper, 1974.

13 Scheff, *Emotions, the Social Bond and Human Reality*, pp. 76–7.

14 Ibid., ch. 5, and especially pp. 115–16.

15 Ibid., ch. 9.

16 G. Ahrne, *Agency and Organization: Towards an Organizational Theory of Society*, London: Sage, 1990.

17 L. Jamieson, *Intimacy: Personal Relationships in Modern Societies*, Cambridge: Polity, 1998.

18 K. Plummer, *Telling Sexual Stories: Power, Change and Social Worlds*, London: Routledge, 1995.

19 Bauman, *Liquid Love*, pp. 9–10. See also R. W. Fevre, *The Demoralization of Western Culture: Social Theory and the Dilemmas of Modern Living*, London: Continuum, 2000.

20 Bauman, *Liquid Love*, p. 15.

21 Ibid., p. 38.

22 Ibid., p. 74.

23 T. Eagleton, *After Theory*, London: Allen Lane, excerpted in the *Guardian Review*, 20 September 2003, pp. 34–5.

Chapter 2   Intimate Connections

1 See for instance V. Gillies, *Family and Intimate Relationships: A Review of Sociological Research*, Families and Social Capital ESRC Research Group Working Papers No. 2, London: South Bank University, 2003; L. Jamieson, *Intimacy: Personal Relationships in Modern Societies*, Cambridge: Polity, 1998.

2 A. Giddens, *Beyond Left and Right: The Future of Radical Politics*, Cambridge: Polity, 1994, pp. 118–19.

3 *The Concise Oxford Dictionary*.

4 See for instance J. Weeks, *Invented Moralities: Sexual Values in an Age of Uncertainty*, New York: Columbia University Press, 1995;

J. Weeks, C. Donovan and B. Heaphy, *Same Sex Intimacies: Families of Choice and Other Life Experiments*, London: Routledge, 2001; and R. Pahl, *On Friendship*, Cambridge: Polity, 2000, for the argument that same-sex relationships and close friendships have created new forms of intimacy which lead to recognition, rights and respect in political life.

5   K. Plummer, *Telling Sexual Stories: Power, Change and Social Worlds*, London: Routledge, 1994, p. 149.

6   J. Burckhardt, *The Civilization of the Renaissance in Italy* (1860), London: Allen and Unwin, 1955, p. 269.

7   Ibid., p. 278.

8   M. Douglas, *How Institutions Think*, London: Routledge and Kegan Paul, 1987.

9   D. Hume, *A Treatise of Human Nature* (1739), ed. L. Selby-Bigge, Oxford: Clarendon Press, 1978, p. 486.

10   Ibid., p. 415.

11   A. Damasio, *Descartes' Error: Emotion, Reason and the Human Brain*, London: Picador, 1995; *Looking for Spinoza: Joy, Sorrow and the Feeling Brain*, London: Heinemann, 2003.

12   Hume, *A Treatise of Human Nature*, p. 483.

13   Ibid., p. 486.

14   Ibid., p. 490.

15   Ibid., pp. 490, 495.

16   J. J. Rousseau, 'A Discourse on the Origin of Inequality among Mankind', (1754) in *The Social Contract and Discourses*: ed. G. D. H. Cole, London: Dent, 1913, p. 186.

17   For a vivid description of the norms and cultures of these clubs, see M. Houellebecq's novel *Atomised* (London: Vintage, 2001). A recent newspaper article claimed that the orderly conduct of such clubs (which boast 500,000 members in the UK) is based on 'flying free from society's restraints on female sexuality' (*Guardian*, 29 August 2003).

18   Rousseau, 'On the Origin of Inequality', pp. 195–6.

19   Ibid., pp. 187–8.

20   Z. Bauman, *Liquid Love: On the Frailty of Human Bonds*, Cambridge: Polity, 2003; R. W. Fevre, *The Demoralization of Western Culture: Social Theory and the Dilemmas of Modern Living*, London: Continuum, 2000.

21   Hume, *Treatise of Human Nature*, p. 571.

22   Ibid., p. 572.

23   Giddens, *Beyond Left and Right*, p. 120.

24   Ibid., pp. 123–4.

25 Bauman, *Liquid Love*, p. 12.
26 Ibid., p. 47.
27 Ibid., p. 50.
28 Ibid., p. 51.

Chapter 3   Sex and Self-improvement

1 T. J. Scheff, *Emotions, the Social Bond, and Human Reality: Part/Whole Analysis*, Cambridge: Cambridge University Press, 1997, pp. 15–16.
2 M. Kundera, *Testaments Betrayed*, New York: Harper-Collins, 1995, pp. 128–9.
3 E. Durkheim, 'Individualism and the Intellectuals', *Revue Bleu*, 4th series, 10, 1898, pp. 7–13.
4 M. Foucault, *The History of Sexuality, Volume I* (1976) in P. Rabinow (ed.), *The Foucault Reader*, Harmondsworth: Penguin, 1984, pp. 302, 306.
5 Ibid., p. 320.
6 M. Foucault, *The History of Sexuality, Volume II* (1979), in Rabinow, *The Foucault Reader*, p. 334.
7 M. Foucault, 'The Subject and Power', in H. L. Dreyfus and P. Rabinow, *Beyond Structuralism and Hermeneutics*, Brighton: Harvester, 1982, p. 208.
8 Ibid., p. 213.
9 K. Starkey and A. McKinlay, 'Afterword: Deconstructing Organisations – Discipline and Desire', in A. McKinlay and K. Starkey (eds.), *Foucault, Management and Organisation Theory*, London: Sage, 1998, p. 231.
10 M. Foucault, 'Sexuality and Solitude', in M. Blonsky (ed.), *On Signs*, Oxford: Blackwell, 1985, p. 367.
11 Ibid., pp. 371, 372.
12 M. Foucault, 'This is Not a Pipe', Berkely, CA: University of California Press, 1983; repr. in Rabinow, *The Foucault Reader*, pp. 237–8.
13 F. Dukelow, ' "Self-Improved Citizens": Citizenship, Social Inclusion and the Self in the Politics of Welfare', Cork: Department of Applied Social Science, University College Cork.
14 B. Cruikshank, 'The Will to Empower: Technologies of Citizenship and the War on Poverty', *Socialist Review*, 23(4), 1994, pp. 29–55; B. Cruikshank, 'Revolutions Within: Self-Government and Self-Esteem', in A. Barry, T. Osborne and N. Rose (eds.), *Foucault and Reason: Neo-Liberalism and Rationalities of Government*,

London, WCC Press, 1996, pp. 301–50; B. Cruikshank, *The Will to Empower: Democratic Citizens and Other Subjects*, Ithaca: Cornell University Press, 1999.

15 N. Rose, 'Inventiveness in Politics', *Economy and Society*, 28(3), 1999, pp. 477–8.

16 T. Blair, *The Third Way: New Politics for the New Century*, Fabian Pamphlet 588, London: Fabian Society, 1998; A. Giddens, *The Third Way: The Renewal of Social Democracy*, Cambridge: Polity, 1998.

17 N. Rose, *Inventing Ourselves: Psychology, Power and Personhood*, Cambridge: Cambridge University Press, 1996, p. 17.

18 Scheff, *Emotions, the Social Bond and Human Reality*, ch. 2; see also J. Hardy, *Jane Austen's Heroines*, London: Routledge, 1984.

19 Scheff, *Emotions, the Social Bond and Human Reality*, pp. 61, 63–4.

20 G. Eliot, *The Mill on the Floss* (1860), New York: Signet Classic, 1965, pp. 498–9.

21 L. Trilling, *Sincerity and Authenticity*, Oxford: Oxford University Press, 1972.

22 D. Lessing, 'Sketches for Bohemia', *Guardian Review*, 14 June 2003.

23 B. Jordan, M. Redley and S. James, *Putting the Family First: Identities, Decisions, Citizenship*, London: UCL Press, 1994, pp. 31–2.

24 Ibid., p. 194.
25 Ibid., p. 195.
26 Ibid., p. 196.
27 Ibid.
28 Ibid., p. 63.
29 Ibid., pp. 63–7.
30 Ibid., p. 64.
31 Ibid., p. 196.
32 Ibid., pp. 141–2.
33 Ibid., p. 142.
34 Ibid., p. 196.
35 Ibid., p. 143.
36 Ibid., p. 14.
37 Ibid., p. 145.
38 Ibid., p. 196.
39 Ibid., p. 199.
40 Ibid., p. 202.
41 Ibid., p. 46.
42 Ibid., p. 47.
43 Ibid.
44 Ibid.

Chapter 4   The Nature of Change

1   See p. 1.
2   Z. Kusá, 'Topics of Inequality and Exclusion in Poor People's Family History Narratives', paper presented to 3rd ESA Conference, 'Twentieth Century Europe: Inclusions: Exclusions', University of Essex, 26–30 August 1997.
3   J. Szalai, 'Power and Poverty: Socialist Second Economy and Self-Protection against Poverty in Hungary', in *Social Capital, Poverty, Mobility and Well-being*, Exeter: Exeter University, Department of Politics, Rusel Papers, Civic Series 5/2002, pp. 6–19.
4   Of all the post-Communist countries of Central Europe, Slovakia was the one with the highest percentages of those who looked back to the 1980s as the best period of their lives – see Z. Ferge, 'Poverty', in *The Social Costs of Economic Transformation in Central Europe*, Vienna: Institüt für die Wissenschaften vom Menschen, 1997, ch. 4.
5   N. Bosanquet, 'Interim Report: Public Spending and the Welfare State', in R. Jowell, S. Witherspoon and L. Brook (eds.), *British Social Attitudes*, London: Gower, 1986; J. Hills and O. Lelkes, 'Social Security, Selective Universalism and Patchwork Redistribution', in R. Jowell, J. Curtice, A. Park and K. Thomson (eds.) *British Social Attitudes*, 16th Report, Aldershot: Ashgate, 1999.
6   M. S. Archer, *Culture and Agency: The Place of Culture in Social Theory*, Cambridge: Cambridge University Press, 1996. Archer argues that sociologists adopted a kind of cultural determinism from anthropology in the 1950s, for instance, T. Parsons, *The Social System*, London: Routledge and Kegan Paul, 1951. This in turn gave way to a structuralist orthodoxy, in which language patterned all thoughts and behaviour, for example in the work of Lévi-Strauss. Subsequently, neo-Marxists dealt in the theory of the manipulated consensus and dominant ideology, as in J. Habermas, *Towards a Rational Society*, London: Heinemann, 1971. Later, the linguistic analogy was used to explain how culture and agency were mutually ordering, as are speech and language – see A. Giddens, *New Rules of Sociological Method*, London: Hutchinson, 1976.
7   J. Elster, *Explaining Technical Change: A Case Study in the Philosophy of Science*, Cambridge: Cambridge University Press, 1983 (see pp. 22–3). Archer explains cultural change in terms of the exploitation of contradictions in the 'cultural system' by individuals in their social interactions.

8   J. Kane-Berman, *South Africa's Silent Revolution*, Johannesburg: South African Institute of Race Relations/Southern Book Publishers, 1997.

9   D. C. North, 'The New Institutional Economics', *Journal of Institutional and Theoretical Economics*, 142, 1986, pp. 230–7; *Institutions, Institutional Change and Economic Performance*, Cambridge: Cambridge University Press, 1990.

10 J. Locke, *Two Treatises of Government* (1698), ed. P. Laslett, Cambridge: Cambridge University Press, 1967; *Second Treatise*, sects. 35–6.

11 Ibid., sects. 37–50.

12 Ibid., sects. 45, 48.

13 Ibid., sects. 11, 93.

14 Ibid., sects. 37, 43.

15 Ibid., sect. 37.

16 Ibid., sect. 50.

17 For instance, J. Dunn, *The Political Theory of John Locke: An Historical Account of the 'Two Treatises of Government'*, Cambridge: Cambridge University Press, 1969; J. Tully, *A Discourse on Property: John Locke and his Adversaries*, Cambridge: Cambridge University Press, 1980.

18 J. Locke, 'Some Considerations of the Consequences of the Lowering of Interest, and Raising the Value of Money', in H. R. Fox Bourne (ed.), *The Letters of John Locke*, Edinburgh: W. Strachan, 1777, ch. 2, pp. 10–46.

19 M. Douglas, *How Institutions Think*, London: Routledge and Kegan Paul, 1987.

20 Ibid., chs 4 and 8.

21 Ibid., pp. 46–8.

22 G. Ahrne, *Agency and Organization: Towards an Organizational Theory of Society*, London: Sage, 1990.

23 Archer, *Culture and Agency*, pp. xv–xvii. She calls this process 'morphogenesis' (see note 7).

24 Ibid., pp. xvii–xxi.

25 B. Jordan, M. Redley and S. James, *Putting the Family First: Identities, Decisions, Citizenship*, London: UCL Press, 1994, p. 39.

26 Ibid.

27 Ibid.

28 Ibid.

29 Ibid.

30 Ibid., p. 40.

31   Douglas, *How Institutions Think*, pp. 91–102.
32   Jordan, Redley and James, *Putting the Family First*, p. 127.
33   Ibid., p. 128.
34   Ibid.
35   Ibid.
36   Ibid., p. 131.
37   Ibid., p. 34.
38   Ibid., pp. 36–7.
39   Ibid., p. 150.
40   Ibid., p. 160.
41   Ibid., p. 116.
42   Ibid., pp. 90–1.
43   Ibid., p. 130.
44   M. Weber, *Economy and Society* (1922), ed. G. Roth and C. Wittich, New York: Bedminster Press, 1968, pp. 8–25.

Chapter 5   On the Move: Mobility as the Basis for Freedom

1   T. Hobbes, *Leviathan* (1651), ed. M. Oakeshott, Oxford: Blackwell, 1966, pp. 97, 122, and 123.
2   G. Marcus, 'Past, Present and Emerging Identities: Requirements for Ethnographics in Late Twentieth Century Modernity', in S. Lasch and J. Friedman (eds.), *Modernity and Identity*, Oxford: Blackwell, 1992, pp. 309–30.
3   A. Smith, *An Inquiry into the Nature and Causes of the Wealth of Nations* (1776), ed. R. H. Campbell and A. S. Skinner, Oxford: Clarendon Press, 1976, Books III and V.
4   Hirschman himself claimed that he was not bent on 'interdisciplinary imperialism', but 'it was because I appreciated the power of the market mechanism, but also believed in the irreplaceability and perfectability of the democratic political process that I was able to develop a "problem-solving" approach which permitted a junction of the political (voice) and the economic (exit) modes of action. The two were not viewed as mutually exclusive; while they were alternatives they could in some situations be combined for best results; moreover, the exit-voice polarity did not yield a systematic intuitive preference for one mechanism over the other, in contrast to more traditional, not unrelated dichotomies, such as Gesellschaft *vs* Gemeinshaft, or universalism *vs* particularism' (*Essays in Trespassing: Economics to Politics and Beyond*, Cambridge: Cambridge University Press, 1981, p. 212).

5 Here Hirschman refers to M. Friedman, *Capitalism and Freedom*, Chicago: Chicago University Press, 1962, ch. 6; and C. Tiebout, 'A Pure Theory of Local Expenditures', *Journal of Political Economy*, 64, 1956, pp. 416–24.

6 A. O. Hirschman, 'Exit, Voice and the State', *World Politics*, 31, 1978, pp. 90–107, repr. in his *Essays in Trespassing*, pp. 246–65, at p. 252.

7 J. Locke, *Two Treatises of Government* (1698), ed. P. Laslett, Cambridge: Cambridge University Press, 1967; *Second Treatise*, sect. 107.

8 D. Hume, *A Treatise of Human Nature* (1739), ed. L. Selby-Bigge, Oxford: Clarendon Press, 1978, p. 539.

9 J.-J. Rousseau, 'A Discourse on the Origin of Language' (1759), in *Oeuvres Complètes*, Paris: NFR Pléiade, 1966, ch. III, p. 203.

10 See for instance C. Lévi-Strauss, 'The Social and Psychological Aspects of Chieftainship in a Primitive Tribe: The Narbikuara of North West Matto Grosso', in R. Cohen and J. Middleton (eds.), *Comparative Political Systems: Studies in the Politics of Pre-Industrial Societies*, Garden City, NY: Natural History Press, 1944, pp. 5–65; J. Middleton and D. Tait (eds.), *Tribes without Rulers: Studies in African Segmentary Systems*, London: Routledge and Kegan Paul, 1958; C. Turnbull, *Wayward Servants: The Two Worlds of African Pygmies*, London: Eyre and Spottiswoode, 1965; E. Service, *The Hunters*, Englewood Cliffs, NJ: Prentice-Hall, 1966; R. Lee and I. De Vore (eds), *Man the Hunter*, Chicago: Wenner-Gremm Foundation 1968; J. Bamberger, 'Exit and Voice in Central Brazil: On the Politics of Flight in Kayapó Society', in D. Maybury-Lewis (ed.), *Dialectical Societies: The Gé and Bororo of Central Brazil*, Cambridge, MA: Harvard University Press, p. 139.

11 M. Douglas, *How Institutions Think*, London: Routledge and Kegan Paul, 1987, pp. 28–9 and 38.

12 See, for instance, D. McKnight, *From Hunting to Drinking: The Devastating Effects of Alcohol on an Australian Aboriginal Community*, London: Routledge, 2002, who says: 'It is one of the striking features of Australian Aborigines that in religious matters the elders are able to form a common front and to organize themselves, but outside the religious sphere they show scant ability for sustained organizations' (p. 60).

13 See the stream of literature and political rhetoric about popular capitalism, stakeholder capitalism and share ownership in the USA and UK, and most recently the announcement of 'baby bonds', to be built on a payment of a lump sum to UK citizens at birth. See also ch. 8, pp. 155–6.

14 For instance, J. M. Buchanan, *The Demand and Supply of Public Goods*, Chicago: Rand McNally, 1968; and *The Economics of Politics*, London: Institute for Economic Affairs, 1978.

15 Tiebout, 'A Pure Theory of Local Expenditures'.

16 W. E. Oates, *Fiscal Federalism*, New York: Harcourt Brace Jovanovich, 1972.

17 A. O. Hirschman, *Exit, Voice and Loyalty: Responses to Decline in Firms, Organizations and States*, Cambridge, MA: Harvard University Press, 1970.

18 M. Olson, *The Logic of Collective Action: Public Goods and the Economics of Groups*, Cambridge, MA: Harvard University Press.

19 In the second edition of his book (1971), Olson refers in a footnote to J. M. Buchanan's seminal 'An Economic Theory of Clubs', *Economica*, 32, 1965, pp. 1–14, and acknowledges that they were simultaneously working on the same issue.

20 Tiebout, 'A Pure Theory of Local Expenditures'.

21 Olson, *The Logic of Collective Action*, pp. 66–131.

22 Douglas, *How Institutions Think*, ch. 3.

23 B. Jordan, *A Theory of Poverty and Social Exclusion*, Cambridge: Polity, 1996, ch. 4.

24 The example chosen by Buchanan, in his 'Economic Theory of Clubs'.

25 The main coalitions addressed by Olson in *The Logic of Collective Action*.

26 O. P. Williams, *Metropolitan Political Analysis*, New York: Free Press, 1971; M. Orbell and T. Uno, 'A Theory of Neighbourhood Problem Solving: Political Action *vs* Residential Mobility', *American Political Science Review*, 66, pp. 471–89.

27 J. Schumpeter, *The Theory of Economic Development* (1911), Cambridge, MA: Harvard University Press, 1936.

28 A. C. Pigou, *The Economics of Welfare*, London: Macmillan, 1920.

29 J. Hills and O. Lelkes, 'Social Security, Selective Universalism and Patchwork Redistribution', in R. Jowell, J. Curtice, A. Park and K. Thomson (eds), *British Social Attitudes*, 16th Report, Aldershot: Ashgate, 1999.

30 A. Casella and B. Frey, 'Federalism and Clubs: Towards an Economic Theory of Overlapping Political Jurisdictions', *European Economic Review*, 36(2/3), 1992, pp. 639–46.

31 A. Cornes and T. Sandler, *The Theory of Externalities, Public Goods and Club Goods*, Cambridge: Cambridge University Press, 1986.

32 R. P. Inman and D. L. Rubinfeld, 'The Political Economy of Federalism', in D. C. Mueller, (ed.), *Perspectives on Public Choice: A Handbook*, Cambridge: Cambridge University Press, 1997, p. 81.

33 Hobbes, *Leviathan*, wrote, 'By SYSTEMS, I understand any number of men joined in one interest, or one business' (p. 214). He grouped together 'public systems' (jurisdictions, agencies and enterprises) and 'private organizations' (firms, corporations and voluntary associations), and thought they should all be regulated by the sovereign, and banned if factious or subversive to the state.

34 B. Jordan and F. Düvell, *Migration: The Boundaries of Equality and Justice*, Cambridge: Polity, 2003.

35 J. Rawls, *Political Liberalism*, New York: Columbia University Press, 1993, p. 181.

36 Ibid., p. 136.

37 J. Rawls, *The Law of Peoples*, Cambridge, MA: Harvard University Press, 1999, p. 39.

38 B. Jordan and F. Düvell, *Irregular Migration: The Dilemmas of Transnational Mobility*, Cheltenham: Edward Elgar, 2002, ch. 9; Jordan and Düvell, *Migration*, ch. 3.

39 Interview 5 (transcript).

40 Interview 6 (transcript).

41 Jordan and Düvell, *Irregular Migration*, p. 228.

42 Ibid.

43 Jordan and Düvell, *Migration*, p. 84.

44 Ibid., p. 85.

Chapter 6   Keep Out: Organizations, Boundaries and Exclusions

1 R. D. Putnam, *Making Democracy Work: Civic Traditions in Modern Italy*, Princeton, NJ: Princeton University Press, 1993.

2 Ibid., chs. 4–6.

3 R. D. Putnam, *Bowling Alone: The Collapse and Revival of American Community*, New York: Simon and Schuster, 2000.

4 J. Coleman, *Foundations of Social Theory*, Cambridge, MA: Harvard University Press, 1990.

5 See for instance, A. Croft, *Great North: A Poem of the Great North Run*, North Shields: Iron Press, 2001.

6 D. C. Mueller, *Public Choice II*, Cambridge: Cambridge University Press, 1989; D. A. Starrett, *Foundations of Public Economics*, Cambridge: Cambridge University Press, 1988; A. Cornes and T. G. Sandler, *The Theory of Externalities, Public Goods and Club Goods*, Cambridge: Cambridge University Press, 1986.

7 Ian Traynor, 'The Privatisation of War', *Guardian*, 10 December 2003, pp. 1–2.

8   From a technical economic standpoint, the goods produced by 'economic clubs' are not pure private goods, because they cannot be exclusively owned and consumed or marketed as discreet units; but they are partially rivalrous (for instance, because of the maintenance costs of providing them), and partially depletable (because utility is lost with extra use by others, i.e. congestion costs). Clubs form to supply those goods which members can consume in non-rivalrous ways, but which are not 'public', because members have the means to exclude others who do not contribute to the costs of supplying them, or who would cause loss of utility through crowding. Hence members' utility is not simply market-related. There must be 'technological externalities' between members – benefits they share, for which outsiders are not compensated and which stem from exclusion as well as cost minimization. Hence a collective relationship, rather than a market mechanism, is adopted by members, who can exercise choice either by leaving to join another club (exit), or by their participation in the governance of the facility (voice).

9   W. A. Niskanen, 'Bureaucrats and Politicians', *Journal of Law and Economics*, 18, 1975, pp. 617–43.

10   J. Cullis and P. Jones, *Public Finance and Public Choice: Analytical Perspectives*, London: McGraw Hill, 1994, pp. 297–302; B. Jordan, *A Theory of Poverty and Social Exclusion*, Cambridge: Polity, 1996, chs 4 and 5. Putnam found that in the USA accelerated mobility and suburban sprawl had made districts more socially homogeneous, sorting populations into 'lifestyle enclaves', and reducing civic engagement (Putnam, *Bowling Alone*, pp. 209–10).

11   'The rich tend to want to be away from the poor, but the poor want to be in the same jurisdiction as the rich', Cullis and Jones, *Public Finance and Public Choice*, p. 300.

12   K. Wicksell, *Finanztheoretische Untersuchungen*, Jena: Fischer, 1896, reproduced as 'A New Principle for Just Taxation', in R. A. Musgrove and A. T. Peacock (eds), *Classics in the Theory of Public Finance*, London: MacMillan, 1958, pp. 72–116.

13   See for instance F. Foldvary, *Public Goods and Private Communities: The Market Provision of Social Services*, Aldershot: Edward Elgar, 1994.

14   Ibid., pp. 63–4. The free-rider problem and the tragedy of the commons (non-contributing members, and over-use of shared facilities by members) are overcome by such systems of governance – see E. Ostrom, *Governing the Commons: The Evolution of Institutions for Collective Action*, Cambridge: Cambridge University Press, 1990.

15 H. Steiner, 'Libertarianism and the Transnational Migration of People', in B. Barry and R. E. Goodin (eds), *Free Movement: Ethical Issues in the Transnational Migration of People and Money*, University Park, PA: Pennsylvania State University Press, 1992, pp. 87–94.

16 R. Nozick, *Anarchy, State and Utopia*, Oxford: Blackwell, 1974.

17 A. O. Hirschman, 'Exit Voice and the State' (1978), in his *Essays in Trespassing: Economics to Politics and Beyond*, Cambridge: Cambridge University Press, 1981, pp. 246–65, at p. 252.

18 K. Polanyi, *The Great Transformation: The Political and Economic Origins of our Time*, Boston: Beacon Press, 1944.

19 B. Jordan and F. Düvell, *Migration: The Boundaries of Equality and Justice*, Cambridge, Polity, 2003, ch. 2.

20 BBC Radio 4, *Sunday*, 26 October 2003, where an Anglican spokesman described this as 'the end of the territorial principle' in the Church of England.

21 BBC World Service, *Pick of the World*, 13 December 2003.

22 M. Barnes et al. (eds), *Poverty and Social Exclusion in Europe*, Cheltenham: Edward Elgar, 2002.

23 B. Jordan, S. James, H. Kay and M. Redley, *Trapped in Poverty? Labour Market Decisions in Low-Income Households*, London: Routledge, 1992.

24 Transcript of interview with Mr and Mrs Itchen, pp. 5–6 and 12.

25 Transcript of interview with Mr Bow, p. 40.

26 Transcript of interview with Mr and Mrs Humber, p. 57.

27 Transcript of interview with Mr and Mrs Rother, pp. 74–5.

28 Transcript of interview with Mr Cherwell, p. 4 and with Mrs Cherwell, p. 28.

29 C. C. Williams and J. Windebank, 'Paid Informal Work in Deprived Neighbourhoods', *Cities*, 17(4), 2000, pp. 285–91.

30 M. Leonard, *Informal Economic Activity in Belfast*, Aldershot: Avebury, 1994.

31 B. Jordan, *Paupers: The Making of the New Claiming Class*, London: Routledge, 1973.

Chapter 7 Organizations and Power

1 T. Scheff, *Emotions, The Social Bond, and Human Reality: Part/Whole Analysis*, Cambridge: Cambridge University Press, 1997.

2 B. Jordan, *Paupers: The Making of the New Claiming Class*, London: Routledge and Kegan Paul, 1973.

3 B. Barry, 'The Continuing Relevance of Socialism', in his *Liberty and Justice: Essays in Political Theory*, vol. I, Oxford: Clarendon Press, 1991, pp. 274–90.

4 A. Ryan, 'Mill and Rousseau: Utility and Rights', in G. Duncan (ed.), *Democratic Theory and Practice*, Cambridge: Cambridge University Press, 1983, pp. 56–7.

5 J.-J. Rousseau 'The Social Contract' (1762) in *The Social Contract and Discourses*, Dent, 1952, pp. 3–15, Book II, ch. 11.

6 D. Hume, *A Treatise of Human Nature* (1739), ed. L. A. Selby-Bigge, Oxford: Clarendon Press, 1978.

7 A. Smith, *An Inquiry into the Nature and Causes of the Wealth of Nations* (1776), ed. R. H. Campbell and A. S. Skinner, Oxford: Clarendon Press, Book V, ch. xi.

8 H. Spencer, *The Man Versus the State* (1884) and *The Social Organism* (1860), in Donald MacRae (ed.), *The Man Versus the State*, Harmondsworth: Penguin, 1969. For a more recent example of an evolutionary explanation of the success and failure of political organizations adapting to economic change, see M. Olson, *The Rise and Decline of Nations: Economic Growth, Stagflation and Social Rigidities*, New Haven, CT: Yale University Press, 1981.

9 C. L. Montesquieu, 'On Politics' (1734), *Oeuvres Complètes*, Paris: NFR Pléiade, 1949, p. 112.

10 Sir James Steuart, *An Inquiry into the Principles of Political Oeconomy*, vol. 1, 1767, p. 278.

11 A. Smith, *The Wealth of Nations*, pp. 594–5. Hirschman points out that the earlier Enlightenment philosophers, such as Spinoza, Vico, d'Holbach and Montesquieu, thought that the 'calm passions' of desire for economic gain could offset the more violent ones of lust for glory and military ambition. Smith and the later thinkers were less confident of this distinction, or of 'the principle of the countervailing passions'. Smith argued that people's interests channelled them towards peace and prosperity through hidden economic laws – see A. O. Hirschman, *The Passions and the Interests: Political Arguments for Capitalism Before Its Triumph*, Princeton, NJ: Princeton University Press, 1977, pp. 20–31 and 100–14.

12 T. Jefferson, 'Notes on Virginia' (1784) in A. Lipscombe (ed.), *The Writings of Thomas Jefferson*, Washington, DC: Jefferson Memorial Association, 1903, vol. 2, argued that citizen's rights were only effective with widespread property holdings, as in the USA. Rousseau, 'The Social Contract', argued against economic dependence, and hence for small independent producers (p. 45).

13 See for instance, D. Begg, S. Fischer and R. Dornbusch, *Economics* (5th edn), London: McGraw-Hill, 1997, where 'Business Organization and Behaviour' is a chapter in the section on 'Positive Microeconomics', and analysed in terms of the supply decision facing a producer. The work of Williamson and Hart (see pp. 152–4 below) is relegated to a box, and its contents not integrated into the main argument (ch. 7, box 7.2).

14 J. Elster, *Making Sense of Marx*, Cambridge: Cambridge University Press, 1985, p. 6.

15 Ibid., pp. 28–9.

16 M. Douglas, *How Institutions Think*, London: Routledge and Kegan Paul, 1987, p. 37.

17 Ibid., p. 43.

18 Jordan, *Paupers*.

19 T. Yamamori, research paper on the origins of the Claimants' Unions' adoption of the Basic Income proposal, as yet unpublished.

20 W. Van Trier, 'Every One a King'. PhD thesis, Sociology Department, University of Leuven.

21 M. Drakeford, *Social Movements and their Followers: The Greenshirts in England*, Basingstoke: Macmillan, 1997.

22 Douglas, *How Institutions Think*, p. 92.

23 O. Hart, *Firms, Contracts and Financial Structure*, Oxford: Clarendon Press, 1995, p. 5 (footnote).

24 M. Ricketts, *The Economics of Business Enterprise: An Introduction to Economic Organisation and the Theory of the Firm*, Cheltenham: Edward Elgar, 2002, p. 199.

25 G. Tullock, 'Rent Seeking as a Negative Sum Game', in J. M. Buchanan, R. D. Tollison and G. Tullock (eds), *Toward a Theory of the Rent Seeking Society*, College Station, TX: Texas A & M University Press, 1986, pp. 3–28, at p. 17.

26 Hart, *Firms, Contracts and Financial Structure*, p. 32.

27 Ibid., p. 29.

28 Ibid., p. 30.

29 Ibid., p. 44.

30 R. H. Coase, 'The Nature of the Firm', *Economica*, 4, 1937, pp. 386–405.

31 Hart, *Firms, Contracts and Financial Structure*, p. 57.

32 Ibid., p. 58.

33 B. Jordan, M. Redley and S. James, *Putting the Family First: Identities, Decisions, Citizenship*, London: UCL Press, 1994, p. 186.

34 Ibid., p. 33.

35　Elster, *Making Sense of Marx*, wrote: 'the presence of non-producible skills prevents us speaking of *the* labour content of commodities, and hence of comparing the labour time expended by an agent and the labour time he receives in the form of commodities. In this case the "labour theory of exploitation" breaks down, as does the labour theory of value' (pp. 201–2). His critique of the concept of exploitation concluded that it was only useful in a general sense (for instance, in broad historical overviews) and could not be a fundamental element in analytical Marxist theory (pp. 204–29).

36　J. Roemer, *A General Theory of Exploitation and Class*, Cambridge, MA: Harvard University Press, 1982, ch. 1.

37　Elster, *Making Sense of Marx*, pp. 167–204.

38　Begg, Fisher and Dornbusch, *Economics*, p. 282.

39　G. Ahrne, *Agency and Organization: Towards an Organizational Theory of Society*, London: Sage, 1990, p. 140.

Chapter 8　Power and World Poverty

1　World Bank, *World Development Report 2000–2001: Attacking Poverty*, Washington, DC: World Bank/Oxford University Press, 2001, p. 3.

2　T. Pogge, *World Poverty and Human Rights*, Cambridge: Polity, 2002, p. 2.

3　A. Sen, *Development as Freedom*, Oxford: Oxford University Press, 1999; J. Stiglitz, *Globalization and Its Discontents*, London: Allen Lane, 2002.

4　World Bank, *World Development Report*, box 3.3, p. 51.

5　For instance, J. McMurtry, *Value Wars: The Global Market versus the Life Economy*, London: Pluto Press, 2002; Oxfam, 'Rigged Rules and Double Standards: Trade, Globalization and the Fight Against Poverty', press release, 24 April 2002.

6　A. G. Frank, *Capitalism and Underdevelopment in Latin America*, New York: Monthly Review Press, 1967; A. Emmanuel, *Unequal Exchange: A Study of the Imperialism of Trade*, New York: Monthly Review Press, 1972.

7　P. Van Parijs, 'Commentary: Citizenship Exploitation, Unequal Exchange and the Breakdown of Popular Sovereignty', in B. Barry and R. E. Goodin (eds), *Free Movement: Ethical Issues in the Transnational Migration of People and Money*, University Park, PA: Pennsylvania University Press, 1992, pp. 155–66.

8　J. Roemer, 'Unequal Exchange, Labour Migration and International Capital Flows: A Theoretical Synthesis', in P. Desai (ed.), *Marxism, the Soviet Economy and Central Planning: Essays in Honor of Alexander Erlich*, Cambridge, MA: MIT Press, 1983, pp. 34–60, at p. 42.

9   Ibid.

10   Van Parijs, 'Commentary', pp. 160–1.

11   Ibid., p. 161.

12   Ibid., p. 164.

13   Ibid., pp. 159–61.

14   R. Boyer, 'The Political in the Era of Globalization and Finance: Focus on Some Regulation School Research', *International Journal of Urban and Regional Research*, 24, 2000, pp. 275–322.

15   International Development Association, *Poverty Reduction Strategy Papers and IDA13*, Washington, DC: International Development Association, May 2001, pp. 11–13.

16   Ibid.

17   World Bank, *World Development Report, 2000–2001*, pp. 34–41.

18   Ibid., p. 85.

19   Stiglitz, *Globalization and Its Discontents*.

20   Ibid., pp. 182–6.

21   G. J. Smith, 'The Transformative Impact of Capital and Labour Mobility on the Chinese City', *Urban Geography*, 21(8), 2000, pp. 670–700.

22   G. Ahrne, *Agency and Organization: Towards an Organizational Theory of Society*, London: Sage, 1990, p. 178.

23   Ibid., pp. 132–3.

24   B. Jordan with C. Jordan, *Social Work and the Third Way: Tough Love as Social Policy*, London: Sage, 2000, pp. 165–7.

25   J. Rawls, *A Theory of Justice*, Oxford: Oxford University Press, 1971.

26   R. Dworkin, 'What Is Equality? Part II: Equality of Resources', *Philosophy and Public Affairs*, 10, 1981, pp. 283–345.

27   World Bank, *World Development Report, 2000–2001*, p. 10.

28   Ibid.

29   Stiglitz, *Globalization and Its Discontents*, Acknowledgements.

30   Sen, *Development as Freedom*, p. 261.

31   Ibid., ch. 1.

32   Ibid., p. 53.

33   Z. Bauman, *Liquid Love: On the Frailty of Human Bonds*, Cambridge: Polity, 2002; R. W. Fevre, *The Demoralization of Western Culture: Social Theory and the Dilemmas of Modern Living*, London: Continuum, 2000; McMurtry, *Value Wars*, Part III.

34   McMurtry, *Value Wars*, pp. 74, 121–5.

35   Bauman, *Liquid Love*, p. 74.

36   J. M. Buchanan and G. Tullock, *The Calculus of Consent*, Ann Arbor,

MI: University of Michigan Press, 1962, pioneered this approach to the study of collective goods, by showing that each kind of institutional structure, from markets in private goods to state allocation of all resources, has its own economic properties, costs and benefits, and that there are trade-offs between the advantages and disadvantages of each. Furthermore, J. M. Buchanan, R. D. Tollison and G. Tullock (eds), *Towards a Theory of the Rent Seeking Society*, College Station, TX: Texas A & M University Press, 1980, show that all collectives, from firms to states, have incentives to try to gain property rights by means other than voluntary exchange (i.e., by exploiting power advantages, instead of increasing productive efficiency).

37 J. Pilger, *The New Rulers of the World*, London: Verso, 2002; G. Monbiot, *The Age of Consent*, London: Harper Collins, 2003.

38 See, for instance W. J. Wilson, *The Truly Disadvantaged: The Underclass, the Ghetto and Public Policy*, Chicago: Chicago University Press, 1989; and *When Work Disappears: The World of the New Urban Poor*, London: Vintage, 1997.

39 Adam Smith pointed out that 'movable property' could act as a discipline on governments, because: 'The proprietor of stock is properly a citizen of the world, and is not necessarily attached to any particular country. He would be apt to abandon the country in which he was exposed to a vexatious inquisition' (*The Wealth of Nations*, p. 800).

40 T. R. Malthus, *An Essay in the Principles of Population* (1798), ed., A. Flew, London: Pelican, 1965.

41 B. Jordan, *The New Politics of Welfare*, London: Sage, 1998.

42 B. Jordan and F. Düvell, *Irregular Migration: The Dilemmas of Transnational Mobility*, Cheltenham: Edward Elgar, 2002, ch. 1.

43 S. Lavenex, *The Europeanisation of Refugee Policies: Between Human Rights and Internal Security*, Aldershot: Ashgate, 2001.

44 B. Jordan and D. Vogel, 'Which Policies Influence Migration Decisions? A Comparative Analysis of Qualitative Interviews with Undocumented Brazilian Immigrants in London and Berlin', Bremen: University of Bremen, Centre for Social Policy Research, 1997.

45 Ibid.

46 Jordan and Düvell, *Irregular Migration*, chs 4 and 5.

47 Ibid., ch. 5.

48 Ibid.

49 Ibid.

50 Page numbers in the following extracts refer to the interview transcripts.

51 Jordan and Düvell, *Irregular Migration*, p. 151.

Chapter 9 Power, Passion and Loyalty

1 J. Buchanan and G. Tullock, *The Calculus of Consent*, Ann Arbor, MI: University of Michigan Press, 1962; J. M. Buchanan, R. D. Tollison and G. Tullock (eds), *Toward a Theory of the Rent Seeking Society*, College Station, TX: Texas A & M University Press, 1980; G. S. Becker, *Human Capital*, New York: NBER, 1964. As Machiavelli pointed out in the *Discourses*: 'in all human affairs one notices, if one examines them closely, that it is impossible to remove one inconvenience without another emerging. . . . Hence in all discussions one should consider which alternative involves fewer inconveniences and should adopt this as the better course, for one never finds any issue that is clear cut.'

2 R. P. Inman and D. L. Rubinfeld, 'The Political Economy of Federalism', in D. C. Mueller (ed.), *Perspectives on Public Choice: A Handbook*, Cambridge: Cambridge University Press, 1997, pp. 73–105; B. R. Weingast, 'The Economic Role of Political Institutions: Market-Preserving Federalism and Economic Development', *Journal of Law and Economic Organization*, 11, 1995, pp. 1–31; A. Casella and B. Frey, 'Federalism and Clubs: Towards an Economic Theory of Overlapping Political Jurisdictions', *European Economic Review*, 36(2/3), 1992, pp. 639–46.

3 A. Cornes and T. Sandler, *The Theory of Externalities, Public Goods and Club Goods*, Cambridge: Cambridge University Press, 1986, ch. 11.

4 M. Douglas, *How Institutions Think*, London: Routledge and Kegan Paul, 1987, pp. 46–7.

5 See for instance E. Evans-Pritchard, *Nuer Religion*, Oxford: Clarendon Press, 1956.

6 Douglas, *How Institutions Think*, pp. 97–9; E. Durkheim, *The Elementary Forms of Religious Life* (1912), Paris: Alcan, 1915.

7 T. Scheff, *Emotions, The Social Bond and Human Reality: Part/Whole Analysis*, Cambridge: Cambridge University Press, 1997, p. 65.

8 Ibid., p. 77.

9 Ibid., p. 78, and N. Elias, *Involvement and Detachment*, Oxford: Blackwell, 1987.

10 Scheff, *Emotions, The Social Bond and Human Reality*, pp. 43–4, 74, 76–7 and 86; and E. Goffman, *Interaction Ritual*, New York: Anchor, 1967.

11 E. Ferri and K. Smith, 'Partnerships and Parenthood', in E. Ferri, J. Bynner and M. Wadsworth (eds), *Changing Britain, Changing Lives: Three Generations at the Turn of the Century*, London: Institute of Education, 2003, p. 115.

12 B. Jordan, M. Redley and S. James, *Putting the Family First: Identities, Decisions, Citizenship*, London: UCL Press, 1994, pp. 114–19.
13 Ibid., p. 106.
14 Ibid., p. 107.
15 Ibid., ch. 5.
16 Ibid., pp. 132–5.
17 J. Lewis, *The End of Marriage? Individualism and Intimate Relations*, Cheltenham: Edward Elgar, 2001, pp. 137, 139.
18 Department for Education and Skills, *Every Child Matters* (Green Paper), London: Stationery Office, p. 7.
19 See, for instance, the Channel 4 TV programme *The Best for My Child*, presented by Fiona Millar, which illustrated this phenomenon. Drawing on her own experience, she showed that parents could join together to take collective action, committing themselves and their children to local comprehensive schools, and raising standards – but that this was a rarely taken option.
20 A. Giddens, 'Family', *Reith Lectures*, BBC Radio 4, 28 April 1999.
21 U. Beck and E. Beck-Gernsheim, *The Normal Chaos of Love*, Cambridge: Polity, 1995, p. 73.
22 J. Ribbens McCarthy and R. Edwards, 'The Individual in Public and Private: The Significance of Mothers and Children', in A. Carling, S. Duncan and R. Edwards (eds), *Families: Morality and Rationality in Policy and Practice*, London: Routledge, 2002.
23 J. Ribbens McCarthy, R. Edwards and V. Gillies, *Making Families: Moral Tales of Parenting and Step-Parenting*, York: Sociology Press, 2003.
24 C. Smart and B. Neale, *Family Fragments*, Cambridge: Polity, 1999.
25 C. Smart, B. Neale and A. Wade, *The Changing Experience of Childhood: Families and Divorce*, Cambridge: Polity, 2001, pp. 45–56.
26 Ibid., p. 77 (Joey, aged 15).
27 J. C. Scott, *Weapons of the Weak: Everyday Forms of Peasant Resistance*, Princeton, NJ: Princeton University Press, 1985; and *Domination and the Arts of Resistance: Hidden Transcripts*, Princeton, NJ: Princeton University Press, 1990.
28 C. C. Williams and J. Windebank, 'Paid Informal Work in Deprived Neighbourhoods', *Cities*, 17(4), 2000, pp. 285–91, at p. 285.
29 C. C. Williams and J. Windebank, 'Why Do People Engage in Paid Informal Work? A Comparison of Higher- and Lower-Income Urban Neighbourhoods in Britain', *Community, Work and Family*, 5(1), 2002, pp. 67–83.
30 M. Leonard, *Informal Economic Activity in Belfast*, Aldershot: Avebury, 1994; 'The Long-Term Unemployed, Economic Activity

and the "Underclass" in Belfast', *International Journal of Urban and Regional Research*, 22(1), 1998, pp. 42–59.

31 M. Leonard, 'Informal Economic Activity: Strategies of Households and Communities', paper presented at the 4th ESA Conference, 'Will Europe Work?', Amsterdam, 18–21 August 1999, p. 6.

32 Ibid., p. 17.

33 Home Office, *Community Cohesion: A Report of the Independent Review Team Chaired by Ted Cantle*, London: Home Office, 2001.

34 B. Jordan with C. Jordan, *Social Work and the Third Way: Tough Love as Social Policy*, London: Sage, 2000, pp. 54–7.

35 B. Jordan, S. James, H. Kay and M. Redley, *Trapped in Poverty? Labour-Market Decisions in Low-Income Households*, London: Routledge, 1992, pp. 88–9.

36 B. Jordan and F. Düvell, *Migration: The Boundaries of Equality and Justice*, Cambridge: Polity, 2003, pp. 150–1.

Chapter 10   Connections and Conclusions

1 D. Triesman, 'Foreword', in the Labour Party, *Turnout in Decline: A Global Picture*, London: Labour Party, 2003, p. 2.

2 Tullock defined rent seeking as an activity where 'an individual . . . invests in something that will not actually improve productivity or will actually lower it, but that does raise his income because it gives him some special position or monopoly power' (G. Tullock, 'Rent Seeking as a Negative Sum Game', in J. M. Buchanan, R. D. Tollison and G. Tullock (eds.), *Towards a Theory of a Rent Seeking Society*, College Station, TX: Texas A & M University Press, 1980, p. 17). He added that the returns to initial investments of this kind, using resources to redistribute income in favour of the rent seeker rather than through efficiency gains, were often greater than those produced by monopoly itself. Theft is a kind of rent seeking, and the contrast between gaining from theft and gaining from voluntary exchange is similar to that between rent seeking and entrepreneurship (G. Tullock, 'The Welfare Costs of Tariffs, Monopolies, and Theft', in *Towards a Theory of a Rent Seeking Society*, pp. 48–9). We have seen (pp. 153–4) that rent seeking is a characteristic activity of both capitalist organizations and political actors – like crime, it is often a form of collective action.

3 Some political theorists argue that electoral politics have become 'an arena of spectacles staged by the mass media', in which 'symbolic dramatizations of pieces of reality' are enacted as 'rituals and

ceremonies' (K. Eder, 'Social Movement Organizations and the Democratic Order: Reorganizing the Social Basis of Political Citizenship in Complex Societies', in C. Crouch, K. Eder and D. Tambini, *Citizenship, Markets and the State*, Oxford: Oxford University Press, 2001, pp. 213–37, at pp. 213–14).

4   In November, 2003, a poll of German citizens chose the post-war Chancellor, Konrad Adenauer, as 'the greatest German of all time' (ahead of Bach, Goethe, Marx, Dürer and so on). This seemed to indicate a remarkable loyalty to the institutions created during the late 1940s and early '50s, though it might also have been a snub by 'Wessies' to the inhabitants of the former German Democratic Republic, most of whom voted for Marx.

5   The tradition in which members of society are imagined as coming together to create political authority, and agree basic social institutions – as in Hobbes, Locke, Rousseau, through to Rawls and Dworkin.

6   W. G. Bennis and B. Nanus, *Leaders: The Strategies for Taking Charge*, New York: Harper and Row, 1985, p. 221.

7   See for instance, J. Dryzek, *Discursive Democracy*, Cambridge: Cambridge University Press, 1990; J. Habermas, *Moral Consciousness and Communicative Action*, Cambridge: Polity, 1990; I. M. Young, *Inclusion and Democracy*, Oxford: Oxford University Press, 2000.

8   For discussion of the larger issues raised by these versions of democracy, and some critical analyses, see J. Bohman, *Public Deliberation*, Cambridge, MA: MIT Press, 1996; J. Johnson, 'Arguing for Deliberation: Some Skeptical Considerations', in J. Elster, *Deliberative Democracy*, Cambridge: Cambridge University Press, 1998; A. Phillips, *Democracy and Difference*, Cambridge: Polity, 1993; and J. Dryzek, *Deliberative Democracy and Beyond: Liberals, Critics, Contestations*, Cambridge: Cambridge University Press, 2000.

9   For a balanced critique of this model of devolution, see P. K. Doherty, *The Management of Participation in an Age of Diversity*, Cork: University of Cork, Department of Applied Social Studies, doctoral thesis, 2003.

10   H. Blears, *Communities in Control: Public Services and Local Socialism*, London: Fabian Society, 2003, argues that 'Decentralisation and mutualisation should be the guiding principles of public service reform. Key parts of the public services should be made into mutual organisations and owned and controlled by local people and their users' (p. 1). However, she acknowledges that her concept of 'mutuality' covers many different forms of ownership, membership and control, and that principles of governance would be problematic,

especially under public-private partnerships: 'One possibility is that every adult voter in the geographical area served by a hospital or primary care trust, school, college, social service – or even parks and leisure facilities – should be given a vote to elect some or all of the non-executive directors as part of a stakeholder board. There might be a form of electoral college with votes distributed among staff, patients, voluntary groups and residents. Some members of governing bodies might be chosen randomly for a prescribed period of office, on the jury service model' (p. 18).

These speculations illustrate the problems of how to establish democratic governance of facilities, with quite different ownership rights and membership stakes among participants, as well as very different capabilities in public discourse. As Doherty, *The Management of Participation in an Age of Diversity*, points out, there are issues of legitimacy, justification and motivation raised by these models of decision-making over public policy.

11 T. Pogge, *World Poverty and Human Rights*, Cambridge: Polity, 2002, p. 24.

12 Ibid., p. 33.

13 J. Pilger, *The New Rulers of the World*, London: Verso, 2002, gives examples of carve-ups between the IMF, the US government and international business corporations, such as the deal under which President Sukarno came to power in Indonesia in 1967.

14 R. P. Inman and D. L. Rubinfeld, 'The Political Economy of Fiscal Federalism', in D. C. Mueller (ed.), *Perspectives on Public Choice: A Handbook*, Cambridge: Cambridge University Press, 1997, pp. 73–105; A. Casella and B. Frey, 'Federalism and Clubs: Towards an Economic Theory of Overlapping Political Jurisdictions', *European Economic Review*, 36(2/3), 1992, pp. 639–46; W. E. Oates, 'An Essay on Fiscal Federalism', *Journal of Economic Literature*, 27, 1999, pp. 1120–49. See B. Jordan and F. Düvell, *Migration: The Boundaries of Equality and Justice*, Cambridge: Polity, 2003, pp. 52–6.

15 J. K. Brueckner, 'Welfare Reform and the "Race to the Bottom": Theory and Evidence', *Southern Economic Journal*, 66(3), 2000, pp. 505–25.

16 W. E. Oates and R. M. Schwab, 'The Theory of Regulating Federalism: The Case of Environmental Management', in W. E. Oates (ed.), *The Political Economy of Fiscal Federalism*, Lexington, MA: Heath-Lexington, 1990, pp. 275–355.

17 World Bank, *World Development Report 2000–2001: Attacking Poverty*, Washington, DC, World Bank/Oxford University Press, 2001, p. 46.

18 BBC Radio 4, *Farming Today*, 29 December 2003.

19 See B. Jordan with C. Jordan, *Social Work and the Third Way: Tough Love as Social Policy*, London: Sage, 2000, chs 5 and 6.
20 Department of Trade and Industry, *Social Enterprise: A Strategy for Success*, London: Stationery Office, 2002.
21 B. Jordan, P. Agulnik, D. Burbidge and S. Duffin, *Stumbling Towards Basic Income: The Prospects for Tax-Benefit Integration*, London: Citizen's Income Study Centre, 2000.
22 Ibid., ch. 3.
23 J. Salt and J. Clarke, 'Foreign Labour in the United Kingdom: Patterns and Trends', *Labour Market Trends*, October, 2000, pp. 473–83.
24 Jordan and Düvell, *Migration*, ch. 5.

Index